# GALLUCCI'S COMMENTARY ON DÜRER'S *FOUR BOOKS ON HUMAN PROPORTION*

# Gallucci's Commentary on Dürer's *Four Books on Human Proportion*

Renaissance Proportion Theory

*Translated with an Introduction
by James Hutson*

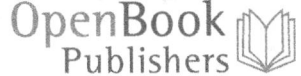

https://www.openbookpublishers.com

© 2020 James Hutson

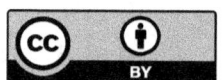 

This work is licensed under a Creative Commons Attribution 4.0 International license (CC BY 4.0). This license allows you to share, copy, distribute and transmit the work; to adapt the work and to make commercial use of the work providing attribution is made to the author (but not in any way that suggests that they endorse you or your use of the work).

Attribution should include the following information:

James Hutson, *Gallucci's Commentary on Dürer's "Four Books on Human Proportion": Renaissance Proportion Theory*. Cambridge, UK: Open Book Publishers, 2020, https://doi.org/10.11647/OBP.0198

Copyright and permission for reuse of many images included in this publication differ from the above. Copyright and permissions information for images is provided separately in the List of Illustrations

In order to access detailed and updated information on the license, please visit https://doi.org/10.11647/OBP.0198#copyright

Further details about CC BY licenses are available at https://creativecommons.org/licenses/by/4.0/

All external links were active at the time of publication unless otherwise stated and have been archived via the Internet Archive Wayback Machine at https://archive.org/web

Any digital material and resources associated with this volume are available at https://doi.org/10.11647/OBP.0198#resources

Every effort has been made to identify and contact copyright holders and any omission or error will be corrected if notification is made to the publisher.

ISBN Paperback: 978-1-78374-887-7
ISBN Hardback: 978-1-78374-888-4
ISBN Digital (PDF): 978-1-78374-889-1
ISBN Digital ebook (epub): 978-1-78374-860-0
ISBN Digital ebook (mobi): 978-1-78374-861-7
ISBN Digital (XML): 978-1-78374-862-4
DOI: 10.11647/OBP.0198

Cover image: Albrecht Dürer, *Adam and Eve* (1507). Oil, 82 1/5 x 31 4/5 in and 82 1/5 x 32 ½ in. Museo del Prado, Madrid. Wikimedia, Public Domain, https://commons.wikimedia.org/wiki/File:Albrecht_D%C3%BCrer_-_Adam_and_Eve_(Prado)_2FXD.jpg

Cover design: Anna Gatti

# Contents

Acknowledgements ix
On the Translation xi

Introduction 1

1. Proportion Theory: Disciplinary Intersections 1
2. Gallucci: Translator, Academician, Pedagogue 26
3. *Ut pictura poesis*: Sister Arts 40
4. Physiognomics: The Science of Passion 50
5. From Microcosm to Macrocosm 58
6. Proportion Studies: Reception and Legacy 67

On the Symmetry of Human Bodies 83

Bibliography 187
List of Illustrations 201
Index of Proper Names 205

*To my wife Piper and son Bishop*

# Acknowledgments

The current study began with my dissertation at the University of Maryland, and continued with an article published in *Storia dell'arte*. I would first like to thank Giles Knox, who introduced me to the study of early modern art theory, followed by Anthony Colantuono, whom I assisted in the paleographical transcription and translation for Orfeo Boselli's *Osservationi della Scoltura antica* [Observations on Antique Sculpture]. It was Colantuono who first recommended that I translate Giovanni Paolo Gallucci's *Della simmetria dei corpi humani* [On the Symmetry of Human Bodies] many years ago at the conclusion of my doctoral study.

This present translation, however, came about more recently. After investigating the shifting landscape of art theory relating to pictorial stylistics, I turned to the more practical application of manuals for artists in their education (thanks to a reader's comments on my first book). I'm indebted to the earlier work elucidating the impact and context of Charles Le Brun's pathognomics by Jennifer Montagu, as well as Jean Julia Chai and her related translation of Giovan Paolo Lomazzo's *Idea del tempio della pittura* [The Idea of the Temple of Painting].

Within my own university, I would like to thank the previous president and provost, James Evans and Jann Weitzel, for allocating resources and funds that allow such publications to exist, as well as the current administration for their continued efforts in advancing scholarship and research. In my own school, I would like to express appreciation for the support of the dean of Arts, Media, and Communications, Joe Alsobrook, and the previous chair of the Art and Design department, John Troy. Their efforts ensured that I had the necessary course release to complete the current manuscript. Finally, several talented students assisted in reviewing the translation as part of their own research and scholarship and should be credited here; their contributions were immeasurable — Cristiano Pennisi, Mattia Forigiani, and Serena Rossi.

# On the Translation

The translation at hand reveals the place of symmetry and proportion in the context of contemporary education of the early modern era, especially the education of artists. In the original contribution and subject of this translation, Giovanni Paolo Gallucci expands on Dürer's nascent interest in the proportions of a diversity of human types and extends this interest in diversity to elaborate systems of physiognomy and humoral readings. Interestingly, the volume's author was not an artist, nor was he an art critic or theorist. As an avid translator, Gallucci worked in a number of fields and was as equally interested in questions of scientific investigation as reinforcing the Counter-Reformation's concerns on doctrinal correctness and the value of *la lingua latina*, or the Latin language, as a galvanizing tool. But above all, Gallucci's passion and legacy can be seen in his lifelong profession as a tutor for the noble youth of Venice. As an educator, he always considered the value of his works in providing mnemonic devices to aid in memorization. This is the key to understanding why a non-specialist would attempt the ambitious task of translating a treatise that, according to experts in the field, was irrelevant to their craft, and why the target language chosen was Italian for a non-academic audience. His writing is then pragmatic in its intention, as are his selection of terms and choice of sentence structure. However, issues arose with the translation for *Della simmetria dei corpi humani* when considering that the source is taken from the Latin edition of the *Four Books on Human Proportion*, rather than the German original. This Latin edition had a number of errors which Gallucci admits hampered his efforts: "This I did, of course, after great effort due to the many mistakes that were in the Latin edition, and because the material itself is difficult to explain, as the author himself affirms."[1]

---

1   Giovanni Paolo Gallucci, "Dedication," *Della simmetria dei corpi humani, libri quattro* (Venice: Domenico Nicolini, 1591; repr. Venice: Roberto Meietti, 1594), 2v, https://archive.org/details/dialbertodurero00gallgoog/page/n4. As noted below, my translations are taken from the 1594 reprint.

The difficulty encountered on the part of the translator can be seen most clearly in his syntax, which often overlooks appropriate punctuation typical for Latin. Moreover, given the direct translation from the Latin edition into the target language, the result is awkward in early modern Italian, not to mention modern English.

As with many late Renaissance authors of his era, Gallucci often uses rather convoluted sentence structures. This is especially true when listing characteristics and their opposites. At the outset of a chapter, he nominally states the subject or body part under discussion only once (e.g. shoulder, head, eyelashes, etc.), and then implies this subject/body part throughout the chapter by describing each passion primarily through verbs and adjectives. As such, I have added breaks for clarity when different topics are included in the same run-on sentences or when required for comprehension in English. Similarly, where Gallucci uses a limited but consistent vocabulary to describe parts of the body and their attributes (e.g. *humido*), I use more nuanced terms that are appropriate to each context (e.g. dewy, misty, wet, moist). Additionally, the terms *imagine, pittura,* and *figura* are often implied or used interchangeably by Gallucci. He also uses the same term for both "eyelashes" and "eyebrows," requiring a careful evaluation of context. When translating the chapter headings, I was consistent in the translation of *imagine* as "figure," while in the chapters themselves, the more appropriate English terms have been used.

The *Della simmetria* was first published in 1591, and reprinted in 1594. This edition focuses only on the original contributions made by Gallucci in the Dedication, Preface, Life of Albrecht Dürer, and Fifth Book. My translation is made from the 1594 reprint, which does not include modernized spelling, accents, and punctuation, nor corrected grammatical or syntactical errors. The original paragraphs used by Gallucci have been retained and, whenever possible, the same sentence structure and punctuation. In the notes, I have discussed the word choices where appropriate and identified the context and sources the translator calls upon to support his arguments. Very often, he will quote directly from these sources without identifying the specific work or even the author. But even though the categories seem esoteric and random at times, he follows consistently the core established in Pseudo-Aristotle's *Physiognomica* when considering height, weight, hair, eye and skin color, relative moisture and temperature, as well as shape and variety of the different body parts. When other authors are cited, I have used the most recent translations available for the sake of clarity.

# Introduction

## 1. Proportion Theory: Disciplinary Intersections

In his treatise on the visual arts written a century before Giorgio Vasari, the Florentine sculptor Lorenzo Ghiberti (1378–1455) would claim that "only proportionality creates beauty."[1] This Renaissance axiom would be universally promulgated in treatises in the visual arts and beyond, forming the foundation on which academic training in the field is built. The belief that beauty is only possible through proper proportion would rarely be challenged, since it had its grounding in venerated classical texts that were reinforced by, and seen as demonstrable in, contemporary workshop practices. Regardless of their medium, painters, sculptors, and architects used human anatomy and proportion as the touchstone for their designs and to illustrate notions of harmony, commensurability, and symmetry. The interest naturally extended beyond the *botteghe*. The subject of human proportion and its relationship to beauty would be taken up repeatedly in early modern era treatises in a range of disciplines, not just the visual arts.[2] In fact, few subjects afford the intersection of so many disciplines, including theories of proportion derived from antiquity and applicable to the visual arts as well as music, anatomical studies, physiognomics and humoral theory, astronomy, astrology and cosmology, theology and philosophy, and even mnemonics and poetry. Given the range of topics, treatises on human proportion, traditionally

---

[1] "la proporzionalità solamente fa pulchritudine." Lorenzo Ghiberti, *I commentarii*, ed. Ottavio Morisani (Naples: R. Ricciardi, 1947), 2: 96.

[2] See, for example Luca Pacioli, *De divina proportione* (Venice: Paganini, 1509), *Summa de arithmetica, geometrica, proportioni et proportionalita* (Venice: Paganini, 1494), and *De viribus quantitatis* (Bologna: unpublished, 1500); Giovanni Battista della Porta, *De humana physiognomia, libri VI* (Vico Equense: Giuseppe Cacchi, 1586).

seen to be written for and the benefit of practicing artists, would find a much wider audience.[3]

By the end of the sixteenth century, there was already a rich body of scholarship dedicated to proportion theory on which to reference and build, testifying to the fertility of the topic.[4] It was within this confluence of topics and a mind for diverse readership that the Italian polymath-translator Giovanni Paolo Gallucci (1538–1621) published his *Della simmetria dei corpi humani* in 1591 (see Fig. 1).

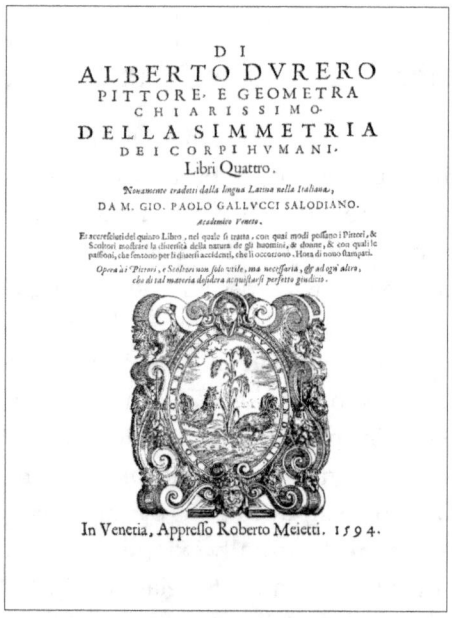

Fig. 1 Giovanni Paolo Gallucci, Title page, 1594. Woodcut from *Della simmetria dei corpi humani, libri quattro* (Venice: Roberto Meietti, 1594), https://archive.org/details/dialbertodurero00gallgoog/page/n4

---

3   Massimiliano Rossi, "Un metodo per le passioni negli Scritti d'arte del tardo Cinquecento," in *Il volto e gli affetti: fisiognomica ed espressione nelle arti del Rinascimento: atti del convegno di studi, Torino 28–29 novembre 2001*, ed. Alessandro Pontremoli (Florence: L.S. Olschki, 2003), 83–102.

4   From antiquity, scholars and artists had access to Vitruvius' *De architectura*, the Pseudo-Aristotelian *Physiognomica*, and Galen's *Doctrines*, while contemporary treatments included Alberti's *De re aedificatoria* and *Della pittura*, Albrecht Dürer's *Die Unterweisung der Messung mit dem Zirkel und Richtscheit* and *Vier Bücher von menschlicher Proportion*, Francisco de Hollanda's *Tractato de pintura antigua*, Giovanni Battista della Porta's *De humana physiognomonia*, and Gian Paolo Lomazzo's *Idea del tempio* and *Trattato*.

The treatise on human proportion was an Italian translation of the Latin edition of the *Vier Bücher von menschlicher Proportion* [Four Books on Human Proportion] (or *Proportionslehre*) by the German artist Albrecht Dürer (1471–1528).[5] The translation reveals the place of symmetry and proportion in the context of contemporary education, especially that of artists. In this new edition, Gallucci reintroduced the popular work in a more accessible language not only for Italian readers, but for those who traveled to study there. Dedicated to Maximilian III, Archduke of Austria, *On the Symmetry of Human Bodies* consists of the original four books by Dürer, published posthumously in 1528, along with a new Dedication and Preface, a short biography of the original author, and an additional Fifth Book. Serving as an epilogue for the encyclopedic treatment on human proportion theory, this last book contextualizes the preceding sections, relating them to other disciplines, and providing a philosophical framework within which to interpret them. The Fifth Book also importantly expands on Dürer's nascent interest in the proportions of the diversity of types of humans and extends this interest in diversity to elaborate systems of physiognomy and humoral readings. This expanded edition in Italian (reprinted in Venice, 1594) would become the most influential version, covering topics that were seen as central to arts education, connoisseurship, patronage, and the appreciation of the *studia humanitatis* in general. With regards to training in the visual arts, apprentices were expected to master more than mere ratios, stereometric measurements, or "ideal" canons. Furthermore, the exercise of copying illustrations like those of Dürer's were not simply ends unto themselves, nor were they merely intended to elevate the artist's social stature.

The study and use of such treatises can be better understood when considering their perceived necessity in the visual arts community. The demand for a new systematization of human proportions began with Leon Battista Alberti (1404–1472), the first art theorist of the Renaissance.[6] Later reiterated by Ghiberti, Alberti sets forth the

---

5   Albrecht Dürer, *Vier Bücher von menschlicher Proportion* (Nuremberg: Hieronymous Andreae, 1528).
6   Alberti dedicates Book II of his *Della pittura* (1435) to the problem of symmetry and harmony in *istoria*, focusing on the relationship of members. Leon Battista Alberti, *On Painting*, transl. John R. Spencer (New Haven; London: Yale University Press, 1966), 70–79.

premise that beauty was dependent on a harmony of parts in all of the arts, stating: "...thus we may say that beauty is a certain agreement and harmony of parts within that to which they belong with regard to a definite number, proportionality, and order, such as concinnity demands."[7] These three interrelated aspects of harmonious congruity described by Alberti (number, proportion, and order) were further discussed in his *Della pittura* [On Painting] of 1435, as he laid out the specific order in which an artist should proceed: "First one must observe that the single members fit together well, and they will fit together well if in relation to the size and measure, character, color, and other similar things they harmonize and form one unified beauty."[8] The harmonious arrangement of the parts of a particular work of art, or "the consonance and mutual integration of the parts," was central to the nature of beauty itself, and as such was defined by harmony and proper proportion.[9]

While this proportion system was most often applied to painting and/or sculpture, the belief that beauty was related to harmonious arrangement was in fact derived from ancient treatments of architecture and music, specifically Vitruvius and the Pythagoreans respectively, who believed such arrangements could be quantified in their value resulting from certain mathematical relationships.[10] These early formulations by Greek thinkers declared that beauty be expressed by the proportions of the parts, the arrangement of those parts, and the size, equality, and number of the parts and their interrelationships.[11] The most detailed and famous exposition for this valuation comes to us from the first-century BCE Roman architect Vitruvius, who, in *De architectura* [On

---

[7] Leon Battista Alberti, *De re aedificatoria*, ed. Giovanni Orlandi and Paolo Portoghesi (Milan: Edizioni Il Polifilo, 1966), 9: 5. Quoted in Erwin Panofsky, *Idea: A Concept in Art Theory* (Columbia: University of South Carolina Press, 1968), 54.

[8] Alberti, *On Painting*, transl. Spencer, 111.

[9] Alberti used various Latin and Italian words to describe the concept: concinnitas, consensus, conspiratio partium, consonantia, concordanza. Alberti, *De re aedificactoria*, 9: 5. Cited in Wladyslaw Tatarkiewicz, "The Great Theory of Beauty and Its Decline," *The Journal of Aesthetics and Art Criticism*, 31.2 (1972), 165–80, at 168, https://doi.org/10.2307/429278

[10] The terms *harmonia* and *simmetria* were connected to the theory after it was developed by the Pythagoreans. Tatarkiewicz, "The Great Theory of Beauty and Its Decline," 167; see also Christopher Celenza, *Piety and Pythagoras in Renaissance Florence, The Symbolum Nesianum* (Leiden: Koninklijke Brill NV, 2001).

[11] Tatarkiewicz, "The Great Theory of Beauty and Its Decline," 169.

Architecture], maintained that beauty in a building is achieved when all of its parts have the appropriate proportions.[12] The same was true in sculpture, painting, and in nature, which is illustrated in that it "has created the human body in such a way that the skull from the chin to the upper brow and hairline makes up one tenth of the entire length of the body."[13] As Vitruvius continued, he presented the proportions for a well-formed human figure that would inspire Leonardo da Vinci (1452–1519) and his *Vitruvian Man* (see Fig. 2).[14]

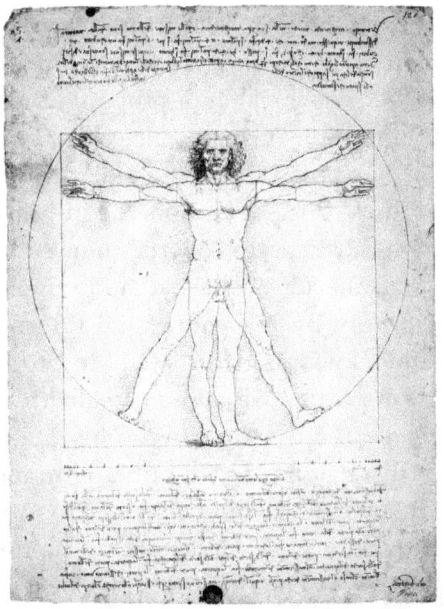

Fig. 2 Leonardo da Vinci, *Vitruvian Man*, ca.1485–1490. Pen and ink, 13 ½ x 9 5/8 in. Gallerie dell'Accademia, Venice. Wikimedia, Public Domain, https://commons.wikimedia.org/wiki/File:Leonardo_da_Vinci-_Vitruvian_Man.JPG

---

12  The treatise on architecture, also known as the *Ten Books on Architecture*, was rediscovered in 1414 by the Florentine humanist Poggio Bracciolini (Marcus Vitruvius Pollio, *The Ten Books on Architecture*, transl. M. H. Morgan (Cambridge, MA: Harvard University Press, 1926)). However, it would not be until ca.1450 that Leon Battista Alberti would finish his seminal treatise based on Vitruvius, *De re aedificatoria*.

13  Vitruvius, *De architectura*, 3: 1. Quoted in Tatarkiewicz, "The Great Theory of Beauty and Its Decline," 169.

14  Vitruvius, *The Ten Books on Architecture*, transl. Morgan, 73–75.

The Roman architect notes that a perfect circle may be formed using the navel of the figure whose arms and legs are extended laying on his back as the central point, his fingers and toes touching the circumference: "And just as the human body yields a circular outline, so too a square figure may be found from it. For if we measure the distance from the soles of the feet to the top of the head, and then apply that measure to the outstretched arms, the breadth will be found to be the same as the height, as in the case of plane surfaces which are perfectly square."[15] The circle and the square were considered perfect by the Pythagoreans and Plato, and thus were considered a reflection of the cosmos; man, in this instance, is understood as the microcosm, reflecting the universe, or macrocosm. In this view, it is possible to present the proper canon of proportions of human bodies in numerical terms, thus resulting in mathematical harmony.[16]

Throughout the Renaissance, artists and theorists had attempted to extrapolate from these ancient authors the ideal proportions for the human figure. Among them were Alberti, followed by Leonardo. Seen in the *Vitruvian Man*, the idealized and nude human figure became the exemplum of beauty by the end of the fifteenth century. Given that beauty was understood as tied directly to proportionality, so the systematization of proportion espoused by Alberti was thus elevated to an empirical science and doctrine.[17] With his anatomical knowledge expanded through dissections carried out later in his career in Milan, Leonardo sought to create a definitive set of proportions for artists to follow and for mathematicians to illustrate the nature of the cosmos.[18] These discoveries made by Leonardo in his proportion illustrations were published in Venice by a fellow mathematician, Luca Pacioli (1446/7–1517) in his *De divina proportione* [On the Divine Proportion] of 1509.[19]

---

15   Ibid., 73.
16   Vitruvius gave measurements for the ideal proportioned human figure as: the length of the head being equal to one-eighth of the total length of the body; the length of the face being equal to one-tenth of the total length of the body. Ibid., 73.
17   Joseph Leo Koerner, *The Moment of Self-Portraiture in Renaissance Germany* (University of Chicago Press: Chicago, 1993), 189; Erwin Panofsky, "The History of the Theory of Human Proportions as a Reflection of the History of Styles," in *Meaning in the Visual Arts* (Garden City, NY: Doubleday, 1955), 55–107, at 93–99.
18   Leonardo returned to Milan in 1506 and, despite a brief sojourn to Florence in 1508, remained there until being called to Rome in 1513 by Leo X. Frederick Hartt and David G. Wilkins, *History of Italian Renaissance Art*, 7th ed. (Upper Saddle River, NJ: Pearson/Prentice Hall, 2011), 468.
19   While Pacioli used Leonardo's proportion studies to illustrate his text, he also published widely on mathematics in works such as *Summa de arithmetica* and *De*

*Introduction* 7

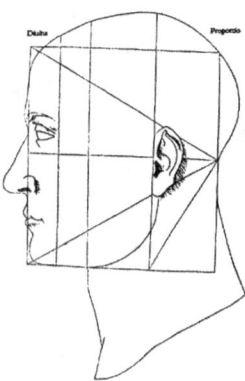

Fig. 3 Leonardo da Vinci, *Proportions of the Human Face*, 1509. Woodcut from Luca Pacioli, *De divina proportione* (Venice: Paganini, 1509), [n.p.]. Wikimedia, Public Domain, https://commons.wikimedia.org/wiki/File:Divina_proportione.png

The ideas of Pacioli were equally influential for Leonardo as they were for contemporary mathematicians.[20] In his treatise on mathematical proportions named for the golden ratio, Pacioli includes three books illustrating the applicability of Euclidian geometry to the visual arts.[21] The diagrams included from Leonardo helped reinforce the text, which assisted in popularizing geometric concepts beyond mathematical circles. The woodcut illustrations included the application of the golden ratio to a human model and Vitruvius' system of integers. Yet, while the first three books provide the descriptive overview with simplistic geometric diagrams illustrating the precepts presented, the illustrations that follow, including the woodcut of the human head illustrated by Leonardo, are mostly dedicated to geometric overlays of the alphabet, polyhedra, and various geometric shapes (see Fig. 3). These illustrations

---

    *viribus quantitatis*. G. M. Biggiogero, "Luca Pacioli e la sua 'Divina proportione,'" *Rendiconti dell'Istituto lombardo di scienze e lettere*, 94 (1960), 3–30.
20  Carlo Maccagni, "Augusto Marioni, Luca Pacioli e Leonardo," in *Hostinato rigore: Leonardiana in memoria di Augusto Marinoni*, ed. Pietro C. Marani (Milan: Electa, 2000), 55–60. See also Alba Ceccarelli Pellegrino, "Sacre Scritture, Divine Proportioni e Honnêteté nell'Architecture di Philibert de L'Orme," in *Il sacro nel Rinascimento: atti del XII convegno internationale. Chianciano-Pienza. 17–20 Luglio, 2002*, ed. Luisa Rotondi Secchi Tarugi (Florence: F. Cesati, 2002), 181–207. For more on the *Divina Proportione* of Pacioli and its connection to Ficino, see Albert van der Schoot, *De ontstelling van Pythagoras: Over de geschiedenis van de goddelijke proportie* (Kok Agora: Kampen, 1998), 95–98, 113–15, 338–39.
21  Pacioli utilized much of Euclid's work, including the theorem $a:b=b:(a+b)$.

were indispensable for proportion studies moving forward, but severely limited in their application of different parts of the human body to demonstrate the ratios inherent in their forms. It would be left to the artist, who would categorize all human types through proportion studies, to continue the work started by Pacioli and visualized by Leonardo.

While the first steps towards a doctrine of proportion had been taken in Italy with Leonardo, the relationship of beauty to a canon of proportions and mathematics was most fully expressed in pedagogical publications in Germany by Dürer. It should be noted that even Leonardo was unable to apply his own proportion and anatomical studies to his work given he painted little, or not at all, during the last decade of his life. Hence, the applicability of the study of proportion to practicing artists was still unclear. Dürer would spend nearly three decades working to remedy this ambiguity. He completed two treatises that would be the dominant basis for art theory in Renaissance Germany; their popularity and influence spreading with their subsequent translations. In 1525, *Underweysung der Messung*, or *Four Books on Measurement*, was published as a practical guide to geometric perspective for students of the arts;[22] and, in 1528, *Vier Bücher von Menschlicher Proportion*, or *Four Books on Human Proportion*, appeared a few months after his death. Taken together, the studies illustrated the Renaissance belief that mathematics formed the firm basis and grounding for the arts. This conviction is confirmed in the 1532 introduction to the Latin edition of the *Vier Bücher* by the translator Joachim Camerarius (1500–1574): "Letters it is true, he had not cultivated, but the great sciences of Physics and Mathematics, which are perpetuated by letters, he had almost entirely mastered. He not only understood principles and knew how to apply them in practice, but he was able to set them forth in words."[23] He did not come to this conclusion alone, for Leonardo was working with Pacioli in Venice at the same time Dürer made his second trip to Italy in 1505–1507.[24] Giovan Paolo Lomazzo's 1584 *Trattato dell'arte della pittura*,

---

22 Albrecht Dürer, *Die Unterweisung der Messung mit dem Zirkel und Richtscheit*, ed. Alvin E. Jaeggli and Christine Papesch (Dietikon-Zuerich: J. Stocker-Schmid, 1966).
23 Jan Białostocki, *Dürer and his Critics 1500–1971: Chapters in the History of Ideas Including a Collection of Texts* (Baden-Baden: V. Koerner, 1986), 28.
24 Enrico Giusti, *Luca Pacioli e la matematica del Rinascimento* (Florence: Giunti, 1994), 16.

*scultura ed architettura* [Treatise on the Art of Painting, Sculpture, and Architecture] attests to Dürer's knowledge of theoretical currents in Venice at the time, especially that of Vincenzo Foppa (1427/30–1515/16) and his drawings.[25] The interest in engaging with these debates on the classical canon can be seen in his *Fall of Man* from 1504 (see Fig. 4), an engraving created prior to his second trip where he demonstrates his understanding of the classical proportions based on statuary in Italian collections, such as the Belvedere Palace. Upon his return, having been in contact with Italian art and theory, Dürer sought to establish and define the mathematical relationships of the human body for the purposes of artistic representation more thoroughly.[26] But the nature and variety of those relationships with beauty were shifting.

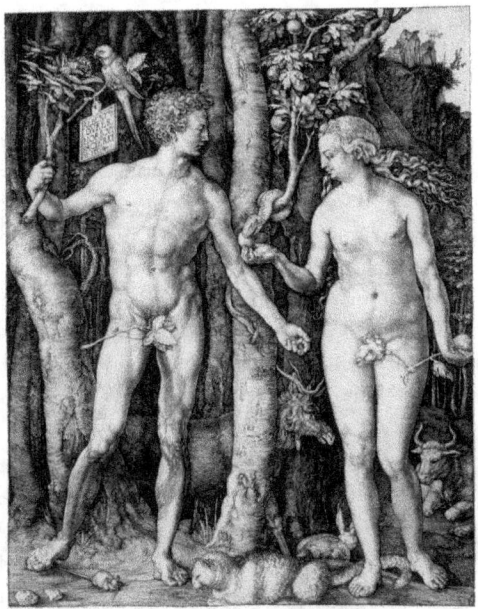

Fig. 4  Albrecht Dürer, *The Fall of Man*, 1504. Engraving, 9 7/8 x 7 5/8 in. Museum of Fine Arts, Boston. Wikimedia, Public Domain, https://upload.wikimedia.org/wikipedia/commons/9/90/Albrecht_D%C3%BCrer_-_The_Fall_of_Man_%28Adam_and_Eve%29_-_Google_Art_Project.jpg

---

25  Katherine Crawford Luber, *Albrecht Dürer and the Venetian Renaissance* (Cambridge, UK: Cambridge University Press, 2005), 106–07.
26  Panofsky, "The History of the Theory of Human Proportions," 56.

Dürer would come to realize that no single canon of beauty could be achieved; there was not a single, universal set of human proportions.[27] In his "Discourse on Aesthetics" — an essay on beauty published as a conclusion to the Third Book of his proportion studies — the artist started questioning the universal nature of beauty and investigating individual types due to variations, not only between men and women, but of different nationalities and races, as well as the infinite variety within each where we find figures that are tall, stocky, lean, noble, rustic, and leonine, each governed by humors. He writes: "Thus one finds among the human races all kinds and types useful for a whole variety of images, according to complexion."[28] The judgment of such a variety of figures as objectively beautiful is also questioned, as is our very ability to make such assertions:

> When we ask, how we shall make a beautiful image, some will say: follow the general taste. Others will not concede that, and neither do I. Without true knowledge, who will give us a reliable standard? I believe there is no one alive capable of perceiving the ultimate ideal of beauty embodied in the least of living creatures, let alone in a human being, which is the special creation of God with dominion over the rest of creation. I do admit that one person conceives and makes a more beautiful image and explains the natural basis of its beauty with more persuasive reasoning than others, yet not to the extent that it might not be yet more beautiful. Such a conception cannot arise in the human mind. Rather, God alone knows that, and if he were to reveal it, man would know it too. Divine truth alone, and no other, contains the secret of what the most beautiful form and measure may be.[29]

Taken together, the acceptance of the diversity of figural types and "infinite number of opinions" on beauty results in not one, but several canons of proportion.[30] Here, we find Dürer shifting away from idealizing, anatomically accurate models to more abstract "types."[31] In fact, the artist seems to have scarcely studied anatomy in detail at

---

27 Giulia Bartrum, ed., *Albrecht Dürer and His Legacy: The Graphic Work of a Renaissance Artist* (Princeton: Princeton University Press, 2002), 172.
28 Albrecht Dürer, "Discourse on Aesthetics," quoted in *Albrecht Dürer: Documentary Biography*, transl. Jeffery Ashcroft (New Haven: Yale University Press, 2017), 878.
29 Ibid., 875.
30 Ibid.
31 Koerner, *The Moment of Self-Portraiture in Renaissance Germany*, 154. For the changing nature of approach in Dürer's figures throughout his oeuvre see Ludwig Justi,

all. He treats the subject only once in his treatise.[32] Instead of detailing the musculoskeletal system, he focuses on the silhouette of the human figure and the ratios, measurements, and projections of the *external* aspects of the form in a total of four books. In these books, he assembles alternate sets of proportions that detail the different shapes and sizes of human figures, for which he took measurements from several hundred individuals.[33] He accumulated no fewer than twenty-six sets of proportions, plus an example of an infant's body with detailed measurements of the head, foot, and hand. Not satisfied with even this, he indicated ways of further varying these many types so as to capture even the abnormal and grotesque by strictly geometrical methods.[34]

The progression of the *Four Books on Human Proportion* reflects the author's own quest to identify a canon of beauty where an ideal is first established, elaborated on in detail, and, finally, questioned. The First Book introduces Dürer's fixed scale for a normal man and a woman, first at seven head lengths tall per figure (see Figs. 5 and 6).

Expanding on his division into fractional parts, he then explains how to proportion figures eight heads in lengths, then nine and ten heads in length. The height of the figures remains the same, demonstrating how the proportions change with each attenuation from stocky to lean (see Fig. 7). Each of the descriptions of the ten sets of proportions is accompanied with three woodcut illustrations representing the figures from the front, side, and back, along with the associated fixed measurements. Instructions on how to use the leading lines of perspective to find and apply the fixed points on a human model are then explained. Then, parts of the body are discussed with instructions on how to draw the hand and foot of a "strong man" (see Figs. 8 and 9), the heads of a man and a woman, and, finally, the book ends with a table of the proportions of a child from the front, side, and back (see Fig. 10). The head of the child is overlaid with a grid divided into the same thirteen units as the previous examples of the man and a woman, signaling greater precision to come.

---

    *Konstruierte Figuren und Koepfe unter den Werken Albrecht Dürers* (Leipzig: K. W. Hiersemann, 1902).
32  This can be found at the outset of the Fourth Book.
33  Bartrum, ed., *Albrecht Dürer and His Legacy*, 172.
34  Dürer, *Vier Bücher von menschlicher Proportion*, Third Book.

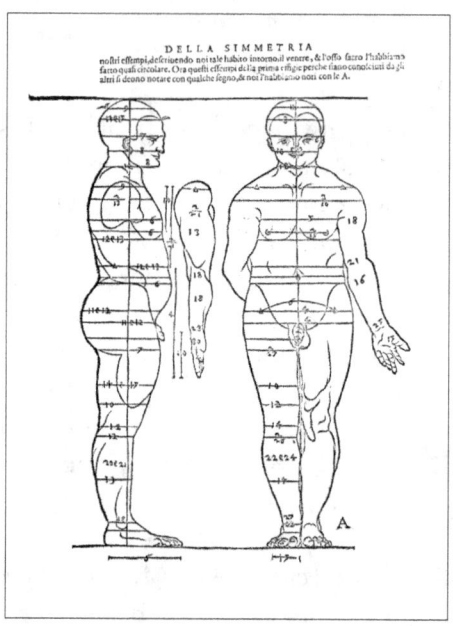

Fig. 5  Giovanni Paolo Gallucci (after Albrecht Dürer), *Proportions of a Man*, 1591. Woodcut from *Della simmetria dei corpi humani, libri quattro* (Venice: Roberto Meietti, 1594), First Book, 4vr, https://archive.org/details/dialbertodurero00gallgoog/page/n21

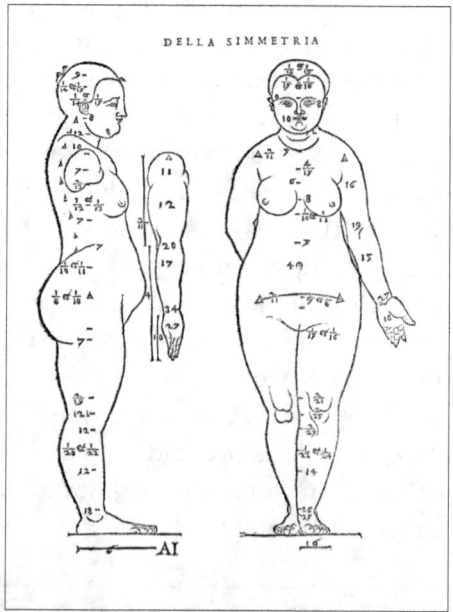

Fig. 6  Giovanni Paolo Gallucci (after Albrecht Dürer), *Proportions of a Woman*, 1591. Woodcut from *Della simmetria dei corpi humani, libri quattro* (Venice: Roberto Meietti, 1594), First Book, 6vr, https://archive.org/details/dialbertodurero00gallgoog/page/n25

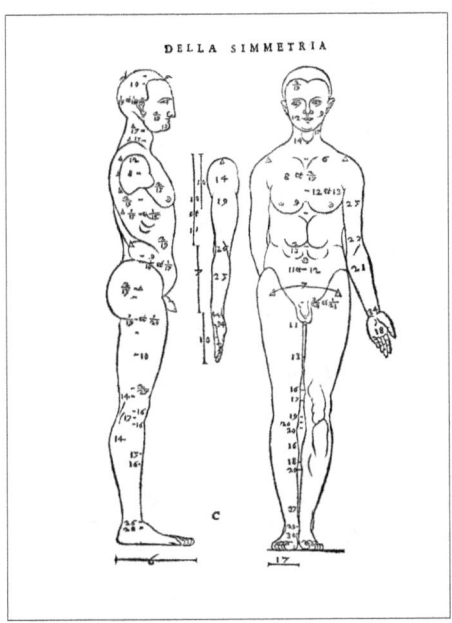

Fig. 7  Giovanni Paolo Gallucci (after Albrecht Dürer), *Proportions of a Man*, 1591. Woodcut from *Della simmetria dei corpi humani, libri quattro* (Venice: Roberto Meietti, 1594), First Book, 11vr, https://archive.org/details/dialbertodurero 00gallgoog/page/n35

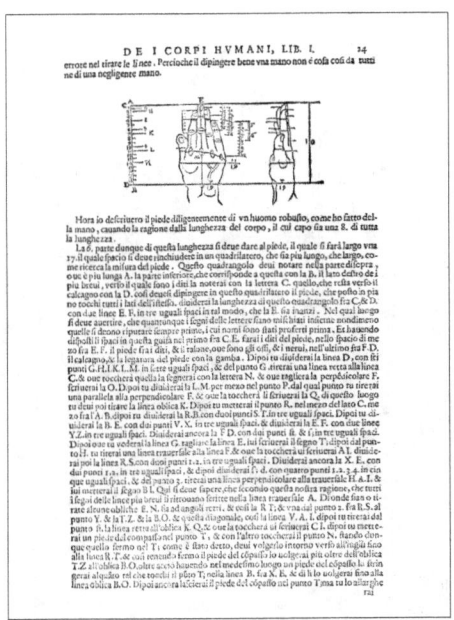

Fig. 8  Giovanni Paolo Gallucci (after Albrecht Dürer), *Proportions of a Hand*, 1591. Woodcut from *Della simmetria dei corpi humani, libri quattro* (Venice: Roberto Meietti, 1594), First Book, 24r, https://archive.org/details/dialbertodurero 00gallgoog/page/n61

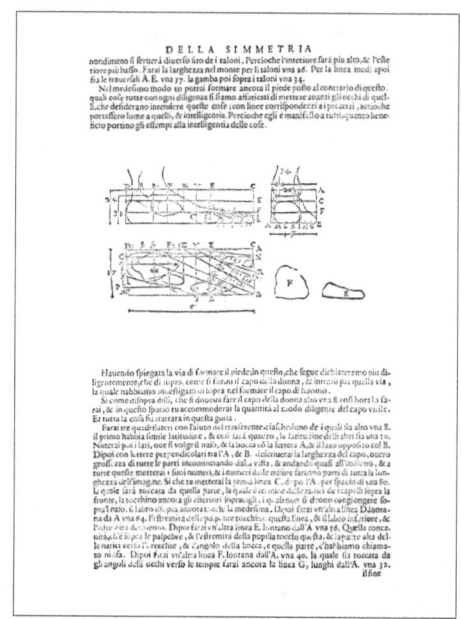

Fig. 9  Giovanni Paolo Gallucci (after Albrecht Dürer), *Proportions of a Foot*, 1591. Woodcut from *Della simmetria dei corpi humani, libri quattro* (Venice: Roberto Meietti, 1594), First Book, 26v, https://archive.org/details/dialbertodurero 00gallgoog/page/n65

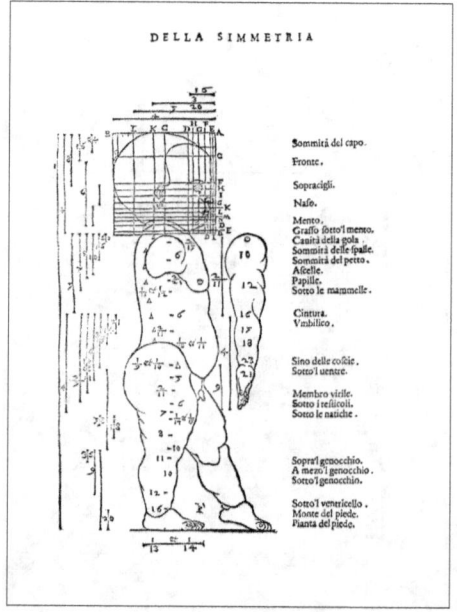

Fig. 10  Giovanni Paolo Gallucci (after Albrecht Dürer), *Proportions of a Child*, 1591. Woodcut from *Della simmetria dei corpi humani, libri quattro* (Venice: Roberto Meietti, 1594), First Book, 29r, https://archive.org/details/dialbertodurero 00gallgoog/page/n71

The Second Book elaborates on the sets of proportions introduced in the first and shows how to construct the normal figures of a man and a woman with a new principle, appending a more elaborate measurement scheme. Laying out his new method, Dürer writes:

> In this book I will teach how to measure the human figure with a rule, which I make either long or short depending on whether the figure be large or small. The rule I always make one sixth of the length of the figure... I then divide the rule into ten equal parts with each part called a *zall*; each *zall* I then divide into ten and call each tenth a *teil*; each *teil* into three and call each third a *trümlein*.[35]

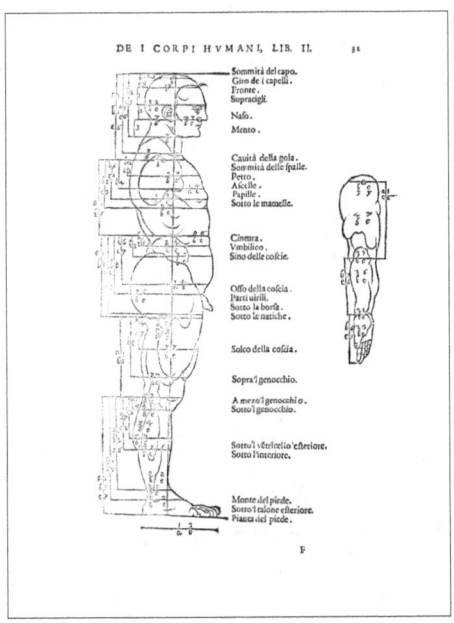

Fig. 11 Giovanni Paolo Gallucci (after Albrecht Dürer), *Proportions of a Man*, 1591. Woodcut from *Della simmetria dei corpi humani, libri quattro* (Venice: Roberto Meietti, 1594), First Book, 31vr, https://archive.org/details/dialbertodurero00gallgoog/page/n75

The overall figure would then be divided into six-hundred *teile*, which is a similar scale also used by Alberti. As in the First Book, he then divides each figure with three vertical lines representing the three sides of the figure, and then divides them further with horizontal lines (see Fig. 11).

---

35  Dürer, *Vier Bücher*, 2: 30v. All translations are my own, unless otherwise specified.

The resulting transections can now be expressed in a series of fractions of the whole height, as he introduced at the outset of the book. This is by far the longest of the books, with descriptions of sixteen figures in total. Here, we find men and women subdivided into fractions, and then shown with extended arms (see Fig. 12); a thin man and two corresponding women, also with arms outstretched, illustrate the various ratios and fractions with different bodily types. Lastly, we are shown two more ways in which to draw men's heads with seven and ten grid sections instead of the thirteen from the First Book.

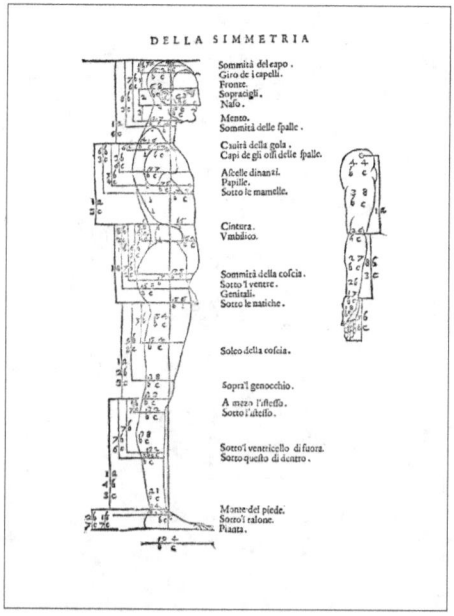

Fig. 12  Giovanni Paolo Gallucci (after Albrecht Dürer), *Proportions of a Man with Arms Outstretched*, 1591. Woodcut from *Della simmetria dei corpi humani, libri quattro* (Venice: Roberto Meietti, 1594), First Book, 46vr, https://archive.org/details/dialbertoduero00gallgoog/page/n105

The Third Book, as has been noted, opens with a discussion "Of the Variety of Figures," including those that are small, stout, large, long, thick, narrow, thin, young, old, lean, fat, ugly, pretty, hard, soft, and so on. Dürer describes these as "Words of Difference," meaning any word with a descriptive quality that "may be divided and differentiated from the one first made."³⁶ Investigating this difference, and the role that proportionality plays within it, Dürer then shows how to distort various figures of men and women, as well as their body parts. He begins with heightening or shortening the body and limbs (see Fig. 13), which continues those original ten sets of proportions outlined in the First Book and how changing the head lengths alter the figures. Next, he alters the proportions of faces and parts of the head in order to demonstrate how a normal face may be distorted to form that of a fool, African, and other "monstrosities" (see Fig. 14). The reasoning behind such exercises, the artist explains, is to ensure that "out of many trials he [the artist] may attain manifold knowledge."³⁷ The variations of faces are distorted by expanding or contracting sections of the grid superimposed over the men's heads. The woodcuts here remove the grid and instead outline the various angles of the ears, brow, nose, and chin.

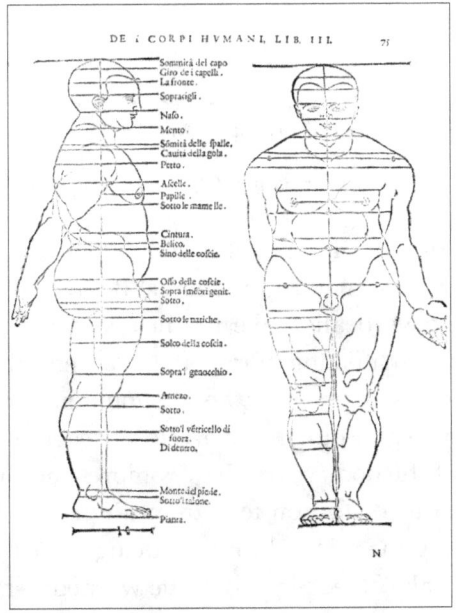

Fig. 13 Giovanni Paolo Gallucci (after Albrecht Dürer), *Proportions of a Man*, 1591. Woodcut from *Della simmetria dei corpi humani, libri quattro* (Venice: Roberto Meietti, 1594), First Book, 75vr, https://archive.org/details/dialbertodurero00gallgoog/page/n161

---

36  Ibid., 3: 70r.
37  Ibid., 84r.

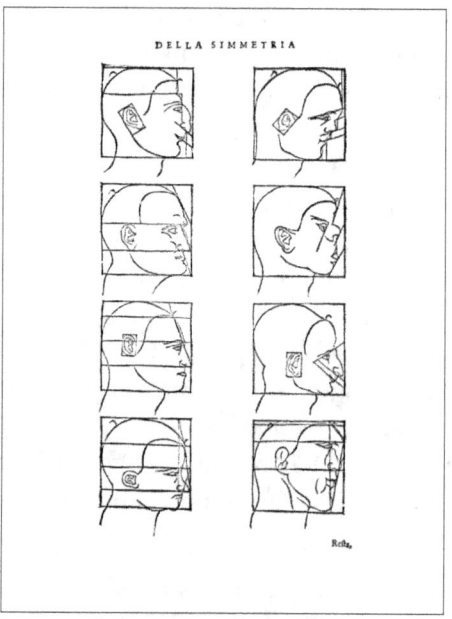

Fig. 14 Giovanni Paolo Gallucci (after Albrecht Dürer), *Faces of a Man*, 1591. Woodcut from *Della simmetria dei corpi humani, libri quattro*, Roberto Meietti, Venice 1594, First Book, 84vr, https://archive.org/details/dialbertodurero00gallgoog/page/n177

Another process of adjusting pions is demonstrated throughtaking the first woman and fourth man from the First Book (see Fig. 15), who are no longer bisected vertically. Like the heads in the previous section, Dürer shows that in making horizontal markers aligned at specific points on the body — eyes, brow, neck, shoulders, breast, hips, knees, ankles, and so on — and moving them closer together or further apart, the proportions of the bodies stretch or compress accordingly. The final illustrations take this distortion to extremes with the figures of a man and a woman using the method for producing monstrous figures, only "for strangeness' sake" (see Fig. 16).[38] The warped perspectival scheme seen to the left of each figure aligns with the various points of the body, such as the top of the head, nose, top of the shoulders, chest, bottom of the breast, bottom of the buttocks, and so on until the bottom of the feet. The figures are narrow, lanky, and attenuated; their necks are greatly elongated along with the mid-torso and legs. These distortions

---

38   Ibid.

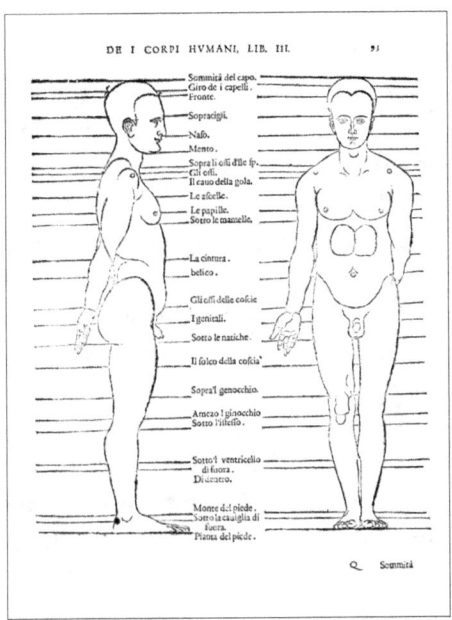

Fig. 15 Giovanni Paolo Gallucci (after Albrecht Dürer), *Proportions of a Man and a Woman*, 1591. Woodcut from *Della simmetria dei corpi humani, libri quattro* (Venice: Roberto Meietti, 1594), First Book, 94vr, https://archive.org/details/dialbertodurero00gallgoog/page/n197

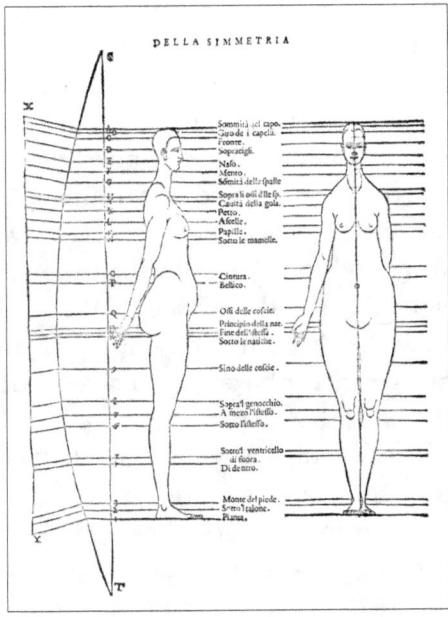

Fig. 16 Giovanni Paolo Gallucci (after Albrecht Dürer), *Proportions of a Woman*, 1591. Woodcut from *Della simmetria dei corpi humani, libri quattro* (Venice: Roberto Meietti, 1594), First Book, 100v, https://archive.org/details/dialbertodurero00gallgoog/page/n207

produce figures that would rarely be used, Dürer admits, which calls into question their usefulness. Gallucci, in his Fifth Book, uses such distortions to elaborate on his physiognomic reading of Dürer's system. Regardless of the seemingly rare use of such figures, editors of the text found it necessary to include an explanation at the end of the text culled from Dürer's own memoranda books. This section became known as the "Aesthetic Excursus," outlining his defense of variety in human figures and of the impossibility of understanding that which is beautiful, which concludes the Third Book.

The Fourth Book explains and demonstrates how to modify the posture of figures described in the First and Second Books. In this introduction, Dürer outlines seven "Words of Difference," specifically bent-at-an-angle, curved, turned, twined, stretched, shortened, and shifted. Each is then illustrated with a series of woodcuts with simple lines angled, curved, transecting one another, and so on. Next, the artist demonstrates how to draw heads in various positions with the methods of perspective outlined in his *Four Books on Measurement*. These are shown in grid overlays from the front, side, below, and at a three-quarter angle. The heads are followed by seven illustrations of human figures (see Fig. 17), each demonstrating one of the "Words of Difference," which bend forward or backward, curved or at an angle. Each figure is first shown from the front and the side bisected vertically with the horizontal markers connecting the two views; for instance, the top of the head may be seen frontally and connected to that seen in profile. The next page finds a contour drawing of the same figure from the front and the side with shadows surrounding them, emphasizing their outlines and how the final version would appear without the overlay. Lastly, Dürer describes the manner in which artists can construct geometric boxes that can be modified according to the qualities discussed earlier (e.g. turned, stretched, and shortened). These imaginary boxes are then used to illustrate the human form and various members of the body (see Fig. 18), all enclosed in box-like sections. This particular method of enclosing the body in imaginary boxes, and how it might be used to assist in foreshortening, was adopted from Italian studies. Lomazzo claims that the practice was invented by Luca Cambiari, but Dürer's publication would become much more influential.

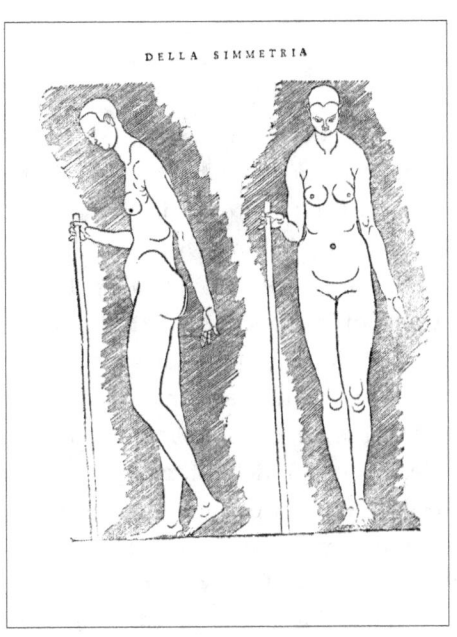

Fig. 17 Giovanni Paolo Gallucci (after Albrecht Dürer), *Proportions of a Man and a Woman*, 1591. Woodcut from *Della simmetria dei corpi humani, libri quattro* (Venice: Roberto Meietti, 1594), First Book, 113vr, https://archive.org/details/dialbertodurero00gallgoog/page/n231

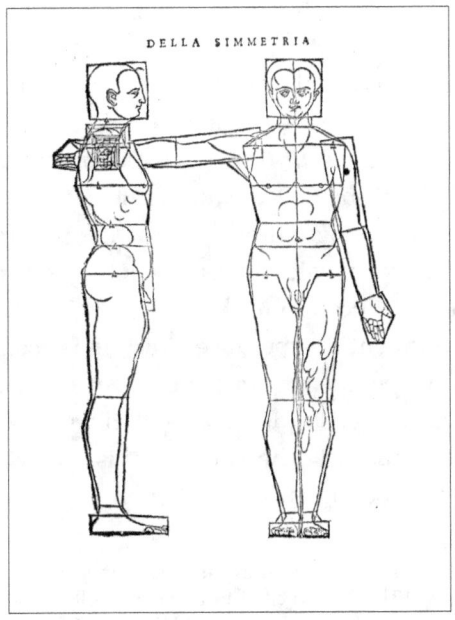

Fig. 18 Giovanni Paolo Gallucci (after Albrecht Dürer), *Proportions of a Man and Body Parts*, 1591. Woodcut from *Della simmetria dei corpi humani, libri quattro* (Venice: Roberto Meietti, 1594), First Book, 113vr, https://archive.org/details/dialbertodurero00gallgoog/page/n241

Part of the treatise's subsequent broad appeal would be due to Gallucci's Italian translation and his additions to the work, which were intended to address the notion of utility in proportion studies. From the outset, Dürer had in fact intended his *Four Books on Human Proportion* to be useful for students of the arts and as a practical reference guide when constructing a variety of figures. In his draft for the introduction to the study, he wrote: "It is most necessary for a man to be competent in some thing by reason of the usefulness which arises therefrom."[39] Yet, while his *Four Books on Measurement* would be accepted for its practicality and clear presentation of perspective exercises, many of those in the corresponding proportion treatise were questioned with regards to their usefulness in daily workshop practice. Not only were the grotesque and monstrous distortions questioned, the very measurement system of Dürer would come under scrutiny in academic institutions as impractical.[40] Additionally, while the "Aesthetic Excursus" attempts to frame what the artist was trying to accomplish with his proportion studies, touching briefly on art theory, metaphysical notions of beauty, astrology, physiognomy and humoral theory, he failed to thoroughly address the significance of his exhaustive enterprise to these various disciplines.

In 1591, Gallucci would address concerns of utility with his translation and additions to the original edition in his expanded version and translation of Dürer's *Four Books* — *Della simmetria dei corpi humani*. More importantly in his new Dedication, Life, Preface, and, principally, his Fifth Book, the pedagogue-translator places the original *Four Books* in the broader context of late sixteenth-century education in various fields of study. The Dedication to the Habsburg Archduke Maximilian opens with the argument that because painting is used to communicate goodness and move people to piety, it is "...surely true that the utility that comes from painting is more divine than would derive from other art, mechanical or liberal."[41] The value of this art, which is capable of expressing "all of the passions that are generated in our souls," extends

---

39 Albrecht Dürer, "Drafts for the Introduction to the Book on Human Proportion (Planned in 1512–1513)," 176f; cited in Elizabeth Gilmore Holt, *Literary Sources of Art History* (Princeton: Princeton University Press, 1947), 279.

40 The so-called "particle" (*Trümlein*) used by Dürer was equal to less than a millimeter, which, Panofsky argues, went beyond artistic usefulness ("The History of the Theory of Proportions," 103–04).

41 Gallucci, "Dedication," *Della simmetria*, 2v.

beyond the theological.[42] The success of *De divina proportione*, for instance, lay in the successful illustration of mathematical principles in the woodcuts of Leonardo. In the same fashion, Gallucci reminds the archduke that astrology, geometry, and all of the liberal arts, are unable to explain their concepts "without using painting to make illustrations with lines, figures, and often even with colors, as can clearly be seen through their books."[43] Thus, at the outset he demonstrates the relevance of the material to various disciplines.

Turning to the translation, Gallucci states that, aside from two Latin editions, the *Four Books on Human Proportion* were nearly impossible to find, and so he took to translating the work "with great effort," as he says, "due to the many mistakes that were in the Latin edition, and because the material itself is difficult to explain."[44] Nevertheless, this was insufficient to explain the great importance of the original Four Books, making it necessary to add a Fifth Book, "which is taught through the authority of philosophers and poets, who, along with those colors and lines, can explain both the natural and the incidental passions of the souls of men."[45] The *paragone* of painting and poetry is further addressed in the following Preface where, citing the authority of Aristotle, Gallucci reiterates a familiar Renaissance axiom: "...painting is a poem that is silent, and poetry is a painting that speaks."[46] This argument structures much of his new Fifth Book, which comprises fifty-eight chapters[47] with descriptions of temperaments, characters, and their respective, "appropriate" body parts often accompanied by excerpts from famous poets, both ancient and modern, to validate Gallucci's assertions. These physiognomic and humoral readings further find their classifications framed in another system — that of astronomy and astrology, as one would expect from Gallucci given his professional preoccupations. In fact, the attempts made to categorize and map the human body were understood by art-theorists, astrologers and natural philosophers as an attempt to reveal the macrocosm of the universe, and thus uncover its "divinely" ordered beauty in the microcosm of man. Such information

---

42  Ibid.
43  Ibid., 3v.
44  Ibid.
45  Ibid.
46  Gallucci, "Preface," *Della simmetria*, [n.p.].
47  Chapter 45 is repeated twice in the numerical sequence that lists only up to Chapter 57.

concerning the structure of the universe was seen as necessary for artists to understand in order to reveal the beauty buried in imperfect material existence.

A complex system, which had evolved to categorize the links between humans and the natural world, assisted artists in understanding these correspondences. Derived from the ancient Greeks, and more specifically the Pythagorean tetractis (where the number four was venerated), all phenomena would be arranged into a series of quadripartite schema; each of which had overlapping relationships that allowed them to be superimposed. Beginning with the macrocosm, the universe was believed to be comprised of four basic elements, which also made up the human body, transformed by way of food through the organs into the four humors. These elements were connected to fluids in a system of associated qualities: hot/warm, dry, cold, and wet/moist. The stars, planets, and seasons were likewise affected by these relationships, as the seasons reflected the ages of man. Thus, the humors corresponded to the four elements of the earthly world, which in turn corresponded to the four ages of man, as well as to the twelve zodiac figures, divided into four groups of three. This correspondence further extends into all areas of the universe and the nature of man: everything was seen as interrelated. Such a complex series of interrelationships required authors to develop mnemonic devices to assist their readers. Gallucci thus uses proportion studies as a structuring conceit for explaining these overlapping classifications to a much wider audience.

Two treatises that used another type of mnemonic machine had, at that time, been recently published, and Gallucci would have been familiar with these. In 1584, Gian Paolo Lomazzo (1538–1592) published his massive encylopedic study on painting, *Trattato dell'arte della pittura, scultura ed architettura*. This exhaustive work has seven chapters, each devoted to one of the seven parts of painting. In order to explain the correspondences between microcosm and macrocosm, the Milanese theorist also published his *Idea del tempio della pittura* [The Idea of the Temple of Painting] in 1590 (a year before Gallucci's *Della simmetria*). The treatise takes the *Trattato*'s divisions and introduces them as a Temple of Painting with seven pillars representing the planetary temperaments as an architectural structure in order to organize the various manners of their governors, such as Michelangelo, Leonardo and Andrea Mantegna. The design of this temple, Lomazzo openly admits, was inspired by Giulio Camillo's *L'Idea del theatro* [The Idea of the Theater] (published posthumously in 1550). Aspiring to encapsulate the whole of the universe, Camillo's theater adapted a Vitruvian plan with a large auditorium divided by seven aisles, each dedicated to one of the planetary deities.[48] These were further divided into seven rows that ascend from floor level to the upper tiers representing the terrestrial and celestial spheres of the world. In each row and aisle were doors painted with significant memories designed to recall a specific location in the universe. The whole of the theater was designed so as to allow the human mind to grasp nothing less than the macrocosm. Camillo would even go on to build examples of this theater in Venice and Paris in the early 1530s.[49] The ascension from the earthly to heavenly realms also inspired Lomazzo in his *Idea del tempio* to adopt the Neoplatonic belief in cosmic influence that implies a harmonious correspondence between various links in a chain.[50]

The organizing principles at play in the *L'Idea del theatro* and *Idea del tempio* would influence many early modern authors.[51] In the case of Gallucci, understanding the universe in the microcosm of man afforded a similar opportunity as conceiving of a subject in architectural terms. He would also adopt a similar Christianized Neoplatonism, even quoting a passage by Marsilio Ficino (1433–1499) directly from Lomazzo.[52] Moreover, while Lomazzo understood his treatise as another type of mnemonic machine, inviting a student of art to experience artists and their corresponding temperaments in architectural terms, Gallucci presented a similar Neoplatonic argument for understanding beauty in the visual arts, but in a more practical fashion. Whereas Lomazzo's

---

48  Giulio Camillo, *L'idea del theatro* (Venice: Agostino Bindoni, 1550), 47–62, https://archive.org/details/bub_gb_R59T2RFRhjkC/page/n10/mode/2up. For commentary, see Frances Yates, *The Art of Memory* (Chicago: University of Chicago Press, 1966), 129–59; Giulio Camillo, *L'idea del theatro*, ed. Lina Bolzoni (Milan: Adelphi, 2015).

49  The version in Venice was able to accommodate two people at a time (Yates, *Art of Memory*, 155–56).

50  Giovanni Paolo Lomazzo, *Idea del tempio della pittura* (Milan: Paolo Gottardo Pontio 1590, https://archive.org/details/bub_gb_YC59KugXgdQC/page/n4/mode/2up; repr. ed. Robert Klein, Florence: Istituto Nazionale di Studi sul Rinascimento, 1974), chapters 9 and 26. See also Panofsky, *Idea*, 95–99.

51  Yates, *Art of Memory*.

52  Gallucci, *Della simmetria*, 5: 124–35, quoting from Lomazzo, *Idea del tempio*, chapter 26.

*Idea del tempio* would serve as the introduction, or as Lomazzo puts it, its "abstract and summary,"[53] for his earlier encyclopedic *Trattato*, so too does Gallucci's *Della simmetria* serve as an indexical epilogue for Dürer's *Four Books*. Placing the technical work of Dürer in its broader intellectual and theoretical context, and using it as a mnemonic device to understand these various disciplines, Gallucci reveals his true intent. First and foremost, Gallucci was a pedagogue and tutor for the Venetian elite, along with his profession as a translator and tutor. His work was, therefore, designed for two distinct, yet interdependent audiences: the amateur-connoisseurs and collectors who patronized the works produced with the guidance of such *trattati*, and the artists who sought to speak to an audience well-versed in classical themes and who expected to see references made to them. Speaking as a non-specialist, the pedagogue creates both an accessible translation of an immensely influential proportion treatise and an indexical reference guide for appending to that a broader understanding of physiognomics, humoral theory, astronomy, and poetics to hang on Dürer's original armature, enlivening and expanding on it in a vivid fashion.

## 2. Gallucci: Translator, Academician, Pedagogue

The life of Gallucci, and his professional interests, greatly shaped the final form of his translation and the framing devices that he chose. While his *Della simmetria* is the only text on the visual arts that Gallucci translates or writes, in this work, he by no means limits its scope of interest to astronomy (one of Gallucci's primary areas of interest). As a pedagogue, translator, and author, he would demonstrate his interest in diverse fields in no less than twenty-two books, pamphlets, and translations, ranging from astrological medicine, astronomy and astronomical instrumentation, mathematics, pedagogy, philosophy, theology, linguistics, optics, the military arts, and the art of memory.[54] His activity can be framed in the context of a group of writers, editors, and translators in the sixteenth century. These *poligrafie* were active in the major publishing centers in Italy (Venice, in the case of Gallucci and

---

53  Lomazzo, *Idea del tempio*, 372.
54  Germana Ernst, "Gallucci, Giovanni Paolo," *Dizionario Biografico degli Italiani*, 56 vols (Rome: Instituto dell'Enciclopedia Italiana, 1925–present), LI (1998), 327–65, 366–74.

of many others).⁵⁵ A true *homo universalis*, the academician and tutor was equally concerned with questions of how scientific investigation could reinforce the Counter-Reformation's concerns on doctrinal correctness and the value of *la lingua latina* as a galvanizing tool for the dissemination of information.⁵⁶ In his extensive oeuvre, which was remarkably produced in under two decades, we can see why he was such a sought after teacher. Many of the works are dedicated specifically to the education of young students and often introduce complicated and ponderous topics, like Dürer's proportion studies or Aristotelian logic. At the end of such works, Gallucci appended synopses, tables, and indexes to aid readers' retention of the material. Though a passionate educator, he always returned to his adoration of astronomy and mathematics and worked diligently to bring the benefits of the sciences to the attention of policy makers, such as popes, cardinals, and high-ranking Church officials. He also dedicated many of his works to them and explained that astronomy should be considered separate from the more superstitious interpretations found in modern astrological divination.⁵⁷

Despite the vast number of extant works we have from Gallucci, little has survived in the way of biographical information. Therefore, despite the important role he played in the fields of science and the arts, little has been published on his life. Most of what is known is derived from the publications to be briefly reviewed here. Born to Giovanni Battista Gallucci in 1538 in Salò near Brescia in Lombardy, Gallucci studied Salò and in Padua before moving to Venice. At the age of twenty-six, Gallucci, along with eighteen others, found the Accademia degli Unanimi on 20 May, 1564, in Gallucci's hometown.⁵⁸ The school was dedicated to promoting harmony among its *literati* members, and its title, "Academy

---

55  See Filippo Bareggi, *Il mestiere di scrivere. Lavoro intellettuale e mercato librario a Venezia nel Cinquecento* (Rome: Bulzoni, 1988); P. Trovato, *Con ogni diligenza corretto. La stampa e le revisionieditoriali dei testi letterari italiani (1470–1570)* (Bologna: il Mulino, 1991); and Paolo Cherchi, *Polimatia di riuso: mezzo secolo di plagio* (Rome: Bulzoni, 1998).

56  Giuseppe Brunati, *Dizionarietto degli uomini illustri della Riviera di Salò* (Milan: Pogliani, 1837), 70–72, https://archive.org/details/bub_gb_v93CFmYBx4kC/page/n4/mode/2up

57  Lynn Thorndike, *History of Magic and Experimental Science*, 8 vols (New York; London: Columbia University Press, 1923–1958), V: 8, 151, 155; VI: 60, 158–60.

58  Camillo Camilli, *Imprese illustri di diversi, coi discorsi di Camillo Camilli, et con le figure intagliate in rame di Girolamo Porro Padouano...*, 3 vols (Venice: Francesco Ziletti, 1586), II: 72–74, 93–95, https://archive.org/details/impreseillustrid04cami/page/n4/mode/2up

of the Unanimous" indicates the nature and motivation of their venture. The emblem of the academy was a swarm of bees accompanied by the motto *idem ardor* ("The same flame").[59] According to Camillo Camilli in his *Imprese illustri di diversi* [Impressions of Famous Men] of 1586, Gallucci would adopt the sobriquet the "the tolerant one" (*tolerante*), a fitting selection given his lasting dedication to educating youth over the course of his career.[60] Moving from Salò to Padua to study at the Università degli Studi di Padova, his first printed work as a student there took the form of a Latin text of an oration held in the cathedral of Padua in 1579 by the acting rector, Dominko Zlatarič (1558–1609) from the Republic of Ragusa (modern day Croatia). Unfortunately, the first edition in Padua was full of errors. Embarrassed, Gallucci condemned it as an unauthorized printing and had the oration reprinted in Venice in September of 1580.[61]

After studying in Salò and Padua, Gallucci settled in Venice, which he would praise as the most vibrant center of intellectual life of the time. He spent the rest of his life devoting himself to private tutoring of young nobles, as well as to writing and printing his books. His pedagogical activity can be demonstrated in works such as his *De formis enthymetatum* [On Types of Syllogism] published in 1586, where he sought to expose his students to the *Rhetoric* of Aristotle.[62] In this work, Gallucci lamented how neglected Aristotle's *Rhetoric* was, and restated the importance of learning Aristotle's precepts for further study in the *studia humanitatis*. As a foundation for further study, he strove in the work to reduce the variety of Aristotelian arguments into specific, easily understood rules.[63] The assertion of the primacy of Aristotle, whom Gallucci refers to as *il Filosofo*, as an ancient authority would remain constant throughout the rest of Gallucci's career. Indeed, in his later works, Gallucci would

---

59 Giovanni Ferro, *Teatro d'imprese*, 2 vols (Venezia: Sarzina, 1623), II: 431; Simone Biralli, *Delle imprese scelte*, 2 vols (Venezia: Giovanni Battista Ciotti Senese, 1600) I: 2; II: 80.
60 Camilli, *Imprese illustri diverse, coi discorsi*, I: 72.
61 In this work, the praises of the young poet are accompanied by a warm eulogy of the Republic of Ragusa (modern day Croatia). Enrico Damiani, "Contributi del dr. Petar Kolendič allo studio delle fonti italiane nella letteratura serbo-croata," *Giornale storico della letteratura italiana*, 100 (1932), 163; Leonardo Cozzando, *Della libraria bresciana* (Brescia: Gio. Maria Rizzardi, 1685), 188.
62 Giovan Paolo Gallucci, *De formis enthymetatum* (Venice: P. Marinelli, 1586).
63 Bongianni Grattarolo, *Historia della Riviera di Salò* (Brescia: Vinc. Sabbio, 1599), 16, 71.

cite Aristotle as validation when he wished to reinforce a declaration. Yet, the philosopher is not referenced as an end unto himself, but as part of a classical education used to frame investigations into other fields, and to discern the legitimacy of these other fields. This interest in foundational education is continued in two short pamphlets that follow *De formis*, each dedicated to the instruction of young students. The first, *De iis in quibus Venetians pueri erudiendi sunt, ut sic suam Rempublicam administrare possint* [On the Manner in Which Venetian Children Are Educated so that They Can Manage Their Republic], explicitly deals with "Venetian youth and the matters in which they are instructed so that they can manage their own Republic" and the importance of education to the future of the Venetian Republic, especially that of the city's future rulers: the aristocracy. The second publication, *De usu tabularum*, demonstrates practical ways in which to accomplish this task through organizational techniques and "use of records." Here, Gallucci introduces a learning strategy that would guide the rest of his career: he insists on the usefulness of drawing up indexes and synopses of authors to be studied. This allows for a greater breadth of information to be covered, while maximizing a pupil's time. The method is drawn from previous scholars who also published on a variety of topics, including the great defender of orthodox Aristotelian logic, Giacomo Zabarella (1533–1589), Marco degli Oddi (1526–1591), professor of medicine at the university of Padua, and the Persian polymath Avicenna (980–1037), whose interests paralleled Gallucci's publishing on a range of topics.[64] Gallucci especially encouraged his students to use the tables given in Avicenna's five-volume medical encyclopedia, *The Canon of Medicine*, given their highly effective facilitation of learning, and their capacity

---

64 Avicenna published on a wide variety of topics, including astronomy, alchemy, geography and geology, psychology, Islamic theology, logic, mathematics, physics, and poetry. See Avicenna, *The Life of Ibn Sina*, ed. And transl. William E. Gohlman (Albany, NY: State University of New York Press, 1974); Avicenna, *Remarks and Admonitions*, ed. S. Dunya and S. Zayid (Cairo: Organisation Générales des Imprimeries Gouvernementales, 1960); Avicenna, *The Canon of Medicine*, ed. I. a-Qashsh (Cairo: [n.p.], 1987); Avicenna, "Essay on the Secret of Destiny," transl. G. Hourani, in *Reason and Tradition in Islamic Ethics* (Cambridge, UK: Cambridge University Press, 1985), 227–48; Avicenna, "The Book of Scientific Knowledge," ed. and transl. P. Morewedge, in *The Metaphysics of Avicenna* (London: Routledge, 2017), 11–109; Avicenna, *The Metaphysics of Healing*, transl. Michael Marmura (Provo, UT: Brigham Young University, 2005); and Avicenna, *The Book of Salvation*, transl. F. Rahman (Oxford: Oxford University Press, 1952).

to help readers memorize learnt material in an orderly way. Over the course of his career, Gallucci would publish such reference guides to assist in the retention and explanation of complex issues pertaining to logic and classical education, which he then applied to the emerging sciences of astronomy, anatomy, physiognomy, and proportion theory.

The interest in including reference guides at the ends of his works, as he did with his translation of Dürer's *Four Books on Human Proportion*, can be seen in many early publications. One of these earlier publications that demonstrate Gallucci's own interests is an edited volume (published 1584 in Venice, on the request of the Bishop of Modena) of various tracts on astrological medicine, including works by the celebrated astrologer Johann Virdung von Hassfurt, Johannes Stadius' translation of the *Iatromathematica* [Iatromathematics] by Hermes Trismegistus, Jacobus Antonius Mariscottus of Florence's translation of the pseudo-Galenic *Prognostica ex egroti decubitu* [Prognosis for the Decubital Sick], as well as Ficino's *Consiglio contro la pestilenza* [Council Against Pestilence] and *De vita libri tres* (or *De triplici vita*) [Three Books on Life].[65] Taken together, the works share the mid-sixteenth-century view that states that the purpose of astronomy is calculative in nature, while astrology would then judge and interpret these findings. The volume concludes with selections from Gallucci's own work on astrological tables and on constructing the "celestial figure, finding the part of fortune and of the liver, dividing the zodiac, essential and incidental dignities of the planets, and the times appropriate for taking medicine."[66] He would follow this interest with his own writing on mathematical and astronomical topics in texts that describe how to build and use observational tools and various types of sundials. In 1590, he published two treaties, dedicated to Pope Sixtus V (1521–1590), on the use of astronomical instrumentation: *Della fabrica et uso del novo horologio universale* [On the Creation and Use of the New Universal Clock] and *Della fabrica et uso di un novo stromento fatto... per fare gli orologi solari* [On the Creation and Use of a New Instrument to Make Sun Dials]. These treatments would be followed by a large-format volume dedicated to Cardinal Francesco Morosini of Venice entitled

---

65   Giovanni Paolo Gallucci, ed. and transl., *Ionnis Hasfurti...de cognoscendis et medendis morbis ex corporum coelestrium positione libri IIII cum argumentis et expositionibus Ioannis Paulli Gallucci Saloensis...quibus accesserunt in eandem sententiam auctores alii...* (Venice: ex officinal Damiani Zenarii, 1584).

66   Thorndike, *A History of Magic*, V: 158.

*Speculum Uranicum* [The Mirror of Urania] (1593), which distinguished the different senses in the theory of the planets and by astrologers.[67] He also provided another method for dividing the zodiac into twelve houses.[68] The following year came a new volume, this time in Italian, entitled *Della fabrica et uso di diversi stromenti di astronomia e cosmografia* in which the author went through the different types of observational instruments, both ancient and modern.[69]

Despite the impact of the above-mentioned works, the text that would make Gallucci a staple in libraries throughout Europe was his *Theatrum mundi et temporis* [Theater of the World and Time] published in Venice in 1588 (reprinted in 1589). The publication came in the wake of an increased interest in celestial mapping in the second half of the century, spurred on by the papacy (especially that of Pius IV and Gregory XIII).[70] In the same manner, the highly influential treatment was dedicated to Sixtus V (Felice Peretti di Montalto), and even invokes the name of the pope in the hope that he would promote the study of celestial science by establishing an astronomical observatory in Rome. The author notes the favorable conditions of clear skies and elevated hills and also claims that the renowned German Jesuit mathematician and astronomer Christopher Clavius (1538–1612) would be on hand to assist in such investigations.[71] Published shortly after the Sixtus V's papal bull, in which astrology and other methods of divination were banned, Gallucci's *Coeli et terrae* [Sky and Earth] (1586) reiterates the importance and nobility of celestial science properly understood and purified from any aspects of superstition.[72] He then discusses the nature and qualities of each planet, their radiation and the influence which

---

67   Giovanni Paolo Gallucci, *Speculum Uranicum in quo vera loca tum octavae sphaerae tum septem plaentarum...ad quodlibet datum tempus ex Prutenicarum ratione colliguntur, una cum regulis fabricandi duodecim coeli domici'ia ex Regiomontano et Alcabitio et dirigendi significatores* (Venice: Damiani Zenarii, 1593), https://www.e-rara.ch/zut/doi/10.3931/e-rara-49833

68   Gallucci, *Speculum Uranicum...*, III: 6.

69   Giovanni Paolo Gallucci, *Della fabrica et uso di diversi stromenti di Astronomia e Cosmographia* (Venice: Ruberto Meietti, 1597).

70   This is especially evident in the creation of the *Galleria delle carte geografiche* in the Vatican and in the *Sala dei brevi*. Jacob Hess, "On Some Celestial Maps and Globes of the Sixteenth Century," *Journal of the Warburg and Courtauld Institutes*, 30 (1967), 406–09, https://doi.org/10.2307/750759

71   Pietro Riccardi, *Biblioteca matematica italiana*, 3 vols (Modena: Società tipografica, 1870–1880), I (1870–1872), part 1, coll. 567–73.

72   Thorndike, *History of Magic*, V: 8, 151, 155; VI: 60, 158–60.

they exert on human bodies through the positions of the zodiac; these, in turn, are discerned by way of their distinguishing characteristics of masculine or feminine, commanding, obedient, or hostile.[73] Not only did particular zodiacal signs affect different bodies in general given propinquity, but, Gallucci enumerates, individual members of the human body were likewise affected.[74] This, in turn, necessitated the drawing up of astrological diagrams (or the figures of constellations in medical practice) in order to ascertain when and what type of treatment to administer. The sign under which a patient was born was also paramount and would determine a variety of preexisting conditions both in body and mind. Though he insisted that the practice among physicians was not contrary to the Council of Trent, nor the papal bull of Sixtus V banning astrological divination, he warned physicians to use the information only as a guide and not to attribute too much authority to it.[75]

The seminal publication would set forth the framing devices that he would extend to his works on the visual arts. The numerous reprints and even a Spanish translation attest to the popularity of the work.[76] In the following century, the work would be published under a different title, clarifying that this *Theater of the World and Time* "explains celestial bodies by means of instruments and figures."[77] The text is divided into six parts and dedicated to the description and mapping of the entire celestial and terrestrial worlds, placing the inferno inside the earth in ten concentric circles.[78] As the first modern celestial atlas, the maps use a coordinate and trapezoidal system of projection that allow for the accurate determination of the star positions, which were derived from the Copernicum catalog. In this and earlier publications, such as *Coeli et terrae*, Gallucci also consulted the celestial models of Ficino.[79] Here,

---

73 Giovanni Paolo Gallucci, *Theatrum mundi et temporis...ubi astrologiae principia cernuntur...nunc primum in lucem editum* (Venice: J. B. Somascum, 1588), 3: 478; Thorndike, *History of Magic*, V: 158–59.
74 Gallucci, *Theatrum mundi...*, 3: 2; 8: 129, 220.
75 Ibid., 3: 2; Thorndike, *History of Magic*, VI: 159.
76 Miguel Perez translated the work into Spanish, which was published in Granada in 1606, 1612, and again in 1617.
77 Giovanni Paolo Gallucci, *Coelestium corporum et rerum ab ipsis pendentium accurata explicatio per instrumenta, rotulas et figuras* (Venice: J. A. Somaschum, 1605).
78 Thorndike, *History of Magic*, V: 60; Gallucci, *Theatrum mundi...*, 2: 10, 15, 38; Rossi, "Un metodo per le passioni negli Scritti d'arte del tardo Cinquecento," 84–85.
79 Ernst, "Gallucci, Giovanni Paolo," 741.

Gallucci intended to offer an informative text that was accessible to non-specialists with simple mathematical demonstrations illustrated with appropriate images; the descriptions are presented as pictures of the items under discussion, and the text is illustrated with forty-eight maps of the Ptolemaic constellations with corresponding mythological figures. The personification of constellations anthropomorphizes the universe, much as in Vitruvian cosmology. The attempt is made, as such, to categorize and relate the heavens and earth through the microcosm-macrocosm pair. Moreover, the very title of Gallucci's work reveals its relationship to other mapping systems that were common around the same time. There were several publications throughout the sixteenth and seventeenth centuries that used *Theatrum* as an encompassing description.[80] Of the most famous and influential of those discussed by Frances Yates was Giulio Camillo's (ca.1480–1544), which was also developed in Venice.[81] In his *L'Idea del theatro*, which was lost after his death, Camillo sought to encapsulate "a complete treatment of its theme."[82] The notion of a "Theater" was widespread in many diverse treatments from calligraphy to women's fashion, and it came to denote an extensive treatment of any given subject. From astrological treatments, Yates also noted that the *Utriusque cosmi historia* [History of the Two Worlds] by Robert Fludd (1574–1637) represented Shakespeare's *Theatrum Mundi* [Theater of the World].[83] The same can be said of Gallucci's *Theatrum mundi et temporis*, whereby the "Theater" sought to encapsulate all of the "world and time."[84] The Venetian system developed by Camillo was not merely an exhaustive treatment. The Theater itself was a "mnemotechnic tool" originally intended to provide orators with well-ordered material for their thoughts.[85] A system of "places and images" had been arranged,

---

80  Aside from Elias Ashmole's *Theatrum chemicum britannicum* of 1652, Father Charles Scribani wrote his *Amphitheatrum Honoris* in 1605. See Anthony Grafton and William Newman, eds, *Secrets of Nature: Astrology and Alchemy in Early Modern Europe* (Cambridge, MA: MIT Press, 2006), 15–16.

81  Yates, *Art of Memory*, 160–72.

82  Richard Bernheimer, "Theatrum Mundi," *The Art Bulletin*, 38.4 (1956), 225–47, at 226, https://doi.org/10.1080/00043079.1956.11408342

83  Yates, *Art of Memory*, 321–41.

84  Gallucci, *Theatrum Mundi*, http://digital.onb.ac.at/OnbViewer/viewer.faces?doc=ABO_%2BZ186392402

85  In the Renaissance, the "memorative art," which was founded by Cicero and Quintilian in antiquity, allowed the augmentation of man's natural power of recall by a discipline extending its scope. Bernheimer, "Theatrum Mundi," 226.

"sufficient for the location and management of all human concepts and of all things in this world, not only those which belong to the various fields of knowledge, but also to the noble arts and the mechanical."[86] Through the careful classification of all knowledge, an ideal ordering of all possible topics, the human mind itself could be made a perfect reflection of the macrocosm. Gallucci would refer again to Camillo's *L'Idea* and the art of memory in 1599 when translating, updating and completing the *Margarita philosophica* [The Philosophical Pearl] (1503) of Gregor Reisch (1467–1525), a popular encyclopedia reprinted several times since the beginning of the century.

The interest in universal mapping, illustrated in Camillo's system, was well-known in Venetian academic circles around mid-century. In 1560, Federico Badoer (1519–1593), founder of the Accademia della Fama, sent a letter to the Procurators of St Mark's concerning the "Program of Universal Knowledge." In the letter, Badoer sets forth that his academy seeks the sole rights to publishing in Venice, and states that he wishes to be put in charge of the library, so that it might better impress visiting dignitaries. The quest for a "universal knowledge" was further elucidated as Badoer continued:

> In short, the whole nobility, and anyone else of whatsoever condition, who comes to listen to the matters under discussion in the Academy everyday, both morning and evening, will obtain two precious and delicious forms of nourishment. One of these is the taste of true virtue, the left hand of God on earth and the empress of the world, served by the twenty queens who are the sciences and faculties. What I mean to say is that not only will everything which the whole of mankind needs to know for necessity, profit, contentment and self-enhancement become attainable, but, as I can readily affirm, everything concerning all the virtues will be attained easily by listening to the discussions and their resolutions.[87]

The same interests were carried on by Gallucci, who went on to found, along with eight others, the second Accademia di Venezia on 21 June, 1593. This academy was established with the intention of continuing the activities of the first, dissolved by the death of its organizer Badoer in the

---

86 Giulio Camillo, "Trattato del'imitatione," in *Opere* (Venice: Domenico Farri, 1581), quoted in Bernheimer, "Theatrum Mundi," 229.
87 David Chambers and Brian Pullan, eds, *Venice: A Documentary History 1450–1630* (Oxford: Blackwell, 1992), 366.

same year.[88] The first head publisher for the new academy was Giovan Battista Ciotti (1560–1625), who would be the printer, publisher, editor, and agent for the poet Giambattista Marino. Ciotti would be followed by Andrea Muschio as publisher.[89] The activities of the new academy were protected by the aristocracy of the city, a relationship maintained from the original, for Badoer had claimed that the "nobility in particular will receive... instruction" as part of the institution's mission.[90] The arrangement would come naturally to Gallucci, for he was already a tutor to young nobles, retained for his vast knowledge and dedicated pedagogy.

Having already gained notoriety for his *Theatrum*, and with a wider acceptance of his discipline in other fields, Gallucci turned his attention to several works that would become some of his most influential publications. Along with his original publications, Gallucci was an accomplished translator, practicing intently. In the late 1580s, he translated into Latin the *Catechismus in symbolum fidei* [The Catechism of the Faith], originally written in Spanish by the Spanish Dominican friar Luis de Granada (1505–1588). In the dedication to Francesco Morosini, the Venetian Cardinal who served as the Bishop of Brescia, he writes that the Latin language is the bond that unites the different members of the Catholic Church, while vernacular languages are limited to the borders of individual countries.[91] Although Granada's work is little known today, Gallucci would call on him in his *Della simmetria*, along with Aristotle, on the relationship between beauty and utility. Ironically, despite his impassioned plea in defense of *la lingua latina*, his greatest success at teaching and popularizing these themes are seen in his vernacular translations of historical and scientific texts. In 1593, he translated a classic manual of optics from the thirteenth century, *I tre libri della perspettiva commune dell' illustriss* [Three Books of the Shared Perspective of Famous Men] by John Peckham (ca.1240–1292).[92] In the

---

88  Johann Gottlob Lunze, *Academia Veneta seu della Fama in disquisitionem vocata* (Leipzig: [n.p.], 1701), 28–33.
89  Michele Maylender, *Storia delle accademie d'Italia*, 5 vols (Bologna: Capelli, 1926–1930), V: 444–46.
90  Rossi, "Un metodo per le passioni negli Scritti d'arte del tardo Cinquecento," 84.
91  Vincenzo Peroni, *Biblioteca bresciana*, 3 vols (Brescia: Bettoni 1818–23), II: 91–94.
92  Giovan Paolo Gallucci, *I tre libri della perspettiva commune dell' illustriss* (Venice: published by the heirs of G. Varisco, 1593).

dedication to the apostolic secretary Giovanni Battista Cucina, Gallucci ingeniously praises the advantages of the optical doctrine presented with a simile relating the clarity provided by faith and ability to discern good and evil to the tools that allow us to discern with our external senses. He encourages his audience to be grateful to those who offer tools that allow us to discern the truth from falsehood, as Peckham communicates clearly and comprehensively every rule of perfect vision. The following years saw the translation of a natural history of India, originally written by the Spanish Jesuit, José de Acosta,[93] along with two martial treatises. The first was a translation from the Spanish of the *Specchio e disciplina militare* [The Mirror of Military Discipline] by Francisco Valdes,[94] followed by a short *Discorso intorno al formare uno squadrone di gente e di terreno* [Discourse on Forming a Squadron of Soldiers on the Field] written by Gallucci himself. The two treaties would be included in an influential collection of texts on the military arts, *Fucina di Marte*, published in 1641.[95]

The successes of his vernacular publications demonstrate their efficacy in disseminating information to a broader audience than Latin afforded, especially as readership shifted. When he turned his attention to the arts, Italian was a natural choice as artists and art collectors from around Europe flocked to Italy in the sixteenth and seventeenth centuries for training and education and/or to purchase works for their collections back home. Reference material for artists and guides for amateur-connoisseurs and patrons were in high demand. Gallucci would capitalize on both markets with one of his most influential vernacular translations, his *Della simmetria*, first published in 1591 and again in 1594. The translation can be situated within the context of other translations carried out in this period by Granada, Peckham, and Valdes. Just the same, given the additions made by Gallucci and the fact that he arguably updated and completed the treatise on proportion (along with the fact that he would also use the art of memory inspired by Camillo's *L'idea*), his translation of the *Four Books on Human Proportion* finds its

---

93   Giovan Paolo Gallucci, *Historia naturale e morale delle Indie* (Venice: B. Basa, 1596).
94   1598 edition available at https://books.google.co.uk/books?id=ghtaAAAAcAAJ&pg=PT1#v=onepage&q&f=false
95   Lelio Brancaccio, *Fucina di Marte: nella quale con mirabile industria e con finissima tempra d'instruzioni militari s'apprestano tutti gli ordini appartenenti à qual si voglia carico essercitabile in guerra* (Venice: Giunti, 1641), 327–65 and 366–74, https://gallica.bnf.fr/ark:/12148/bpt6k51208j.image

counterpart in his translation of the *Margarita philosophica* of 1599. As in his *Margarita*, Gallucci again appends new sections, including a Dedication, Preface, short biography of the original author, and the Fifth Book, which, as stated on the title page of the Fifth Book, aims to teach "...the way painters are able to express the passions of the body and soul in the figures of men and women with lines and colors, whether they be natural or incidental, according to the opinion of philosophers and poets."[96]

The connection to the volume's original author is made clear, as well as the contemporary religious environment in Europe. In his Dedication to the Habsburg archduke, Gallucci celebrates painting's ability to penetrate into the most intimate parts of our soul through the eyes: "...as windows to our soul, while locked in this prison, penetrates into the most secret parts, eliciting pain, joy, desire, and fear." The great emotional appeal and strength of painting is further associate with the power of religious iconography, as Gallucci cites images of the Holy Fathers, Michelangelo's *Last Judgment*, and the works of Dürer. He demands: "Who does not burn of the love of Christ our Lord having seen his life represented with diligence...?"[97] The utility of this enterprise is thus defended in post-Tridentine terms as a powerful tool for the Church's use. Moreover, the decision to dedicate the translation to Maximilian III was a strategic consideration by the translator. Although the importance of the archduke can be understated by modern historians (due to the fact that he did not attain the title of King of Poland), his position as the Archduke of Austria, as well as a contender to the Polish crown, ensured that he was not merely a figurehead. In addition to his own political importance, given the proximity of Austria to Venice, he was also influential through his brother Rudolf II, who ruled as the Holy Roman Emperor throughout Gallucci's most prolific period.[98] In currying favor with the neighbors to the North, Gallucci translated one of the most famous German publications into Italian and upheld the importance and ideas of its original author. The connection of the dedicatee of the *Della simmetria* to Dürer's greatest patron later in his career, the Holy Roman Emperor Maximilian I, would have been intentional on the part

---

96  Gallucci, *Della simmetria*, 5: 124v.
97  Ibid., 2v.
98  Paula S. Fichter, *Emperor Maximilian II* (New Haven: Yale University Press, 2001), 202.

of Gallucci and would also not have gone unnoticed by his intended audience. As he notes in his Life of Albrecht Dürer, the artist was sought after by many kings and princes, "and, in particular, by Maximilian..."[99] Yet the connection between Venice and the ruling Habsburg line goes beyond Dürer working for Maximilian I. In fact, Maximilian II had an important influence on Venice, and was in turn affected by the politics of Venice, having negotiated peace with the Turks in 1567. The Eastern power was a continued threat to Venetian trading in the Mediterranean.[100] Throughout much of the sixteenth century, the Austrian Habsburgs were at war with the Turks, while all of Italy was armed against the increasing threat to religion and trade.[101] Moreover, the connection between the two political powers was further evinced through art and artists. Just as Dürer had traveled to Venice and worked there, from 1557 onward the Venetian Jacopo da Strada (1515–1588) stayed at the court of Maximilian II and acted as an art consultant and courtier.[102] In as much as can be inferred, there was a maintained Venetian presence and interest in the Germanic courts throughout the sixteenth century, clarifying the dedication by Gallucci and conscious connection with Dürer.[103]

While the Dedication praises Dürer, his original work, and his connection to the Habsburgs, pointing to the role art of art in promoting religious causes, the following Preface establishes the theoretical structure of the treatise. At the outset of the Preface, he emphasizes "the similarity that painting has with poetry" in that "...painting is a poem that is silent, and poetry is a painting that speaks."[104] Whereas one uses words and the other images, each seeks to imitate natural and imaginary

---

99  "Egli s'acquistò il favore, & liberalità de i Rè, & Prencipi, & in particolare, di Massimilano..." Gallucci, "Life of Albrecht Dürer," Della simmetria, 4r.
100  Fichter, Emperor Maximilian II, 76, 98.
101  Ibid., 124; Michael Hughes, Early Modern Germany, 1477–1806 (Philadelphia: University of Pennsylvania Press, 1992), 64–65.
102  Elisabeth Scheicher, Die Kunst- und Wunder Kammer der Habsburger (Vienna: Molden, 1979), 137–40; Dirk Jacob Jansen, "The Instruments of Patronage: Jacopo Strada at the Court of Maximilian II, A Case Study," in Kaiser Maximilian II. Kultur und Politik im 16. Jahrhundert, ed. F. Edelmayer and A. Kohler (Vienna: Verlag für Geschichte und Politik, 1992), 182–202. Maximilian also brought to his court Giuseppe Arcimboldo and Bartholomäus Spranger. For more on Habsburg patronage, see Karen Jutta MacHardy, War, Religion and Court Patronage in Habsburg Austria (New York: Palgrave Macmillan, 2003).
103  This was continued by his son Rudolf II, who was a significant patron of the arts as well. Hughes, Early Modern Germany, 65.
104  Gallucci, "Preface," Della simmetria, [n.p.].

subjects. In order to accomplish this, the painter and poet alike need to know how to appropriately characterize various types of figures, and must be able to comprehend the virtues and passions of the human soul. This requirement is couched in terms of physiognomics, where the extreme diversity of the appearance of individuals is connected to their natural inclinations and how their character and psychological disposition can be related to various animal traits: "For instance, the man who has some similarities with the members of the lion is robust and strong, as seen from experience, but if he has legs similar to that of the deer, he is shy."[105] Therefore, talented painters should make themselves familiar with the different body parts, their functions, and the natural disposition of each. The Fifth Book is devoted to laying out the appropriate figures and their various members based on character traits and disposition. In this way, the Fifth Book acts as a very useful index that follows and supplements Dürer's original *Four Books*.

Gallucci's *Della simmetria* thus merges his expertise in pedagogy — as seen in his early publications concerned with the education of young Venetians, such as *De usu tabularum* — with his passion and ability in scientific and technical matters; matters that in turn constituted an interest of his patrons. In the various topics Gallucci touched on in his fairly short career, he would commonly include additional synopses, indexes, columns, and tables to assist the reader in gleaning more from the work with reference guides. The Fifth Book provides such an indexical reference where the work of the original author is contextualized, directing readers to the appropriate book after finding the character or body part to be represented. For artists, this was a very user-friendly manual that could be referenced as needed in the workshop as a practical guide. In the descriptions, Gallucci also includes excerpts from the most famous ancient and modern literary works. The summary of these classical sources could also function as a sort of study guide that would assist artists in engaging scholars in conversations. On the other hand, the canonical works associated with the visual arts provided a range of students another mnemonic device to remember their classical studies as part of their education. Finally, those interested in patronizing or appreciating the arts would find the material edifying and would gain a greater understanding and prestige in their circles.

---

105 Ibid.

Gallucci is still known primarily as an pedagogue and translator, while his numerous publications on astronomy and astronomical instrumentation cement his legacy in the history of natural science. The importance of celestial cartography at the dawn of the seventeenth century and the discoveries of Galileo Galilei (1564–1642), a contemporary of his, provide the historical backdrop to locate him in the intellectual milieu of his day. Yet, that same environment saw a dynamic exchange of ideas across disciplines. Gallucci saw the applicability of his own field of study and others to that of the visual arts. In fact, it would be impossible to fully understand a subject such as painting without drawing on various interpretative strategies. In the case of *Della simmetria*, these would include the relationship between the sister arts of poetry and painting; physiognomy and its ability to reveal the "passions of the soul;" and cosmology as revealed through proportion theory.

## 3. *Ut pictura poesis*: Sister Arts

The relationship between poetry and painting was well established by the time of Gallucci's translation. Of the various disciplines with which students of the visual arts must be familiar, poetry was considered necessary for both the insight that it provided to the *affetti dell'animo* and its role as the acknowledged sister art of painting. As Gallucci opens in his Preface, "...painting is a poem that is silent, and poetry is a painting that speaks."[106] The Renaissance axiom was attributed to Horace in his *Ars Poetica* and became central to art theory and education from the fifteenth century onward. In his *I commentarii* [Commentaries] (1447), Lorenzo Ghiberti (1378–1455) was among the first theorists to extend Vitruvius' instructions for the education of the architect to the painter and sculptor.[107] Vitruvius had specified the disciplines in which an architect should be knowledgeable in his *De architectura* by stating:

> Let him be educated, skillful with the pencil, instructed in geometry, know much history, have followed the philosophers with attention,

---

106 Though most famously cited from Horace's *Ars Poetica*, the oft-repeated Renaissance axiom "Poema pictura loquens, pictura poema silens" ("poetry is a speaking picture, painting a silent [mute] poetry") is first recorded by Plutarch. Plutarch, *De gloria Atheniensium*, ed. C. J. Thiolier (Paris: Presses de l'Université de Paris-Sorbonne, 1985), 3.347a.

107 Julius von Schlosser, *Lorenzo Ghilberti's Denkwürdigkeiten (I commentarii)*, 2 vols (Berlin: Bard, 1912), I: 102.

understand music, have some knowledge of medicine, know the opinions of the jurists, and be acquainted with astronomy and the theory of the heavens.[108]

The painters and sculptors of the fifteenth century were to aspire to gain the knowledge that the ancients saw as necessary to carry out their trades, encompassing the branches of the *quadrivium*: music, arithmetic, geometry, and astronomy. Ironically, it was Leon Battista Alberti (1404–1472), whose primary educational concern was that artists should learn geometry, who bundled Vitruvius' specifications into one general recommendation that artists be as knowledgeable as possible in all of the liberal arts. Unwittingly, Alberti would influence the addition of the *trivium* to complete the seven branches of learning with the addition of grammar, logic, and, most importantly, rhetoric. He suggested an artist cultivate associations with poets and orators, who "are full of information about many subjects" and could aid the painter in "preparing the composition of an *'historia.'*"[109] As the first theorist of the Renaissance to demonstrate a pragmatic understanding of art education, Alberti advised "the studious painter to make himself familiar with poets, orators and other men of letters, for he will not only obtain excellent ornaments from such learned minds, but he will also be assisted in those very inventions which in painting may gain him the greatest possible praise."[110]

The paralleling of the aims of both poetry and rhetoric with painting and sculpture found the two inextricably intertwined towards the end of the century with the Horatian creed of *ut pictura poesis* firmly establishing painting as mute poetry.[111] Following tradition, Gallucci cites Aristotle's *Poetics* to confirm the assertion, stating that the two arts "...live together

---

108 Vitruvius, *I dieci libri dell'architettura di Marcus Vitruvio*, transl. Daniel Barbaro (Venice: Francesco de'Franceschi Senese & Giovanni Chrieger Alemano Compagni, 1567), 1: 1, quoted in Vitruvius, *The Ten Books on Architecture*, transl. Morgan, 5f.
109 Cecil Grayson, ed., *Leon Battista Alberti on Painting and Sculpture: The Latin Texts of "De Pictura" and "De Statua"* (London: Phaidon Press, 1972), 95. Pomponio Gaurico's ideal sculptor (De sculptora, 1504) would be "very instructed in all of the arts and also cultured in literature." See also Guarico's debate with sculptors on the necessity of the study of literature as opposed to art in Paola Barocchi, ed., *Scritti d'arte del cinquecento*, 3 vols (Milan: Riccardo Ricciardi, 1971–1977), II: 130, 1315ff.
110 Grayson, *Leon Battista Alberti on Painting and Sculpture*, 97.
111 Rensselaer Lee, *Ut Pictura Poesis: The Humanistic Theory of Painting* (New York: W. W. Norton, 1967). Also see Elizabeth Hazelton Haight, "Horace on Art: Ut Pictura Poesis," *The Classical Journal*, 47.5 (1952), 157–62, 201–02.

in balance, because both... imitate natural and artificial things — one with the words, represents things to the ears, while the other one with its colors in the eyes of mortals."[112] The interrelationship of painting and poetry had further elevated the status of the artist, while simultaneously placing greater demands on him. The Venetian theorist and dramatist Lodovico Dolce (1508–1568) argued in his dialogue *L'Aretino* (1557) that: "painters have always been appreciated for it appears that they surpass the rest of humanity in intellect and spirit."[113] For Dolce, "well-developed intelligence" and knowledge of historical narrative and poetry were essential for the facility in *invenzione*, mastery of one's subject, and adherence to the laws of propriety.[114] Moreover, like Alberti, Dolce did not find it necessary for the artist to be a man of letters. He suggests instead that the artist merely "keep in close touch with poets and men of letters."[115] In the same fashion, Gallucci's audience, which included readership outside of arts practitioners, were made familiar with the field of the visual arts, while simultaneously reinforcing their own education and standard humanist reading list. Expertise and first-hand knowledge of the creative process is not a prerequisite for a full appreciation of *Della simmetria*. In fact, the primary goal of the work was, arguably, to introduce new topics of study while referencing and reinforcing the standard educational curriculum that developed over the last two centuries.

The curriculum of this liberal education expected from families of means was codified in Italy in the sixteenth century and was only slightly modified in the seventeenth.[116] It commenced with education in elementary and then grammar schools where students would first gain a command of the vernacular followed by a working knowledge of Latin. After the desired level of literacy had been achieved, usually between twelve and fourteen years of age, artists would then be apprenticed to a local master, while upwardly mobile students would

---

112 Gallucci, "Preface," *Della simmetria*, [n.p.]; Aristotle, *Poetics*, transl. Stephen Halliwell (Cambridge, MA: Harvard University Press, 1995), 1: 2.
113 Mark Roskill, *Dolce's "L'Aretino" and Venetian Art Theory of the Cinquecento* (New York: New York University Press, 1968), 11.
114 Roskill, *Dolce's "L'Aretino,"* 11, 129.
115 Ibid., 129.
116 See Charles E. Little, "The Italians and Their Schools," *Peabody Journal of Education*, 10.4 (1933), 206–44.

continue in the university with law or letters.[117] The impetus behind the new curriculum came from humanists who sought to reform the late medieval education system based on Greco-Roman classics. This programmatic definition of the sequence of studies would become known as the *studia humanitatis*. It would be first published in 1472 in the posthumous work by Pier Paolo Vergerio (1370–1444/1445) in his treatise *De ingenuis moribus ac liberalibus studiis* [On the Manners of a Gentleman and Liberal Studies], which included grammar, rhetoric, poetry, history, and moral philosophy.[118] Further refinement resulted in a normative syllabus that divided grammar education into two schools. The lower, or elementary school, utilized grammar manuals, such as Cato's *Disticha* and Vives' *Colloquia*, and also included repetitive drills in basic grammatical structure. The upper school built on basic grammar by learning Cicero's letters as an introduction to rhetoric, and Virgil as an introduction to poetry. It often added another poet, such as Terence, Horace, or Ovid, along with a historian, such as Caesar, Sallust, or Valerius Maximus. A few pedagogues even augmented the core curriculum with some Greek, and logic, or excerpts from Aristotle. Upon leaving grammar school, one would have achieved a firm foundation for reading and writing in Latin, as well as an extensive repertoire of ancient rhetoricians and poets.[119] The canonicity of such syllabi is demonstrable through a quick review of the bibliography utilized in later treatises, such as Gallucci's. Every author mentioned above is called upon to support various assertions. Knowledge of the entirety of these author's works, and in which volume quotations are derived, is a presumed prerequisite for a full understanding of the arguments set forth. Aristotle is the philosophical authority most often cited, though Seneca and Plato are referenced; Cicero is repeatedly

---

117 Apprentice painters came above all from families of painters and artisans in the allied crafts, although the sons of men in unrelated trades became painters as well. Additionally, painting offered a socially and economically respectable alternative for the sons of upper class families which had come down in the world, such as Michelangelo, Titian, and Rubens. Gabriele Bleek-Bryne, "The Education of the Painter in the Workshop," in *Children of Mercury: The Education of Artists in the Sixteenth and Seventeenth Centuries*, ed. Jeffrey M. Muller (Providence, RI: Brown University, 1984), 28–39.
118 Pier Paolo Vergerio, *De ingenuis moribus ac liberalibus studiis* (Venice: [n.p.], 1472).
119 Charles Dempsey, "Some Observations on the Education of Artists in Florence and Bologna in the Later Sixteenth Century," *The Art Bulletin*, 62 (1980), 557–69, at 561, https://doi.org/10.2307/3050053

referenced for rhetoric, and Sallust, Catullus, Horace, Ovid, and Virgil for poetry; and, finally, Plutarch and Pliny for history.

The organization of the new additions in *Della simmetria* cleverly interweaves these various literary traditions to assist in elucidating the original goals of Dürer's proportion studies. In the Preface, dedicated to "showing the similarity that painting has with poetry," Gallucci introduces the interpretative schema for his new translation and argues that painters and poets should learn from the other's field, stating: "In addition, since the poet cannot imitate well with words that man whose actions he does not fully know, thus the painter cannot imitate well that body whose parts are not entirely visible."[120] Poetry assists the painter in selecting what is appropriate to communicate what was intended, for he "also needs to know what action is appropriate for whatever virtue."[121] Understanding the bodily types, expressions, and psychological disposition of different characters is necessary to ensure decorum and propriety, which primarily consists of two main things: "one is in knowing how to suitably form all kinds of bodies; the other in knowing for what type of person each of those is appropriate."[122]

In his Fifth Book, Gallucci categorizes various types of characters, personalities, genders, and dispositions, along with the appropriate features to illustrate each in fifty-eight chapters. In supporting his assertions, ancient and modern poets, philosophers, and rhetoricians are called upon as authorities. In addition to Homer, we also find Anacreon, Catullus, Ovid, Horace, Virgil, and other ancient poets read alongside Petrarch, Dante, Ariosto, and Tasso from the early modern era. For instance, in opening his discussion with the "Differences of Humans with Respect to Countries, Sex and Age," the build, complexion, and appearance of men and women from various countries is discussed. Men from "Egypt, and other places in the south" are smaller than men in the north, and, as Tasso describes Arabs in Book 17 of *Gerusalemme liberata* [Jerusalem Delivered], "They have women's voices, bodies short and thin,/ and long, black locks of hair, and swarthy skin."[123] After discussing the appropriate build for men that approximate a lion, he continues on with what is

---

120 Gallucci, "Preface," *Della simmetria*, [n.p.].
121 Ibid.
122 Ibid.
123 Gallucci, *Della simmetria*, 5: 125v; Torquato Tasso, *The Liberation of Jerusalem*, transl. Max Wickert (Oxford: Oxford University Press, 2009), 17: 21.

appropriate for women and effeminate men should be that of a leopard or panther. He then calls upon Homer for confirmation of his description in the *Iliad* where the Trojan prince Paris is treated: "When, advancing together, the two armies/ came near, Alexandros, like a god, appeared wearing/ a panther skin on his shoulders, and his curved bow..."[124] In the following chapter on "The Beauty of Women," there is a compendium of references on the characteristics on feminine beauty, specifically related to complexion, build, facial features, hair, and breasts. Describing this ideal, Gallucci calls on Homer, Ariosto, Tasso, Petrarch, Catullus, and Seneca, who all confirm the complexion should be "lily-white" or "alabaster," limbs should be "lustrous" and soft, hair like "golden tresses flowing in the wind," and, finally, "unripe apple-breasts."[125] This lengthy section reiterates the themes, leaving no doubt to the veracity of the translator's claims for his audience. At the same time, readers are called upon to remember from what chapter, book, and section the excerpt is derived. Hence, in each section Gallucci attempts to draw on both modern and ancient poets to demonstrate the consistency in their descriptions and to support his own conclusions, while refreshing and reinforcing the reader's knowledge of this bibliography.

These poetic citations, however, go beyond physiognomic descriptors. While the confirmation of physical appearance in various personages is demonstrable in *Della simmetria*, there are broader implications for the association between the sister arts here with regards to the theoretical superstructure. In point of fact, the publication of the translation and commentary coincided with the Ariosto-Tasso debate and considered the merits of epic poetry over chivalric romances. Applicable to the arguments that would preoccupy artists and academicians in the following century, apologists on both sides would argue for the supremacy of one over the other. The different narrative styles were bound up in the *Orlando furioso* [The Frenzy of Orlando] (1532) by Ludovico Ariosto (1474–1533) and the later *Gerusalemme liberata* (1581) by Torquato Tasso (1544–1595). The chivalric romance of Ariosto, which was characterized by "micronarratives" of an interlaced

---

124 Homer, *Iliad*, transl. Barry Powell (Oxford: Oxford University Press, 2014), 3: 13–16.
125 Petrarch, "Canzone 350," *The Complete Canzoniere*, transl. A. S. Kline ([n.p.]: Poetry in Translation, 2001), 487; Homer, *Iliad*, transl. Powell, 3: 35–37; Ludovico Ariosto, *Orlando Furioso*, transl. Guido Waldman (Oxford: Oxford University Press, 2008), "Canto 10," 95–96; 103; Tasso, *The Liberation of Jerusalem*, transl. Wickert, 4: 29–31.

structure and myriad digressions, found a counterpoint in the epic of Tasso, a "macronarrative" with a linear progression leading towards an inevitable conclusion. The works represented two equally viable approaches to art, poetry, and rhetorical structure. Ariosto offered an entertaining mixture of "heroic and erotic actions"; his descriptions of characters and their actions were appreciated for the emotions that they could elicit, inspiring artists well into the following century. Tasso, on the other hand, provides a "seemingly seamless master discourse," and a compelling model for history painting, especially of religious scenes.[126] Both poets are given seemingly equal treatment by Gallucci, each being called upon for their perspective on all manner of heroic and dramatic themes. However, if we consider the goal of Gallucci and his understanding of Dürer's goal in the *Four Books*, the epic works and theoretical treatises of Tasso are more influential.

Gallucci laments at the outset of his work that so many artists in his own day work without precepts, which Dürer had attempted to establish, but were forgotten by the end of the century. He states:

> For without any precept, which would certainly guide students, they instead propose their own or copy the drawings of others. Thus, all of this profession, which is truly worthy of science and practice, they reduce to practice alone, and, as a result, like so many amputees going about limping and blind people groping, deprive their histories of the variety of many colors in order to satisfy the ignorant and vulgar.[127]

Instead of groping blindly, students of painting need firm rules founded on verifiable principles from the study of nature and mathematics, as well as academic disciplines in poetry, philosophy, and the like. With that in mind, and the defense of this "noble art," Gallucci opens his Dedication with a defense of the power of art to move individuals to piety when viewing religious scenes, especially of martyrs: "Who does not burn of the love of Christ our Lord having seen his life represented with such diligence, and in art in the many drawings of our Albrecht Dürer?"[128] Hence, imitable actions should be the goal of art, especially in post-Tridentine Italy. The new requirement is clearly

---

126 Valeria Finucci, "Introduction: Ariosto, Tasso, and Storytelling," in *Renaissance Transactions: Ariosto and Tasso*, ed. Valeria Finucci (Durham and London: Duke University Press, 1999), 1–3.
127 Gallucci, "Preface," *Della simmetria*, [n.p.].
128 Gallucci, "Dedication," *Della simmetria*, [n.p.].

related by the ecclesiastical authorities who would first elaborate on the pronouncements of the council.[129] Reform-minded clerics, such as Archbishops Carlo Borromeo and Gabriele Paleotti, demanded clarity and simplicity in artworks that would, above all, inspire their viewers to pious action through contemplation and reflection laid out in treatises like *Discorso intorno alle immagini sacre e profane* [Discourse on Sacred and Profane Images] (1582).[130] Calling on the authority of Aristotle in the *Discorso*, Paleotti cites that imitation is inborn in man; as such, paintings that are closer to sense-perceptible reality are more persuasive: "Whence those paintings that imitate the live and true more in such a manner that deceives animals, and sometimes even men, like those Pliny relates like Zeuxis and Parrhasius, are always more worthy of status and commendation as they have delighted onlookers so much more."[131] The rhetorical nature of the artist's charge is aided by the mimetic properties of his medium. The closer he approximates the visible world, the more compelling his art will be to the viewers to inspire them to action through the pious display they see on the canvas.

In as much as the goals of painting were to depict human action to inspire piety, so too was poetry defined as the imitation of human action. Tasso confirmed this in his own definition of the goals of epic poetry when writing in his *Discorsi del poema eroico* [Discourses on the Heroic Poem] of 1594:

> Therefore, I would say instead that poetry was none other than the imitation of human actions, which properly constitute imitable actions;

---

129 Regina Pörtner, *The Counter-Reformation in Central Europe: Styria 1580–1630* (Oxford: Clarendon Press, 2001).

130 A facsimile edition of the *Discorso* is available at https://books.google.co.uk/books?id=BiWvs5txQmAC&printsec=frontcover&source=gbs_ge_summary_r&cad=0#v=onepage&q&f=false. The specific impact these publications had on art *en fin du siècle* has been difficult to determine. Boschloo attempted to connect the writings of Gabriele Paleotti to the reform of painting in the Carracci Academy in the early 1580s, but was only able to present a hypothetical connection between the two parties. A. W. A. Boschloo, *Annibale Carracci in Bologna: Visible Reality in Art after the Council of Trent*, 2 vols (The Hague: Govt. Pub. Off., 1974). For another example of reformatory decrees on art production, see Carlo Borromeo, "Instructiones fabricate et supellectilis ecclesiasticae," in *Trattati d'arte del cinquecento, fra manierismo e controriforma*, ed. Paola Barocchi, Scrittori d'Italia 221, 3 vols (Bari: Laterza, 1961), III: 1–112.

131 "onde quelle pitture che più imitando il vivo e vero, per modo che ingannano gli animali e tal volta gli uomini, come racconta Plinio di Zeusi e di Parasio, tanto più sempre sono state degne di commendazione e maggiormente hanno dilettato i riguardanti." Barocchi, ed., *Trattati d'arte*, III: 220.

and the others were not imitated in and of themselves, but incidentally, nor as the principal part [of the poem], but as accessory. In such manner one can imitate not only the actions of beasts, such as the battle of the unicorn with the elephant, or of the swan with the eagle, but natural events, such as tempests at sea, pestilences, deluges, conflagrations, earthquakes, and other such things.[132]

Gallucci, as mentioned, opened his translation reiterating the importance of understanding "which action is appropriate for whatever virtue."[133] Inspiring virtuous action should be the goal of the painter as it is the poet, and the same expectations were then translated into art theory from Tassian poetics. Early modern artists, in fact, understanding the united goals of the sister disciplines, would take such definitions and apply them to the visual arts, especially that of painting — replacing "pittura" for "poesia." Nicolas Poussin (1594–1665), the artist who would use Gallucci's translation in his own unfinished treatise on art, demonstrates its applicability in his *Osservazioni sopra la pittura*, or *Definition of Painting and of the Imitation Proper to It*. Here, Poussin quotes directly from Tasso's *Discorsi* and the definition that, like poetry, "Painting is none other than the imitation of human actions..."[134] The relationship between these goals was further elaborated on by Tasso, who in demonstrating the analogy between the exemplary actions of epic poetry and the goals of painting, compared the ideal virtues in epic verse to images that the intellect paints in the mind's eye of the readers:

> Their own intellect is the painter who goes on painting in their souls, based on this similitude, the forms of strength, of temperance, of justice, of faith, of piety, of religion, and of every other virtue, which is either acquired through much exertion, or infused by divine grace.[135]

---

132 Torquato Tasso, *Discorsi del poema eroico*, ed. Ettore Mazzali and Francesco Flora (Milan: Ricciardi, 1959; repr. Rome: Biblioteca Italiana, 2004, http://www.bibliotecaitaliana.it/testo/bibit000856), 77; quoted in Jonathan Unglaub, *Poussin and the Poetics of Painting: Pictorial Narrative and the Legacy of Tasso* (Cambridge, UK: Cambridge University Press, 2006), 11–12.
133 Gallucci, "Preface," *Della simmetria*, [n.p.].
134 Giovan Pietro Bellori, *Le vite de pittori, scultori e architetti moderni*, ed. Evelina Borea and Giovanni Previtali (Turin: Einaudi, 1976), 478; Giovan Pietro Bellori, *The Lives of the Modern Painters, Sculptors and Architects*, transl. Helmut Wohl and Alice Sedgwick Wohl (New York: Cambridge University Press, 2005), 338.
135 Tasso, *Discorsi del poema eroico*, 71; quoted in Unglaub, *Poussin and the Poetics of Painting*, 19.

Tasso claims that epic poetry "paints" the forms of strength, faith, and other virtues, upon the minds of its readers. In like fashion, Gallucci often uses the term "paints" as opposed to "says" when explaining how poets describe, or "paint" a picture of an image for the reader. Finally, the related goals of poetry and painting, especially relating to the potential for capturing emotions and virtues, would be recorded by one of the last great art theorists and biographers, Giovan Pietro Bellori (1613–1696). In his famous lecture delivered to the Accademia di San Luca in 1664, Bellori would define painting as the imitation of human action, and in his speech he encourages the painter to emulate the poet in crafting a universal representation of different emotional traits. In addressing this relationship, he writes:

> We must further consider that since painting is a representation of human action, likewise the painter must retain in his mind the exemplar of the emotions that accompany these actions, much as the poet preserves [in his mind] the idea of the wrathful, the fearful, the sorrowful, the joyful, and thus of laughter, of weeping, of fear, and of temerity.[136]

The two disciplines share the goal to display human action in order to reveal a truth behind the appearance of humankind. Human action and activity are highlighted in order to communicate ideals of behavior and belief, and to reveal the underlying nature of the universe. Importantly, Bellori exhorts artists to be knowledgeable of these emotional exemplars and their corresponding actions that make their psychological states known to the viewer. As a matter of fact, the importance of human activity and its ability to convey meaning moves beyond depicting humans. As noted, Tasso points out that painters and poets even represent gods, natural disasters, and animals from the perspective of human activity and often assign to them human attributes. What Gallucci, Bellori, and Tasso all agree on is that while the art forms of painting and poetry have the ability to represent any range of natural or fantastic phenomena, human action is their principle and proper enterprise. The ability to identify an individual character through appearance and classify a figure's movements led to the development of two interrelated disciplines in the Renaissance. Building on the

---

[136] Bellori, "L'Idea del pittore, dello scultore e dell'architetto scelta dalle bellezze naturali superior alla Natura," *Le Vite de pittori...*, 20.

importance of human action and particularities to interpret an infinite range of real and imagined things, the discipline of physiognomics emerged as a mechanism by which to discern the judgment of human character from individual features, while the theory of pathognomics grew alongside to assist in interpreting how expressive movements of figures reveal their passions.

## 4. Physiognomics: The Science of Passion

The dialectic on human expression, especially the ancient theory of physiognomic typology, occupied authors throughout the sixteenth century. The considerations consumed Dürer's studies at the outset of the century as he assembled his twenty-six sets of human proportions, as well as Gallucci, at the end of the century, with his attempt to contextualize Dürer's studies. Drawing upon the ancient and the revived science as applied to the visual arts, *Della simmetria* attempted to prepare artists for the two complementary aspects of the discipline: "the diagnostic significance ascribed to the morphology of human faces and the communication of emotions by means of the dynamic mimicry of the features."[137] For Gallucci, that meant providing an accessible index or reference to represent a range of characters and emotional states. This quantitative and taxonomic reference guide walked the reader through the creative process for various figures for history paintings. When a character, or their type, was known for a particular narrative, the reader could turn to the corresponding description where Gallucci directs the reader to the relevant book in which Dürer outlines the mathematical armature on which to hang the appropriate *affetti*.[138] These physiognomic case studies include quick axiomatic references for appropriate musculature and complexion, as well as attitude, facial features, hair, beard, and eye color, and even the lines of the face. Examples range from particular body parts (such as ears, hands, and lips) — appropriate to jealous, angry, or loquacious men — to very specific character combinations, such as "The Figure of a Man, Who Is

---

[137] Avigdor W.G. Posèq, "On Physiognomic Communication in Bernini," *Artibus et Historiae*, 27.54 (2006), 161–90, at 161, https://doi.org/10.2307/20067127

[138] As with his other references to ancient and modern authors, the specific chapter, page, and line is not indicated, only the specification of which book to review (e.g. Book Two).

by Nature Cold and Wet, Therefore, Meek and Humble, Feeble, Slow, Quiet, and Effeminate."[139] The range of characteristics and passions are illustrated in a comparative method: after describing the characteristics relating to a particular temperament, the opposite is then described as a binary distinction.

The comparative approach can be illustrated with the "Figure of a Cheerful Man" described by Gallucci. Once an artist has properly proportioned the figure, based on Dürer's formula, a quick reference relates that: "The figure principally consists of the appearance of the forehead and eyes, which all ancient writers agree upon, demonstrate this passion through its opposite when the brow cringes, showing pain and severity."[140] Here, he cite as his authority Ariosto, quoting the effects of joy from the chivalric epic *Orlando furioso*: "'So strange a sight smoothed Jocondo's brow and cleared his eyes. He became more jocund, as his name implied, and his glumness turned to gaiety. He became happy again, filled out, took on colour, looked once more like a cherub from paradise.'"[141] Along with the forehead and eyes, this passion is identified through the fleshy and flushed face of the figure. As with each description, Gallucci then provides the contrary emotion, "A Melancholic and Grieved Man," whereby we are told that: "the forehead must be wrinkled like a newly plowed field with relaxed eyebrows that appear to quiver, but with fixed and stern eyelids. In all aspects he should appear troubled, having discomfort in everything."[142] As with all of the passions, the initial description of figures experiencing emotions cite only the momentary response to an external stimulus. Behind such evaluations, though, lies the belief that a figure's appearance is also tied to their character. Thus, anyone's character can be known if following certain diagnostic criteria set forth in many earlier physiognomic treatises.

The advent of natural physiognomy can be traced to antiquity, where a number of treatises provided important technical handbooks.[143] The

---

139  Gallucci, *Della simmetria*, 5: 130r.
140  Ibid., 132v.
141  Ibid.
142  Ibid., 132r.
143  In addition to the Pseudo-Aristotelian *Physiognomica* of the third BCE, Polemo Rhetor of Laodicea wrote his *Physiognomonia* in the second century CE, as well as an anonymous Latin handbook entitled *de Physiognomonia* from the ca. fourth century CE. Elizabeth Evans, "Physiognomics in the Ancient World," *Transactions of the American Philosophical Society*, 59.5 (1969), 1–101, https://doi.org/10.2307/1006011

most important ancient work, and first of its kind to treat the subject, was the *Physiognomica* attributed to Aristotle (though now agreed to be by an anonymous third century BCE author). Reprinted and illustrated in several Renaissance editions, the author, referred to as Pseudo-Aristotle, relates that careful observers can ascertain the nature of men and women through certain physiognomic signs, such as: movements and gestures of the body, color, characteristic facial expressions, growth of hair, smoothness of the skin, the voice, the condition of the flesh, the parts of the body, the build of the body as a whole, etc. Important for later writers on the subject, the author relates humans to animals, dividing the whole animal kingdom into two physical types — male and female.[144] In all species the female is tamer, gentler, less powerful, easily trained, and more manageable, but, at the same time, more deceitful and mischievous. Their heads are smaller and faces narrower; furthermore, the female's neck thinner, chest weaker, and sides smaller. At the same time, her hips and thighs are fuller, though thin-legged and with more delicate feet. Males are the opposite of all of these things, including being hotter and dryer due to their humoral disposition. After a comparison of humans with their animal counterparts to determine character based on appearance, Pseudo-Aristotle considers the signs of psychological comportment in the cases of courage, cowardice, good disposition, dullness of sense, shamelessness, etc. These signs are drawn from observation of human behavior; for example, in the case of "courage," he lists: coarse hair, upright carriage of the body, size and strength in the bones, sides, and extremities, a stomach that is broad and flat, a sturdy, not overly fleshy neck, a chest that is broad and fleshy, the calves of the legs are larger towards the ankles, a gleaming eye, neither too wide nor too closed, a rather dry skin, and a sharp forehead, straight and not large, neither very smooth nor very wrinkled.[145] The belief that the characters of animals were universal and stable was uncontested. For instance, asses were insensitive to pain; deer, cats, and hares were timid; bulls were strong; lions courageous and magnanimous, and so on. Yet, since antiquity and the publication by Pseudo-Aristotle, artists and writers were warned that no one would resemble an animal in its

---

[144] Pseudo-Aristotle, *Physiognomica*, 4: 809a; Aristotle, *Minor Works*, transl. W. S. Hett (London: William Heinemann, 1936), 107.

[145] Pseudo-Aristotle, *Physiognomica*, 4: 807a–b.

entirety; it was necessary to clarify which features of the beast indicated which characteristics.[146] Following these principles, Renaissance thinkers like Gallucci presumed as Pseudo-Aristotle wrote: "that soul and body react on each other; when the character of the soul changes, it changes also the form of the body, and conversely, when the form of the body changes, it changes the character of the soul."[147]

Evidence of the use of the classification laid out in the *Physiognomica* may be seen in both Dürer's original text and Gallucci's later additions. In his "Aesthetic Excursus" in the Third Book, for instance, Dürer relates the differences in figures based on race, along with their temperament and physiognomy. He writes: "Thus one finds among the families of men all manner of type, which may be used for diverse figures according to temperament. As such, the strong are firm in body as with lions, while the weak are softer and less rugged and strong."[148] In his Fifth Book, Gallucci addresses the same subject and states: "Nevertheless, if it is possible, painters are obliged to represent men with the limbs of a lion, while that of a leopard is appropriate for women and effeminate men."[149] Following the introduction to nationalities and genders, where men and women are associated with animals, instructions on how to paint specific passions further illustrate the scheme. The complexion, build, facial features, and behavior of various temperaments are identified that range from strong, angry, or ingenious to loquacious, drowsy, or libidinous. This is followed by which body parts are appropriate to which passions (e.g. legs, knees, chest, fingernails, etc.) and their movements. The Fifth Book culminates in a theoretical defense of the nature of beauty, citing Marsilio Ficino's (1433–1499) *Commentary on Plato*.[150]

The treatise joined a growing body of literature by the end of the century on the applicability of the system to the visual arts, such as Lomazzo's 1584 *Trattato dell'arte della pittura, scultura ed architettura*. While the Milanese painter had little to say concerning facial expressions, nearly an entire book is dedicated to physiognomics. Beginning with a Horatian

---

146 Jennifer Montagu, *The Expression of the Passions: The Origin and Influence of Charles Le Brun's Conférence sur l'expression générale et particulière* (New Haven: Yale University Press, 1994), 23.
147 Pseudo-Aristotle, *Physiognomica*, 4: 808b; Aristotle, *Minor Works*, transl. Hett, 107.
148 Dürer, *Vier Bücher*, 3: 70r.
149 Gallucci, *Della simmetria*, 5: 125r.
150 Marsilio Ficino, *Commentary on Plato's Symposium on Love*, transl. Sears Jayne (Dallas, TX: Spring, 1985), 88.

introduction, Book Two, "Del sito, posizione, decoro, moto, furia, e grazia delle figure," addresses the movements related to expressing the passions and concludes with eleven passions that are divided into those that are desirable and irascible.[151] These temperaments affect the body in various ways that are also restated in the *Della simmetria*: joy expands the posture of figures, and expands the heart, while fear contracts figures and, likewise, grief retracts inwards; fear also brings coldness, a quick-beating heart, loss of voice, and paleness.[152] Gallucci had also commented on the effects of fear on the body: "The timid man pulls his limbs as tightly to his body as possible, as when all the men are, for any reason, alarmed by any serious fear; this comportment makes it look as though they are shrinking into themselves, looking for a narrower place to hide. They look like they are running away and are pale overall."[153] This observation is confirmed through a number of citations that follow from various poets, including Ariosto, Homer, Ovid, Virgil, and Tasso.[154] In a similar fashion, Lomazzo follows the account of these general passions with descriptions of nearly a hundred more in greater detail, wherein a few general remarks on typical features are followed by accounts drawn from ancient and modern poets.

Such physiognomic treatments developed within the context of a variety of fields publishing on the relationship between character and appearance. These took the form of iconographic manuals, anatomical texts, emblemata, and whole treatises dedicated to the subject. The first was in the form of a special chapter dedicated to physiognomy in *De sculptura* [On Sculpture] in 1504 by the humanist and amateur sculptor Pomponoi Gaurico (1482–1620). The treatment was followed in 1522 with a complete treatise on astrology, chiromancy and physiognomy in one volume entitled *Introductiones Apotelesmaticae* [Introduction to Apotelesmatics] by the German chiromancer John Indagine. Chiromancy or palmistry (the interpretation of one's character from the lines and other features on their hands) is discussed in the first section and physiognomy the second. This text formed the basis for physiognomics indebted to astrology. In 1548, Paolo Pino (1534–1565)

---

151 Giovanni Paolo Lomazzo, *Trattato dell'arte della pittura, scultura ed architetta* (Milan: Paolo Gottardo Pontio, 1584), 2.2: 3–4, 102–03.
152 Ibid.
153 Gallucci, *Della simmetria*, 5: 125v.
154 Ibid., 125v-125r.

briefly touches on physiognomics and its importance for artists in his *Dialogo di pittura* [Dialogue on Painting], citing Gaurico.[155] The same year finds Francisco de Hollanda (1517–1585) mentioning Gaurico in some observations on physiognomics in *Tractato de pintura antigua* [Treatise on Ancient Painting].[156] Later in the century, several important works on the subject were published. Francesco Bocchi (1548–1618) in his *Eccellenza della statua del San Giorgio di Donatello* [Excellence of the Statue of *Saint George* by Donatello], written in 1571 and published in 1584 in Florence, would move beyond a general discussion of the subject to be the first to specifically articulate the role of physiognomics to expression in the visual arts.[157] But the most influential treatise on the subject was Giovanni Battista della Porta's (1535–1615) *De humana physiognomonia* [On Human Physiognomy], originally published in 1588, later translated into Italian (like *Della simmetria*, making the text more widely accessible to artists) as *Della fisionomia dell'huomo* [On the Physiognomy of Man] in 1598 and reprinted in 1608.[158] Drawing heavily on the classification techniques described in Pseudo-Aristotle's *Physiognomica*, Della Porta assigned the variety of human types based on their similarity to the features of certain animals, claiming that a man's resemblance to an animal indicates that he shares those behavioral habits. As he writes: "For instance an individual's similarity to a lion would indicate an ardent personality, resemblance to a hare would show that a person is easily frightened, a likeness to a cock stands for liberality, while canine traits suggest avarice, etc."[159] The human-animal comparative method would influence the most famous of these publications on the passions and physiognomy. Published after a series of lectures delivered at the French Academy, *Méthode pour apprendre à dessiner les passions* [Method for Learning to Draw the Passions] of 1668 by Charles Le Brun (1619–1690) illustrates the main points through a series of drawings comparing human and animal faces (based on the *Physiognomica*). In all, the French academician describes twenty-two

---

155 Barocchi, ed., *Trattati d'arte del Cinquecento*, I: 136.
156 Francisco de Hollanda, *De la pintura antigua por Francisco de Hollanda, versión castellana de Manuel Denis (1563)*, ed. E. Tormo (Madrid: Ratés, 1921), 70–74.
157 Francesco Bocchi, "Eccellenza della statua del San Griogio di Donatello," in *Trattati d'arte del Cinquecento*, ed. Barocchi, 3: 127–94.
158 Giovanni Battista della Porta, *Della fisionomia dell'huomo* (Venice: Presso C. Tomasini, 1598).
159 Della Porta, *Della fisionomia dell'huomo;* cited in Posèq, "On Physiognomic Communication in Bernini," 162.

passions, along with the "mixed passions," including: Joy, Hope, Anger, Fear, Love, Astonishment, and so on. Each one was illustrated and paired with a description of the particular passion.[160]

Such passions and physiognomic types were also dictated by humoral disposition. As with physiognomics, the medical theory of the humors was also concerned with the study of the relationship between the body to mental characteristics.[161] Since antiquity, the blending (*krasis*) of the humors was assumed to determine physical, as well as psychological disposition (*complexio*).[162] In the period under investigation, writers used the terms "temperament" and "humor" interchangeably due to the fact that they identified the dominant elemental properties inside the body, which in turn affected psychological disposition and complexion. For instance, if the hot wetness of fire predominated, an individual was choleric, and thus quick to fierce action and emotion; if the hot wetness of air was prevalent, that individual was sanguine, loving of pleasure and cheerful; if the cold wetness of water abounded, the person was phlegmatic, and thus slow in both mind and body; and if the cold dryness of earth was most common, the person was melancholic, depressed and solitary. Understanding which humor was dominant was necessary for both poets and artists. The Italian sculptor Orfeo Boselli (1597–1667) discusses the necessity of humoral balance in his treatise *Osservazioni della scoltura antica* [Observations on Ancient Sculpture], noting that although true health — both mental and physical — derives from a perfect humoral equilibrium, this rarely occurs; one humor will predominate and the artist will need to understand the external symptoms to correctly capture all individual personalities. Boselli advises the sculptor to be mindful of these dominant humors:

> Now, when these [humors] are in equilibrium, the soul is the perfect master of the natural powers, and according to the external forces is angered, perturbed, or rejoices. Because in the composition of the body one of the elemental humors often has the upper hand, one face thus

---

160 Montagu, *Expression of the Passions*.
161 Michael Kwakkelstein, "Leonardo's Grotesque Heads and the Breaking of the Physiognomic Mould," *Journal of the Warburg and Courtauld Institutes*, 54 (1992), 127–36, at 128, https://doi.org/10.2307/751484
162 George Sarton, "Remarks on the Theory of Temperaments," *Isis*, 34 (1943), 205–08, https://doi.org/10.1086/347791

has a naturally melancholic physiognomy, another glad and another majestic. For this reason, one can conclude that, in the face, one of these [humors] will be expressed either naturally, or through external causes. Therefore, in making the face, one should first think of which of these affects is underlying, and throw oneself into expressing that one.[163]

Whether the figure to be created was of sanguine, phlegmatic, melancholic, or choleric personality, the dominance of one humor in the body was the cause, externally influencing appearance seen through skin tone; thus, the term "complexion" also came into widespread use when discussing artistic style in relationship to humoral balance. When Lomazzo became blind and turned to writing, he instructed artists to blend their colors to ensure that the skin of phlegmatics is paler, melancholics swarthier, sanguine figures rosier, and cholerics yellower.[164] Thus, in addition to physical characteristics shared with the animal kingdom, temperament could be ascertained through an individual's complexion.

Nonetheless, the centrality of taxonomic classification to physiognomics means that another aspect underpinning physiognomic studies is often overlooked: the relationship between the microcosm and the macrocosm. While physiognomy lists diagnostic criteria, answering the *what, when* and, *where* of physical appearance, cosmology answers the *how* and *why*. Why are some men prone to anger with a quick temper and ugly, while others calm, cheerful and handsome? Why are some predisposed to illness and malady, while others healthy? How is temperament, complexion and attractiveness related to the time of year and one's age? According to ancient and early modern writers, the answers to these questions lie in our relationship to the cosmos.

---

163 "...hora quando queste sono in equilibrio, è l'anima perfetta signora delle potenze naturali, e secondo li accidenti si altera, si turba, si ralegra: ma perche nella compositione del corpo li elementary humori per il più sempre, una parte prevale più dell'altra in loro, quindi è che un Volto è di fisonomia naturale mesto, l'altro lieto, l'altro Maestoso, onde si può concludere, che sempre nel Viso una di queste potenze, o naturalmente; o acidentalmente sia da esprimersi. Però nel far la faccia si deve prima pensare a quale di questi affetti soggiaccia, et alla espressione di quello che dimonstra totalmente buttarsi." Orfeo Boselli, *Osservazioni della scoltura antica dai Manoscritti Corsini e Doria e altri scritti*, ed. Phoebe Dent Weil (Florence: S.P.E.S., 1978), 23v–24r.

164 Gian Paolo Lomazzo, *Scritti sulle arti*, ed. Roberto P. Ciardi, 2 vols (Florence: Centro Di, 1973–1974), II: 262–69.

## 5. From Microcosm to Macrocosm

At the outset of his treatise, Gallucci established that human proportions (or microcosm) reflect the harmony of the universe (or macrocosm). The Vitruvian pairing, where the universe could be numerically calculated and revealed through the human body, illustrates the perceived interrelationship between the cosmos and the human body. This worldview connected the balance and constitution of figures with the theory of the four elements and humors. These physiognomic and humoral readings find their classifications framed in terms of astronomy and astrology, appropriate given the translator's background. Furthermore, the attempts made to categorize and map the human body, in the case of Dürer and others, were understood by art-theorists, astrologers and natural philosophers as an attempt to reveal the macrocosm of the universe. Through this process, the "divinely" ordered beauty in the microcosm of man is also revealed. Such information concerning the structure of the universe was seen as necessary for artists to understand in order to reveal the beauty buried in an imperfect material existence. In fact, Dürer himself had related the connected concerns of astrology and humoral theory in his "Aesthetic Excursus:"

> If one wished to create some strange Saturnine or Martial figure, or represent the charming loveliness of Venus, and you practice the aforementioned teachings, then by their aid you will know what standard and style you should employ for each. Through their bodily proportions, a varieties of men can be shown, whether fiery, airy, watery, or earthly in temperament. Thus, the power of art, as mentioned, masters each [type] in every work.[165]

While the microcosm-macrocosm pair could be represented — and, thus, determined — numerically, the interrelationship between the universe and the human body sympathetically affected all matter; therefore, all things could be found to be connected to man. This system of relationships was expressed early on by Ficino, who demonstrated the applicability of Vitruvian cosmology to Neoplatonism. In fact, the body measurements given by Ficino in Speech V Chapter VI of his *Sopra lo amore o Convito di Plantone* [Plato's Symposium on Love] are derived,

---

165 Dürer, *Vier Bücher*, 3: 70r.

in part, from the canon of Vitruvius, where we find that: "eight heads will make the length of the body; this same length the spread of the arms to the side and likewise of the legs and feet will also measure," and where the face is divided into three lengths of the nose.[166] Elaborating on the notion of the balance and constitution of figures, Ficino then enumerated the three steps that were to be taken to ensure matter's acceptance of beauty — order, mode, and form. Within each of these steps, the appropriateness of type and the balance of each were critical to prepare matter so that it might result in something pleasant and harmonious. But, as he continues, the theory of the four elements and humors are cited as the actual basis for this beauty:

> The basis of these three conditions is the harmonious constitution of the four elements in such a way that our body most resembles heaven, the substance of which is harmonious, and does not rebel against the formation of the soul due to an excess of some humor. In such a way, the splendor of heaven easily appears in the body as similar to heaven. And this perfect form of man, which the spirit possesses, will be more integral in peaceful and obedient matter...[167]

The body and the universe, from microcosm to macrocosm, are here related not by geometrical relationships, but rather metaphysical balance. The same elements that made up the physical universe also constituted the human body. The conception has its origin in Greek cosmology, where Plato's *Philebus* finds Socrates voicing the thesis that the elements in man's body are derived from elements in the body of the cosmos; whatever man has, the cosmos must also have. Therefore, Socrates posits: "Whence can a human body have received its soul, if the body of the universe does not possess a soul?"[168] As the world, and subsequently the universe, is balanced by the four elements (earth, air, fire, and water), so to is the human body, and subsequently the soul, balanced by the four humors (black bile, yellow bile, phlegm, and blood).[169] For physicians, who derived their ideas from Hippocrates and Galen, restoring health

---

166 Ficino, *Commentary on Plato's Symposium on Love*, transl. Jayne, 93.
167 Ibid., 93–94.
168 David E. Hahm, *The Origins of Stoic Cosmology* (Columbus, OH: Ohio State University Press, 1977), 138.
169 See Allen G. Debus, *The Chemical Philosophy: Paracelsian Science and Medicine* (New York: Science History Publications, 1977); Walter Pagel, *Paracelsus: An Introduction to Philosophical Medicine in the Era of the Renaissance* (Basel: S. Karger, 1958).

meant reducing the excesses through the introduction of opposites in processes, such as bloodletting.[170] For artists, philosophers, and those concerned with astronomy and astrology, balance and harmony in the universe, human body, and art resulted in order, health, and beauty. Therefore, according to Ficino, if the proper preparation for beauty, which includes these concerns, is observed, then the "splendor of heaven easily appears in the body as similar to heaven."[171]

The interconnected nature of man and the universe naturally extended to heavenly bodies, and, as such, astronomy and astrology became intertwined with human proportion. For those interested in mapping the cosmos, such as Gallucci, the microcosm-macrocosm pairing allowed the extension of the knowledge of man to that of the universe, as they were self-reflective.[172] This was made possible through the dispersion of the same four elements throughout the universe, as well as the belief that the universe was organized in a similar fashion to man. Plato's *Timaeus*, for instance, had argued that: "The visible universe is a living creature, having soul (*psyche*) in body and reason (*nous*) in soul… Man is also composed of reason, soul, and body; but his body will be dissolved back into the elements, and the two lower parts of his soul are also mortal. Only the divine reason in him is imperishable."[173] In a model that would also appeal to Christian thinkers, the human body is derived from the elements and will return to them after death. The constitution of these elements can be found in the different planets and these in turn influence the makeup of bodies born under their astrological agency. The manner in which celestial bodies affected earthly ones reflected the organization of the cosmos. For as Elias Ashmole (1617–1692), antiquarian and founding member of the Royal Society, related in his *Theatrum chemicum britannicum* [The Theater of British Chemistry] (1652): the universe is divided into supercelestial, celestial, and natural

---

170 Hippocrates, *On the Nature of Man*, transl. W. H. S. Jones (Cambridge, MA: Harvard University Press, 2014), 3–4.
171 Ficino, *Commentary on Plato's Symposium on Love*, transl. Jayne, 94.
172 Alex Wayman, "The Human Body as Microcosm in India, Greek Cosmology, and Sixteenth-Century Europe," *History of Religions*, 22.2 (1982), 172–90, at 174, https://doi.org/10.1086/462918
173 Francis MacDonald Conford, *Plato's Cosmology: The Timaeus of Plato* (Indianapolis: Hackett Publishing Company, 1997), 38; see also Richard Broxton Onians, *The Origins of European Thought about the Body, the Mind, the Soul, the World, Time and Fate* (Cambridge: Cambridge University Press, 1954).

realms; the sublunary world being the final recipient of divine ideas transmitted by the planets and stars.[174]

The applicability of this belief to the arts was already demonstrated in treatises on art. Case in point, Lomazzo related proportions to astrology in Chapter XXVI of his *Idea del tempio* when he followed the Ficinian definition of beauty and importance of humoral theory with a detailed list of each planet and their appropriate corresponding proportions. The material is again derived from Ficino, in this case his *De triplici vita* [Three Books on Life].[175] Citing the works of "mathematicians and astrologers," Lomazzo notes: "But when it comes to fashioning the bodies, beauty is taken from the qualities that make all our bodies dissimilar, changing from one to the other more or less..."[176] This diversity is caused by the elements and planets: "There can be, however, only four main types of dissimilarity, in accordance with the number of elements and the strength of their qualities, which the mathematicians assert are the bases of all the forms or rather types of human bodies."[177] Each planet is associated with a particular quality inherent in the elements, and is thus transferred to earthly bodies. For instance, the hot and dry nature of fire causes Martian types to have larger limbs, whereas the cool and humid nature of water restricts the size of Lunar types. The same is true for Jovian types (where air produces full-bodied figures) and Saturnine types (where earth produces straight and concave limbs).[178]

---

174 Elias Ashmole, *Theatrum chemicum britannicum*, ed. A. G. Debus (New York: Johnson Reprint Corporation, 1967; facsimile of London, 1652, https://archive.org/stream/theatrumchemicum00ashm?ref=ol#page/n6/mode/2up), 446; Newman and Grafton, eds, *Secrets of Nature*, 16.

175 Lomazzo, *Idea del Tempio*..., 26: 83–86. The seven pillars of Lomazzo's "temple of painting" correspond to seven artists (Michelangelo, Gaudenzio Ferrari, Polidoro da Caravaggio, Leonardo, Raphael, Mantegna, and Titian) and are related to the seven planets where they derive their celestial influences; Marsilio Ficino, *Three Books on Life*, ed. and transl. Carol V. Kaske and John R. Clark, Medieval and Renaissance Texts and Studies 57 (Binghamton, NY: The Renaissance Society of America, 1989), 293–97.

176 "Ma venendo alla temperature dei corpi ella si cava dalla qualità, per le quail tutti i corpi nostri vegono ad essere tra se dissimili, trasferendosi l'una al'altra più e meno..." Lomazzo, *Idea del Tempio*..., 26: 85.

177 "Ma non possono però essere se non quattro principali maniera di dissimiglianza secondo il numero degli elementi e la forza delle loro qualità, che i mathematici affermano essere come fondamenti di tutte le forme over maniera dei corpi umani." Ibid.

178 Ibid., 26: 85–86.

Furthermore, as man was seen as a microcosm in astrological terms, it was already asserted that the twelve zodiacal signs affected different parts of the body.[179] Enumerated in his *De triplici vita*, Ficino's model of human life held that there were thousands of lines of influence connecting every organ, part of the body and soul to a particular star and planet.[180] The nature of this exchange is likened to the transmission of light. As he notes:

> ...every spirit is therefore instantly moved one way or the other and formed by these things. And however it turns out, such in turn in some degree it makes the mind, and absolutely such, the quality of the body. Then, as soon as it is opportunely exposed to the Graces through things pertaining to them, being also naturally in accord with those things, it immediately gains wondrous gifts of the Graces through their rays, which both flourish everywhere and are akin to it.[181]

This symbolism was carried on in the seventeenth century by Robert Fludd in his *Utriusque cosmi historia* (1617–1621). As seen in the title page of his work illustrating the macrocosm-microcosm (see Fig. 19), the right foot is in Leo, while the left in Libra. The right hand is in Gemini, the left in Capricorn, and the head is at the Pisces-Aries cusp. The five classical planets are said to rule these signs. Thus, the cusp of Pisces-Aries corresponds to Jupiter and Mars; for Capricorn, Saturn; for Gemini, Mercury; and for Libra, Venus. In addition, Leo is ruled by the Sun, but none of the five members are found in Cancer, which is ruled by the Moon. Fludd shows the Sun and Moon above, along with the other planets, in the macrocosm; man, of course, is in the microcosm. The fact that man has these five chief members, arranged in such a correspondence, led to the pentagram becoming adopted as the special symbol of man as microcosm.[182] Hence, the influence of the zodiacal spheres on different parts of the body is appropriate in their convenient juxtapositions. Their assigned adjacency or propinquity in space allowed for an appropriate understanding of the different areas of the body to correspond to different parts of the universe.[183]

---

179 Wayman, "The Human Body as Microcosm," 173.
180 Anthony Grafton, *Cardano's Cosmos: The Worlds and Works of a Renaissance Astrologer* (Cambridge, MA: Harvard University Press, 1999), 184.
181 Ficino, *Three Books on Life*, ed. and transl. Kaske and Clark, 297.
182 Wayman, "The Human Body as Microcosm," 185.
183 Ibid., 179–80.

Introduction 63

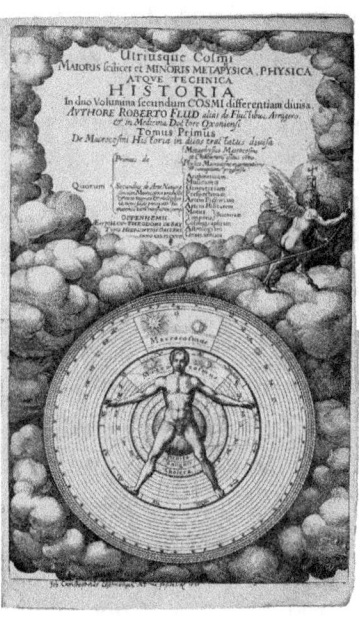

Fig. 19 Robert Fludd, Title page, 1617. Engraving from *Utriusque cosmi historia* (Oppenheim: Johann Theodor de Bry, 1617). Wikimedia, Public Domain, https://commons.wikimedia.org/wiki/File:Robert_Fludd_Utriusque_ cosmi.jpg#/media/File:Robert_Fludd_Utriusque_cosmi.jpg

Importantly, the interest in astrology demonstrated by Lomazzo paralleled a shift in arts education seen in the Accademia del Disegno. While the study of mathematics and anatomy formed the core of the Academy's studies, around 1590 (the same year as the publication of Lomazzo's *Idea*) natural philosophy joined the program for the second generation of members. As part of the original curriculum, the mind and eye had been trained to discover the mathematical relationships of the parts of the body to one another, which would enable the artist to depict ideal human forms of perfect proportions. With an understanding of the mechanics of the body, the artist could animate his ideal forms and set them convincingly in motion. Yet, external movements of the body were but visible manifestations of the internal movements of the soul: pose, gesture, and facial expression, and all aspects of physiognomy (including hair color, skin tone, and texture), were dictated by the various humors and emotional states to which men were subject. According to these principles, men of sanguine, melancholic, choleric, and phlegmatic temperaments had their own pathological traits and idiosyncrasies. The artist would have to be able to distinguish men of different humors when subject to various emotional states (*affetti dell'animo*), which dictate the external movements of the body.[184] Thus, natural philosophy, which encompassed such branches of knowledge as physiognomy and astrology, became part of the curriculum. A general knowledge of the discipline was expected since it formed a context for narrower discussions of physiognomy, because certain correspondences existed among all natural things. It was thus that the humors corresponded to the four elements of the sublunary world, which in turn corresponded to the four ages of man, as well as to the twelve zodiacal figures divided into four groups of three. These twelve zodiacal figures were each associated with one of the twelve gods and goddesses of the ancient world, and so the correspondences continued.[185]

The delay in the inclusion of natural philosophy and astrology in arts education relates to the acceptance of the discipline itself, since astrology had only recently been acknowledged as part of natural philosophy. As late as 1547, the mathematician and astrologer Girolamo Cardano (1501–1576) found it necessary to argue for its acceptance in his *Libelli*, which included the *Astrologicorum aphorismorum segmenta septum*.[186] In his impassioned plea, Cardano also wished to elevate and classify astrology as an art (not a science) and compared its revival in the Renaissance to that of medicine in Galen's time.[187] The classification by this astrologer is indicative of the perceived difference in the roles of astrology and astronomy at the time. Elaborated on by Ashmole in his *Theatrum chemicum britannicum*, the two distinct disciplines are described as such: "In the operative part of this Science [i.e., alchemy] the Rules of *Astronomie* and *Astrologie* (as elsewhere I have said) are to be consulted with... So that Elections (whose Calculatory part belongs

---

184 Karen Barzman, "The Florentine Accademia del Disegno: Liberal Education and the Renaissance Artist," in *Academies of Art between Renaissance and Romanticism*, ed. A. W. A. Boschloo (S'Gravenhage: SDU Uitgeverij, 1989), 14–30, at 23.

185 Of the last two specific parts of the curriculum, notably the study of inanimate forms and the teaching of architectural principles, Barzman found little record listing specifics. Ibid., 23–25.

186 Girolamo Cardano, *Peroratio, Opera*, 5: 90–92; Germana Ernst, "Veritatis amor dulcissimus," in *Secrets of Nature*, 45–46.

187 Anthony Grafton and Nancy Siraisi, "Between the Election and My Hopes," in *Secrets of Nature*, 105–06.

to *Astronomie*, but the Judiciary to *Astrologie*) are very necessary to begin this work with."[188] The view that the purpose of astronomy was to be calculative in nature, while astrology would then judge and interpret these findings, emerged slowly at the outset of the fifteenth century. Nevertheless, the two disciplines still worked hand in hand to increase mankind's understanding of the universe and their relationship to it.[189] The interpretation is evidenced in the publications of Gallucci himself, for while he is primarily remembered for his work in astronomy and astronomical instrumentation, he helped edit publications on astrology. For example, he edited and published a series of pseudo-Galenic pamphlets on astrological medicine in 1584 with texts by Johann Virdung von Hassfurt, Hermes Trismegistus, as well as Ficino's *De triplici vita*.[190] The editions demonstrated the applicability of astrological explication to medicine and astronomy as he ardently defended the usefulness of astronomy devoid of superstition.

As influential as these texts were, the text that made Gallucci a preeminent author throughout Europe, would be his *Theatrum mundi et temporis*. *Theatrum* provides the keenest insight into his mnemonic framing devices and interpretation of *Della simmetria*. As noted above, the publication came in the wake of an increased interest in celestial mapping in the second half of the century, spurred on by the papacy.[191] The work is even dedicated to Sixtus V. Divided into six parts, the text is dedicated to the description and mapping of the entire celestial and terrestrial worlds.[192] The first modern celestial atlas uses maps with a coordinate and trapezoidal system of projection that allow for the accurate determination of the star positions, which are derived from the Copernicum catalog.[193] Illustrated

---

188 Ashmole, *Theatrum chemicum britannicum*, 450; quoted in Newman and Grafton, eds, *Secrets of Nature*, 16.
189 Newman and Grafton, eds, *Secrets of Nature*, 9.
190 The volume itself concluded with brief booklets and astrological indexes by Gallucci. *De Cognoscendis, Et Medendis Morbis Ex Corporum Coelestium Positione Libri IIII*. Ernst, "Giovanni Paolo Gallucci," 740–41.
191 This is especially evident in the creation of the *Galleria delle carte geografiche* in the Vatican and in the *Sala dei brevi*. Hess, "On Some Celestial Maps and Globes of the Sixteenth Century," 406–09.
192 Massimiliano Rossi, "Un metodo per le passioni negli Scritti d'arte del tardo Cinquecento," in *Il volto e gli affetti: fisiognomica ed espressione nelle arti del Rinascimento: atti del convegno di studi, Torino 28–29 novembre 2001*, ed. Alessandro Pontremoli (Florence: L.S. Olschki, 2003), 83–102, at 84–85.
193 Ernst, "Giovanni Paolo Gallucci," 741.

with forty-eight maps of the Ptolemaic constellations and corresponding mythological figures, these personifications anthropomorphize the universe, much as in Vitruvian cosmology. The attempt is made, as such, to categorize and relate the heavens and earth through the microcosm-macrocosm pair. Inspired by other mapping systems, such as Camillo's Theater discussed earlier, Gallucci's "Theater" seeks to encapsulate all of the "world and time."[194] The original Theater described and then built after the description of Camillo itself was merely a "mnemotechnic tool," originally intended to provide orators with a well-ordered structure for their thought.[195] A system of "places and images" had been arranged, "sufficient for the location and management of all human concepts and of all things in this world, not only those which belong to the various fields of knowledge, but also to the noble arts and the mechanical."[196] Through the careful classification of all knowledge and an ideal ordering of all possible topics, the human mind itself could be made a perfect reflection of the macrocosm. Gallucci sets out the interrelated disciplines one must be familiar with in order to successfully capture an appropriate passion and portray it in an equally appropriate body, which includes proportion and anatomical theory; physiognomics and humoral theory; astronomy, astrology, and natural philosophy; theology; and even mnemonics and poetry. Given the overwhelming and interconnected nature of the topic, a mnemonic device borrowed from his own discipline is understandably suitable.

Examined together, we are able to identify the applicability of the device to the visual arts. For instance, should an artist wish to portray a figure who is happy, all of these influential forces need be considered. As Gallucci writes, "A painter wanting to make a joyful and cheerful man must make the face large, plump, moist, and quite fleshy."[197] Therefore, the figure is sanguine, has a rosy complexion due to the abundance of blood, which is affected by the hot-wetness of Jupiter, spring and childhood. This physiognomy, or "passion," would be appropriate for representing youthful figures and maidens, such as the Christ Child or

---

194 Gallucci, *Theatrum Mundi...*; quoted in Bernheimer, "Theatrum Mundi," 226.
195 In the Renaissance the "memorative art," which was founded by Cicero and Quintilian in antiquity, allowed the extension of man's natural power of recall by a discipline extending its scope. Bernheimer, "Theatrum Mundi," 226.
196 Camillo, "Trattato del'imitatione,"; quoted in Bernheimer, "Theatrum Mundi," 229.
197 Gallucci, *Della simmetria*, 5: 132v.

angels. Alternatively, a choleric figure would be shown with a yellowish complexion, due to the excess of yellow bile, and is appropriate for soldiers or young men — such as Ariosto's Rinaldo — who are irascible and quick to violence because they are under the influence of Mars, the god of war. The predominance of hot-dryness blows them about, with their passions compelling them. On the other hand, melancholic figures are swarthy with a dark and cool complexion due to the dominance of black bile and the cold-dry influence of Saturn on their systems. This type is appropriate for mature figures, but those especially whose dark and gloomy dispositions reveal something of their character, like Judas. And finally, phlegmatic figures are represented as pale, since illness is accompanied by an abundance of phlegm; this type is appropriate for elderly figures, like St Jerome, made sluggish and feminine through their proximity to the cold-wetness of the Moon and Venus. Furthermore, they also grow smaller later in life, their frames shrinking, until they are the size of women. In this way, gender, build, facial features, and character were understood as influenced by humoral theory; and astrological agency was adeptly outlined in a treatise that found an audience among artists and aspiring connoisseurs.

## 6. Proportion Studies: Reception and Legacy

Renaissance treatises expanded to address a wider range of subjects in the sixteenth century, often within a humanist framework. Though information on these early modern discourses, including use and readership, is scarce, their relative success can generally be discerned through the number of editions and translations published of each treatise, and the frequency and nature of citations found in later works that make reference to them. With this in mind, both the original *Vier Bücher* by Dürer and the later Italian translations by Gallucci achieved notable acclaim. Dürer's treatise on human proportion was, in fact, the German artist's most popular book, which can be attested to in the number of editions and translations that followed the original posthumous 1528 edition. Of these twelve translations, the Latin edition by Camerarius would be printed in two parts in Nuremberg in 1532 and 1534, followed by a second Latin edition printed in Paris in 1537 and a third in 1557. The same year as the last Latin edition, Louis Meigret

(1550–1558) translated the work into French. This fact is not surprising given the two prior Latin editions printed there. Italy, however, would remain a center for arts patronage and production and there Gallucci would write his translation in 1591, publishing it in Venice, as well as the second edition being printed in Venice in 1594. These would be followed by a Spanish translation by Luiz da Costa in Madrid, ca.1599, and da Costa's translation into Portuguese, which was never printed. The second German edition appeared in Arnheim in 1603; the second French edition in the same city in 1614, followed by the final translations into Dutch in 1622 and a second edition in 1662.[198]

Though the vernacular translations, especially French and Spanish, expanded readership of the *Four Books*, the most influential translation for artists and art education was Gallucci's own from 1591/1594. The Italian editions were highly influential in two ways: first, as a translation of Dürer's treatise into the target language of those living in the region responsible for dictating trends in the art world; and, second, as an interpretative device for the original author's ideas. In the Dedication to Maximilian, Gallucci states that the translation was necessary, for "…even though it was printed twice, one cannot find a copy anymore, except with someone whose kept them as dear as oriental pearls, and in the most honored places of their studies. Now, so as to ensure that this valuable work would not remain dead, and to allow every painter to take advantage of it (given that only a few prefer the Latin language), I have translated it to our Italian language."[199] Though the text was widely known — having reached a greater readership through its translation from German into Latin — by the second half of the sixteenth century, it was rare to find or own. Compounding the problem of availability were the reading skills of the intended audience. Though artists were expected to have a grammar school education, and hence the ability to read in Latin, since the fifteenth century, the reality remained that few practicing artists were fluent in *la lingua latina*.[200] Even artists highly regarded for their academic acumen, such as Nicolas Poussin, preferred the Italian version. In fact, Poussin would make extensive use of Chapter LVII in the Book Five of Gallucci's publication in his own *Osservazioni*,

---

198 William Martin Conway, transl., *The Writings of Albrecht Dürer* (London: Owen, 1958), 229–30.
199 Gallucci, "Preface," *Della simmetria*, 2v.
200 Dempsey, "Some Observations on the Education of Artists," 557–69.

printed by Giovan Pietro Bellori (1613–1696) in his Life of the artist.[201] There was also an extensive reutilization of the chapter in a section on physiognomy in Vincenzo Carducci's (ca.1578–1638) *Diálogos de la pintura* [Dialogues on Painting] (1633).[202] These authors excerpted sections from Gallucci's original contribution to the treatise in the last book. The translator had explained at the outset that he "...was not satisfied with [only the original *Four Books*] and found it very necessary to add a fifth book for students of this faculty, which is taught through the authority of philosophers and poets, who, along with those colors and lines, can explain both the natural and the incidental passions of the souls of men."[203] Many works following in the wake of Gallucci's publication utilize Dürer's system for laying out ratios and proportions for human anatomy, as well as Gallucci's classification system for understanding utilize Dürer's system in terms of physiognomy.

The treatise taken as a whole greatly expanded the artistic discourse and availability of information on human anatomy in Italy, and remained the version most often cited in later treatises, though it is virtually unknown today.[204] In fact, "Studies on the problem of proportions are generally received with skepticism or, at most, with little interest."[205] Such was Erwin Panofsky's estimation of proportion studies in 1955. Though the direction and interest in the topic has shifted somewhat since then, studies of treatises (such as the one currently under review) are still rare.[206] The lack of recognition for *Della simmetria* in particular is in part due to the dismissal of the work

---

201 Anthony Blunt, "Poussin's Notes on Painting," *Journal of the Warburg Institute*, 1 (1938), 344–51, https://doi.org/10.2307/750002; Bellori, *Le vite...*, 460–62.
202 Vincente Carducho, *Dialogos de la Pintura. Su defense, origen, esencia, definicion, modos y differencias*, ed. F. Calvo Serraller (Madrid: Ediciones Turner, 1979), 396–404; Rossi has also suggested that copies were also in the private collections or available to several artists in the seventeenth century. Rossi, "Un metodo per le passioni negli Scritti d'arte del tardo Cinquecento," 83–84.
203 Gallucci, "Preface," *Della simmetria*, 2v.
204 Bartrum, ed., *Albrecht Dürer and His Legacy*, 240; Enrico Castelnuovo, "Dürer scrittore e scienziato," in *Dürer e l'Italia*, ed. Kristina Herrmann Fiore (Milan: Electa, 2007), 97–103, at 98.
205 Panofsky, "The History of The Theory of Human Proportions," 55–107.
206 None of the treatises on human proportions from the period discussed have been translated into English. Treatments are limited to articles. See Jane Andrews Aiken, "Leon Battista Alberti's System of Human Proportions," *Journal of the Warburg and Courtauld Institutes*, 43 (1980), 68–96, https://doi.org/10.2307/751189; Rossi, "Un metodo per le passioni negli Scritti d'arte del tardo Cinquecento," 83–84; Rudolf Wittkower, "The Changing Concept of Proportion," *Daedalus*, 89.1 (1960), 199–215.

as a mere translation of another author's work, while the original sections, which are the focus of this study, remain almost completely overlooked.[207] Another reason for this oversight is the critical milieu in which Gallucci published. Whereas the number of publications on art was quite paltry from Alberti to Vasari, the late sixteenth century witnessed an explosion on various specialized topics, not least among them art.[208] Looking forward to the seventeenth century, most of the authors were also no longer practicing artists, but were professionals in a variety of disciplines, including medicine, astronomy, law, and letters.[209] As such, the usefulness of their treatments for working artists was questioned, even in their time. Compounding this situation is the perception that treatises like Gallucci's were "inspired by the haste of contemporary taxonomy" prevalent in the period demonstrated in other encyclopedic treatments, such as Lomazzo's *Trattato dell'arte della pittura, scultura ed architettura* of 1584.[210] These seemingly self-indulgent, lengthy, and ponderous lists appear distanced from everyday practical matters of the craft and of interest only to amateur-connoisseurs and aristocratic dilettantes (like the author's own pupils).

In the mid-sixteenth century, a further complication developed that would tarnish the reputation of Dürer and the usefulness of his study. The development of a canon of proportions based on arithmetic ratios was the consequence of the belief in the relationship between beauty and harmony sought in arts education since the early fifteenth century. Yet, as the system had been established and disseminated through treatises like Dürer's, another current of thought sought to undermine the premise that beauty could be attained purely through harmony, symmetry, and mathematics. This can be illustrated in the figure of the sculptor-theorist Vincenzo Danti (1530–1576). Only the first book of Danti's essentially Albertian treatise on *disegno* ("drawing") was ever published (1567),

---

207 Rossi, "Un metodo per le passioni negli Scritti d'arte del tardo Cinquecento," 83–84.
208 Anthony Blunt, *Artistic Theory in Italy 1450–1600* (Oxford: Oxford University Press, 1962).
209 For instance, Giulio Mancini and Francesco Scannelli were physicians by profession, while Giovan Pietro Bellori, perhaps the most significant writer on art of the century, was an academic, librarian, and antiquarian.
210 "Non siamo, evidentemente, in presenza del libro che Dürer avrebbe potuto aggiungere, ma piuttosto di un'interpretazione estrema, radicale, ispirata alla furia tassonomica contemporanea che cerca e rilancia precedenti di forte sintonia." Rossi, "Un metodo per le passioni negli Scritti d'arte del tardo Cinquecento," 99.

but we know that eight of the remaining thirteen books were devoted to the subject of anatomy. Danti's telling title of his treatment, *Trattato delle perfette proporzioni* [Treatise on Perfect Proportions], indicates that he was centrally concerned, like Dürer, with the perfect proportions of the human form, and, therefore, with the mathematical relationships of the parts of the body from one to another. Nevertheless, he writes explicitly of a *misura intelletuale*, or "intellectual measure."[211] The perceived interrelationships of forms in Danti's conception were not to be measured with instruments. On the contrary, they could be discerned by the eye of a trained intellect, the greatest instrument of all.

The understanding and circulation of such an ability was well known after the apotheosis of Michelangelo Buonarroti (1475–1564). In his biography of the "divine" artist of 1553, Ascanio Condivi (1525–1574) noted that Michelangelo intended to write a treatise on proportion himself, drawing upon the years of anatomical study and the dissection of corpses, "with a brilliant theory which he arrived at through long experience." Extending the critique of Dürer's rigid, mathematical conception of human proportions, Condivi reassures that:

> I know very well that, when he reads Albrecht Dürer, he finds his work very weak, seeing in his mind how much more beautiful and useful in the study of this subject his own conception would have been. And, to tell the truth, Albrecht discusses only the measurements and varieties of human bodies, for which no fixed rule can be given, and he forms his figures straight upright like poles; as to what was more important, the movements and gestures of human beings, he says not a word.[212]

The understanding that "no fixed rule can be given" for proper proportions is consistent with Danti's concept of the *misura intelletuale*, a belief that Michelangelo's biographers considered Michelangelo to have possessed.

Proceeding from the disparaging judgment of Dürer's theory of proportions by Michelangelo, according to Condivi and Vasari (*Le Vite*, 1568), many theorists later in the century vigorously and consciously

---

211 Margaret Davis, "Beyond the 'Primo Libro' of Vincenzo Danti's 'Trattato delle perfette proporzioni,'" *Mitteilungen des kunsthistorischen Institutes in Florenz*, 26.1 (1982), 63–84, esp. 68.

212 Ascanio Condivi, *The Life of Michelangelo*, transl. Alice Sedgwick Wohl (University Park, PA: Pennsylvania State University Press, 1999), 98–99.

criticized the earlier attempts to place artistic representation on a scientific, especially a mathematical basis.[213] Leonardo da Vinci had taken pains to determine the motions of the body according to the laws of strength and weight, even to fix numerically the changes of measurement induced by these movements.[214] He also contributed anatomical studies to Pacioli's proportion treatise, while Dürer sought to master "foreshortening" through geometrical construction. All these theoreticians agreed that the proportions of the human body at rest could be ascertained and fixed within an agreed upon mathematical canon of human proportion, and that this was necessary for beauty.[215] The belief was replaced by repeated warnings against overvaluing the theory of proportions that had been diligently established for posterity. Even though the artist was recommended to be familiar with established canons, he was instructed to disregard them, especially if attempting to reproduce the effects of movement in the human body, as Condivi noted.[216] Such was the recommendation of Raffaello Borghini (1537–1588) in his *Il Riposo* of 1584, for he noted that:

> As for measurements... it is necessary to know them; but one must bear in mind that it is not always advisable to observe them. For we often make figures bend, rise, or turn where the arms are now stretched out and now contracted; so that, in order to give the figures gracefulness, it is necessary to extend the measurements in some part and to shorten them in some other part. This cannot be taught; but the artist must judiciously learn it from nature.[217]

To achieve the desired effect of "gracefulness" in figures to be produced for a given composition, the artist was required to alter the canon, which was important to internalize for just this reason. If a particular pose or gesture was desired, accepted precepts would offer a conceptual starting

---

213 Condivi, *The Life of Michelangelo*, transl. Wohl, 98–99.
214 Leonardo da Vinci, *On Painting*, transl. Martin Kemp and Margaret Walker (New Haven; London: Yale University Press, 1989), 117–43.
215 Luca Pacioli, *De divina proportione*. Dürer, *Vier Bücher*.
216 Condivi, *The Life of Michelangelo*, transl. Wohl, 98–99.
217 "Le misure... è cosa necessaria à sapere; but considerar si dee, che non sempre fa luogo l'osseruarle. Conciosiacosa che spesso si facciamo figure in atto di chinarsi, d'alzarsi, e di volgersi, nelle cui attitudini hora si distndono ed hora si raccolgono le braccie di maniera, che à voler dar gratia alle figure bisogna in qualche parte allungare ed in qualche altra parte ristringere le misure. La qual cosa non si può insegnare; ma bisogna che l'artefice con giudicio del naturale la imprenda." Raffaello Borghini, *Il Riposo* (Florence: Giorgio Marescotti, 1584), 150.

point for the artist, which would then be tempered by "nature" and improved upon by *invenzione*.

By the turn of the century, the usefulness of mathematics for practicing artists was rejected in academic institutions. Federico Zuccaro (ca.1542–1609), co-founder and first *principe* of the Accademia di San Luca, attests to the hatred for mathematics in his *L'Idea di pittori, scultori et architetti* [The Idea of the Painters, Sculptors, and Architects] of 1607; for, as he set forth, "the art of painting does not derive its principles from the mathematical sciences..." since "painting is not their daughter, but the daughter of Nature and *Disegno*."[218] In response to those "mathematical rules" established by Dürer, Zuccaro notes that "such rules neither serve nor suit our actions [as artists]."[219] In fact, he states that the German artist produced the studies "as a joke, a pastime, and to give diversion to those minds that are inclined to contemplation rather than to action..."[220] Such pursuits should be "left to those sciences and speculative professions of geometry, astronomy, arithmetic, and the like..." as they require "proofs."[221]

Much as Borghini had stressed, the artist need only be familiar with "the basic principles and instructions acquired from his predecessors, or also from nature itself, becomes a skillful man through mere natural judgment with proper care and observation of the beautiful...without any aid from or need for mathematics."[222] Relating the qualities cited by Condivi, Zuccaro calls instead for the quality discussed as *giudizio dell'occhio* ("judgement of the eye"); he states, as "you make yourself

---

218  "Ma dico bene e so, che dico il vero, che l'arte della pittura non piglia i suoi principi, nè ha necessità alcuna di ricorrere alle mattematiche Scienze, ad imparare regole e modi alcuni per l'arte sua, nè anco per poterne ragionare in speculazione; però non è di essa figliuola, ma bensì della Natura e del Disegno." *Scritti d'Arte di Federico Zuccaro*, ed. Detlef Heikamp (Florence: L. S. Olschki, 1961), 249–50.

219  "perchè oltre gli scorci e forma del corpo sempre sferico, cotali regole non servono ne convengono alle nostre operazioni..." Ibid., 250.

220  "Sicchè il Durero per quella fatica, che non fu poca, credo, che egli a scherzo, a passatempo e per dar trattenimento a quelli intelletti, che stanno più su la contemplazione, che su le operazioni, ciò facesse, e per mostrare, che il Disegno e lo spirito del pittore sa e può tutto ciò, che si presuppone fare." Ibid., 251.

221  "Dirò bene, che queste regole mattematiche si devono lasciare a quelle scienze e professioni speculative della geometria, astronomia, arimmetica, e simili, che con le prove loro acquietano l'intelletto." Ibid.

222  "Sicchè il pittore, oltre i primi principi ed ammaestramenti avuti da' suoi predecessori, oppure dalla Natura stessa, dal giudizio stesso naturale con buona diligenza ed osservazione del bello e buono divento valent' uomo senz' altro ajuto o bisogno della mattematica." Ibid., 250.

so familiar with these rules and measures in working, that you have the compass and the square in your eyes, and judgment and practice in your hands."[223] Zuccaro then returns to the Aristotelian tradition cited in Aquinas that the artist's goal should be that of mimesis, a truth to nature: "But we, professors of *Disegno*, have no need of other rules than those which Nature herself gives for imitating her."[224]

Thus, ironically, the same period that so zealously guarded artistic freedom against the restrictions of mathematical systems, also attempted to systematically organize art in such a way that even the most gifted had to learn and even the most untalented could learn.[225] Therefore, even though Zuccaro denied that an artist must observe the laws of proportion, he, nonetheless, admitted that they must be known. The same can be said of Danti, who wrote in his proportion study that an artist should reject the mathematical schematization of the form and movement of the body; Danti, nevertheless, admitted that the anatomical method was unconditionally valid, since somehow a "scientific" approach to art had to be found. He stated expressly that his *vera regola*, or "true rule," would be useful to those "born to art," as well as to those not born to it, thus supporting the notion that art could be learned.[226] Although a single proportion and canon was not championed as the norm of beauty, which had been customary earlier in the century, even Lomazzo, who espoused the idea of the *figura serpentinata*, also recounted Dürer's detailed proportions in both of his treatises.[227] Begrudgingly then, studies on human proportion were seen as necessary even by their most ardent critics.

Despite the condemnation of proportion studies by all manner of writers on art, their proliferation did not slow, nor was their perceived benefit for arts education seriously doubted. Moreover, by the end of

---

223 "Ma conviene, disse egli, che tu ti facci sì familiari queste regole e misure nell' operare, che tu abbi nelli occhi il compasso e la squadra: e il giudizio e la pratica nelle mani." Ibid.
224 "Ma noi altri professori del Disegno non abbiamo bisogno d'altre regole, che quelle, che la Natura stessa ne dà, per quella imitare." Ibid., 251.
225 Giovanni Battista Armenini, *On the True Precepts of the Art of Painting*, transl. Robert Baldick (New York: Vintage Books, 1977).
226 Vincenzo Danti, "Preface," *Il primo libro del Trattato delle perfette proporzioni* (Perugia: Bartelli, 1830), [n.p.]; Danti, *Il primo libro*, chapter 16.
227 Lomazzo, *Trattato dell'arte della pittura*, 1: 5–8; 4: 3. Rossi, "Un metodo per le passioni negli Scritti d'arte del tardo Cinquecento," 97–98.

the sixteenth century, the theory of proportions and anatomy had been well-developed: with several treatises dedicated solely to the issue, and with dozens of treatments mentioning the theory in passing.[228] In each of the treatises dedicated solely to proportion theory, their pedagogical application was a paramount concern. The widely available canons of proportions were necessary for young artists to initially internalize in order to derive poses, actions and emotions of figures in *istorie*, or history paintings. After these had been mastered, the mature artist could then modify each set of ratios to befit a given character or narrative. By its very nature then, the original purpose of Dürer's publication was arguably both pedagogical and referential.[229] This is confirmed when considering that before he died the artist was obsessed with compiling the typological sets for posterity and the benefit of young painters.[230] The same function was retained by Gallucci, but was circulated within a very different artistic environment due to the perceived decline in the arts around mid-century.

Those artists living in the wake of the High Renaissance, as related by critics like Mancini, were discussed as living in the "the age of senescence and decrepitude."[231] The notion of art as a biological organism was applied by Vasari to illustrate the continual march towards perfection in his *Lives*: "The arts, like men themselves, are born, grow up, become old and die."[232] Nevertheless, such a "decline" in the arts did not prevent one of the greatest periods of publication on art of the

---

228 Of those available in the sixteenth century: Luca Pacioli, *De divina proportione* (1509); Vincenzo Danti, *Trattato delle perfette proporzioni* (1567); Juan Valverde, *Historia de la composicion del cuerpo humano* (1556) (Italian edition published 1560); Andreas Vesalius, *De humani corporis fabrica libri septum* (1543).

229 Concerned with individual aesthetic judgment, Dürer had questioned the usefulness of his studies: "In the rigid postures in which they are drawn up on the foregoing pages," he says of his numerous, elaborate paradigms, "the figures are of no use whatever." Erwin Panofsky, *Dürers Kunsttheorie: vornehmlich in ihrem Verhältnis zur Kunsttheorie der Italiener* (Berlin: De Gruyter, 2011), 81 ff.

230 Joseph Leo Koerner, "Albrecht Dürer: A Sixteenth-Century Influenza," in *Albrecht Dürer and His Legacy*, ed. Bartrum, 18–38, at 22.

231 Mancini, *Considerazioni sulla Pittura*, ed. Adriana Marucchi and Luigi Salerno, 2 vols (Rome: Accademia Nazionale dei Lincei, 1957), I: 105; quoted in Philip Sohm, *The Artist Grows Old: The Aging of Art and Artists in Italy 1500–1800* (New Haven: Yale University Press, 2007), 137.

232 Giorgio Vasari, *Le vite de' più eccellenti pittori scultori e architettori: nelle redazioni del 1550 e 1568*, ed. Rosanna Bettarini and Paola Barocchi, 6 vols (Florence: Sansoni, 1966–1987), II: 31.

early modern period.²³³ One explanation for the spike in literary interest, surprisingly, was the belief in art academies, such as the Accademia di San Luca in Rome (founded in 1593 by Federico Zuccaro), that art had sunk into *pratica* and needed reform through a thorough reintroduction and reinforcement of theory.²³⁴ Though the reasons varied, most of the publications emerging at the end of the sixteenth century were designed to rectify this imbalance in the production of art and overvaluing "practice." In like fashion, we find that in his Preface, Gallucci does not spare criticism for contemporary painters who proceed without precepts and rely solely on practice without theory:

> For without any precept, which would certainly guide students, they instead propose their own or copy the drawings of others. Thus, all of this profession, which is truly worthy of science and practice, they reduce to practice alone, and, as a result, like so many amputees going about limping and blind people groping, deprive their histories of the variety of many colors in order to satisfy the ignorant and vulgar.²³⁵

The pedagogue laments that "modern painters" have deviated from the canon established by Dürer, producing figures of nine or ten head-lengths. These artists ignore the proportions "in every kind of body" that the artist had "toiled over in his studies."²³⁶ In this way, Gallucci can be seen to have the same instructive goals as Giovanni Battista Armenini, Lomazzo, and, later, Zuccaro, as the translation of the quintessential treatment on human proportions for artists offered a perfect supplementary text to an artist's education in an academic or workshop setting.

---

233 Sohm has pointed out that there was a spike in publications in the 1560s, and then later in the 1580s and 1590s. Sohm, *The Artist Grows Old*, 140.

234 Ibid.

235 "come tanti Volcani vanno zoticando e come orbi vanno e tentoni e per sodisfare all'ignorante volgo riempiono di più colori che nel caos originario." Gallucci, "Preface," *Della simmetria*, 7r.

236 "Et questa sono le misure universali, che si usano da i moderni pittori, le quali dicono essi, havere comprobate, si col natuale, si con le statue antiche più scelte. Veddino non dime no come le misure del nostro Durero, sono più esquistite, & più certe, che queste misurando quelle ciascheduna particella, quantunque piccola, & queste solo i membri principali, oltre acciò dando quelle misure ad ogni sorte di corpi, che si possa ritrovare fra gli huomini, & queste solo a quelli che costano di nove, & diece teste. Non rincresca dunque alli studiosi l'affaticarsi nelle misure del Durero, come più certe, & in questi discorsi, c'hanno forza di spiegare le nature de gli huomini, accioche imitado bene la natura come deono, ne portino quel frutto, che menitano le loro fatiche." Gallucci, *Della simmetria*, 5: 144v.

In point of fact, it was in the first academy established for the arts, the Florentine Accademia del Disegno, that the need for such texts already existed when Gallucci entered the discourse on proportion studies in 1591. Founded as an instrument of liberal education, the Florentine Academy codified existing principles of theory and practice in a formal program for artists of all ages.[237] *Disegno*, the theoretical principle uniting the three *arti di disegno*, was embraced as the guiding principle of the new institution. In the Introduction to the second edition of the Lives, Giorgio Vasari, one of the founders of the organization, defined *disegno* as the realization of the *idea*, which is born in the intellect.[238] Through endless study and practice, and the application of measured judgment, the hand could be trained to reproduce the inventions of the intellect. This notion of *disegno* called for the union of theory and practice; the mind had to be exercised as well as the hand in order to lead to perfection in art. The curriculum of the Academy was a progressive sequence of study, beginning with foundation sciences and exercises, and then advancing to related disciplines and activities. In the sixteenth century, mathematics was recognized as the foundation of knowledge, as a means for rationalizing the external world, and, therefore, study commenced with mathematics to provide the artist with the conceptual key for comprehending the world around him. Since Florentine art was primarily concerned with the human figure, anatomy followed mathematics and was complemented by drawing the figure from life. Natural philosophy came next, along with the study of inanimate forms like drapery; all of these studies intended to aid the artist in the composition of *istoria*. Knowledge of one subject conditioned comprehension of the next, and together they constituted a coherent theory of art. This codification of the curriculum was drawn directly from Renaissance traditions and earlier theorists, such as that of Alberti, while towards the end of the century unpublished manuscripts of Leonardo's art theory started to circulate in Florence.[239]

In a letter from 1591 to his brother in Genoa, the painter Giovanni Battista Paggi (1554–1627) summarized the curriculum of the

---

[237] Barzman, "The Florentine Accademia del Disegno," 14.
[238] Vasari, *Le vite de' più eccellenti pittori scultori e architettori*, ed. Bettarini and Barocchi, I: 168–69.
[239] Barzman, "The Florentine Accademia del Disegno," 15.

Academy and began by affirming the Albertian dictum that theory begins with first principles, which, for the arts of *disegno*, meant the mathematical sciences.[240] He asserted that contemporary artistic theory was grounded partly in arithmetic and partly in geometry.[241] From these sciences the artist would gain a knowledge of perspective and symmetry. The rigorous drafting of three-dimensional forms, such as regular and irregular polyhedra, according to the rules of geometry, provided fundamental exercises necessary for developing a facility of the hand. In addition to this, the study of mathematics was thought to develop measured judgment in both action and intellect.[242] Dürer, like Alberti and especially Leonardo, understood the importance of a firm grounding in mathematics for artists, which informed his publication in 1525 of Die Unterweisung der Messung mit dem Zirkel und Richtscheit [Instructions for Measuring with Compass and Ruler], the guide to geometrical and perspective constructions. The treatise was to be read in tandem with the *Vier Bücher*, as it offered a mathematical foundation for the study of human proportion to benefit the education of the young artist.[243]

This sequence was adopted by the Accademia as the next part of the curriculum with anatomy and life drawing, particularly for the painter and sculptor. In order to discern the mathematical relationships of the parts of the body, one studied mathematics first and then anatomy in great detail, followed by life drawing. This process would enable the artist to recognize and then produce ideal human forms whose beauty was the result of harmonious proportions. After anatomy, the artist turned to the study of the human figure from life. According to Alberti, although the beauty of the body's planes and surfaces could be grasped from ancient sculpture, it was best mastered from nature directly.[244] Alberti had urged artists to study human anatomy in a systematic fashion, concentrating on those parts of the body responsible for mobilization. The study of bone

---

240 Carroll William Westfall, "Painting and the Liberal Arts: Alberti's View," *Journal of the History of Ideas* (1967), 487–506, https://doi.org/10.2307/2708607
241 Giovanni Bottari, *Raccolta di lettere sulla pittura, scultura ed architettura scritte da' più celebri personaggi dei secoli XV, XVI, e XVII*, ed. Stefano Ticozzi, 8 vols (Milan: Giovanni Silvestri, 1822–1825), VI: 83.
242 Hence the Academy's teachings were modeled on the universities, where one would read and comment on authoritative texts, such as Euclid and Vitruvius. Barzman, "The Florentine Accademia del Disegno," 15.
243 Dürer, *Die Unterweisung*, ed. Jaeggli and Patesch.
244 Alberti, *On Painting*, transl. Spencer, 3: 55–60.

structure, musculature, and the flesh stripped of skin would follow each other sequentially. Of course, these internal anatomical components had to be mastered in addition to those external features studied in life drawing classes. They had to be understood in their individual appearances and functions, and in their proportional relationships to one another, in order for the artist to fully comprehend the mechanics of mobility. Annual dissections were carried out at the Academy from its inception in 1563, but the interest in anatomical dissection accelerated in the wake of Michelangelo.[245] There was a pervasive notion that the perfection of the "divine" Michelangelo's art, which celebrated and ennobled the human form, lay in his profound knowledge of anatomy. Academy members sought to perfect their own art by way of a solid grounding in this science.[246] The goal of such a rigorous series of studies was to effectively relate the emotional state of figures to be represented in works of art. Based initially on Alberti's recommendations, and then reinforced by the prescripts of Leonardo, the artist was trained to have their works communicate mutely, with their inner thoughts and passions, or *affetti dell'animo*, made visibly manifest.[247] This exhortation remained a central theme in the publications surrounding Gallucci's work. In fact, the proposed theory of physiognomy in *Della simmetria* is a primary leitmotif used as a literary precept to effectively express the "passions that [men and women] perceive."[248] The same interest had already been expressed by Lomazzo in his *Trattato* in such chapters as "Delle passion dell'animo e loro origine e differenza [On the Passion of the Soul, and Their Origin and Difference]" and "Dell'amicizia et inimicizia [On Friendship and Enmity]".[249]

---

245 Karen Barzman, "Perception, Knowledge, and the Theory of Disegno in Sixteenth-Century Florence," *From Stuio to Studiolo: Florentine Draughtsmanship under the First Medici Grand Dukes*, ed. Larry J. Feinberg (Oberlin and Seattle: Allen Memorial Art Museum and University of Washington Press, 1991), 37–48, at 41.

246 Although dissections were held only annually in the hospital of Santa Maria Nuova, the corpse was probably viewed for longer than the medical professionals would have advised in order to have the maximum number of students view it. Barzman, "Perception, Knowledge, and the Theory of *Disegno*," 37–48.

247 Ibid., 41.

248 Rossi, "Un metodo per le passioni negli Scritti d'arte del tardo Cinquecento," 86; Ernst, "Gallucci, Giovanni Paolo," 740–43.

249 See especially chapter 3 of Lomazzo's *Trattato* ("Delle passioni dell'animo e loro origine e differenza"), and chapter 18 ("Dell'amicizia et inimicizia de i moti e loro accoppiamenti"). Lomazzo, *Trattato dell'arte della pittura*, 3: 103, 153; Rossi, "Un metodo per le passioni negli Scritti d'arte del tardo Cinquecento," 101.

Yet, in order to divine the internal passions, or *affetti*, of figures, the stages of anatomical study were organized to build one upon the next. Knowledge of the internal structure of human bodies and their mechanics preceded the study of live models. Only after the mathematical components of the parts had been analyzed could the artist move to assembling multiplicity into a unified whole. And only then could he begin producing numerous drawings from a live nude model. There were many supplementary materials at the disposal of students at the Academy to assist in the process of creating proportional human figures. Along with sculptures and plaster casts, supplementary texts on anatomy would be used to further investigations that started with geometrical construction, dissections and life drawing. These texts would have included Danti's *Trattato delle perfette proporzioni*, which was incomplete, but available by 1567, as well as the now lost *Il Microcosmo* [The Microcosm] by Pietro Francavilla, which discussed physiognomy, various humors and temperaments along with human anatomy.[250] Of extant examples, Juan Valverde's *Historia de la composicion del cuerpo humano* [History of the Composition of the Human Body] was widely circulated and translated into Italian in 1560, while the encyclopedic treatment *De humani corporis fabrica libri septum* [On the Fabric of the Human Body in Seven Books] by Andreas Vesalius of 1543 was the most influential for the arts and medicine. Appended to this list must be Gallucci's *Della simmetria*, as its influence is demonstrable among artists in the following century. The illustrations that accompanied these texts would have provided excellent models for copying by young artists, as Alessandro Allori (1535–1607) claims in his own treatise.[251] Evidence of this use comes not only from examples artists have left to posterity, but also information associated with art academies. According to the statues of the Roman Accademia, a library was created with donated books from its members. The volumes would be attached by chains to counters where members could consult the various texts. Designed

---

250 Barzman, "Perception, Knowledge, and Theory of *Disegno*," 47. Baldinucci noted that the treatise covered these topics in his *Notizie*: Filippo Baldinucci, *Notizie de' professori del disegno*, ed. F. Ranalli and Paolo Barocchi, 7 vols (Florence: Eurografica S.p.A, 1974), III: 71.

251 Ciardi discusses Allori's text and recommendations for artists in: Roberto P. Ciardi, "Le regole del disegno di Alessandro Allori e la nascita del dilettantismo pittorico," *Storia dell'arte*, 12 (1971), 267–84; Barzman, "Perception, Knowledge, and Theory of *Disegno*," 47.

to accommodate both academicians and practicing artists of various educational backgrounds, the collection was furnished with treatises on general, as well as specialized topics. In an inventory requested in 1624 by Simon Vouet, the library had grown to around forty volumes, an impressive collection for a single institution dedicated to teaching art. Included in the works were the authors: Alberti, Dürer (Gallucci's translation), Lomazzo, Ripa, Castiglione, Flavio, Heron, Euclid, and Ovid.[252] Inasmuch as library patrons would read *Della simmetria* alongside other art treatises, ancient and modern poets, so too would they with Gallucci's own volume, a microcosm itself of arts libraries and a compendium of knowledge.

Gallucci's translation of Dürer's *Vier Bücher* deliberately attempted to connect with the intellectual and political interests of the original author. Through an association with one of the greatest patrons of the artist, Maximilian I, the polymath-translator demonstrated that his association with Dürer was political, as well as theoretical. In doing so, the *Della simmetria* is a testament to the applicability of astronomy and astrology to the arts and vice versa. Gallucci's interest in mapping the universe through Vitruvian cosmology naturally lent its mnemonic tool to the theory of human proportion. In turn, the anthropomorphizing of astronomical phenomena can be seen to have been influenced by Dürer's systematization and schematization of the human form, which the artist then translated to his own astrological maps.[253] Furthermore, the publications surrounding that of Gallucci's, which also utilized universal mapping systems, like Lomazzo's *Trattato* and *Idea*, demonstrate that the translation was reflective of the dominant interests of art theory late in the cinquecento. As proportion studies evolved, we find that the intent of Dürer, both as represented in his own work and as illustrated in Gallucci's translation, foretold the evolution

---

252 Karl Noehles, *La Chiesa dei SS. Luca e Martina nell'opera di Pietro da Cortona* (Rome: Ugo Bozzi Editore, 1970), 336–38 Pietro Roccasecca, "Teaching in the Studio," *The Accademia Seminars*, ed. Peter Lukehart (New Haven; London: National Gallery of Art, Yale University Press, 2009), 123–60, at 142.

253 In 1515, Dürer published his forty-eight wood engravings of the classical constellations. Roberta J. M. Olson, "...And They Saw Stars: Renaissance Representations of Comets and Pretelescopic Astronomy," *Art Journal*, 44.3 (1984), 216–24, at 220, https://doi.org/10.1080/00043249.1984.10792549. Gallucci also connected the work produced by Dürer for Maximilian to astronomy: "Vi sono gli Encomi di Massimiliano, & l'immortali opera dell'historia Astronomica..." (Gallucci, "Life of Albrecht Dürer," *Della simmetria*, 4r).

of art theory. For by the century's end, beauty in human proportion theory had metamorphosed from a general "notion" in the artist's mind that related to "harmonious arrangements," to a regularized concept that is formed and infused in matter through a specific stratagem. The emphasis on quantifying and, subsequently, qualifying mathematical interrelationships between objects, resulted in a continued effort to distill a universally valid set of harmonious relationships in the parts of human anatomy. The resultant canon of proportions that derived from the study of Vitruvius was coupled with the incorporeal conditions of universal Forms. In the tradition of Ficino adopted by Dürer, Lomazzo, and Gallucci, a system was developed whereby the intellective faculty for "universal knowledge" gave the human mind the ability to perceive, comprehend, and expectantly, express all of Creation. In a similar fashion, proportion theory became a way in which to train artists to express not only the motions and emotions of figures in their works, but offered a metaphysical basis for the construction of perceived or intended visual phenomena. The epistemological model allowed the whole of the universe to be comprehended in the microcosm of man and, resultantly, be reproduced in art, as man had the intellective and creative power of Nature to create imbued by God. It is no wonder then that treatises like Gallucci's remained a favorite reference for artists until the modern era. The specificity and taxonomic interest in listing increasingly specific parts of the human body, appropriate to different passions, shows just how discerning early modern viewers and collectors were. It also reveals the daunting task of artists, who were expected to master these various interrelated physiognomies and correspondences. Unlike their more privileged counterparts, artists often did not advance as far in their grammar studies and thus required additional resources to construct elaborate pictorial conceits; a highlight or summary of the most salient points or themes in the *studia humanitatis* assisted in bolstering the claims of the visual arts as liberal. In short, Gallucci's *Della simmetria* reveals the perceived benefits of symmetry and proportion in the context of contemporary education, but especially that of artists. As seen in the following sections of his original contribution to Dürer's earlier enterprise, the author would expand on this interest in diversity of human types to elaborate systems of physiognomy and humoral readings.

# On the Symmetry of Human Bodies

*By Albrecht Dürer,
Illustrious Painter and Geometrician.
Translated by James Hutson*

# On the Symmetry of Human Bodies,

## Four Books.

*Newly translated from the Latin language into Italian,*

*By M. Giovanni Paolo Gallucci Salodiano,*

*Venetian academician.*

And elaborated on in the Fifth Book, wherein he addresses the manners in which painters and sculptors represent the diversity of the nature of men and women, and with what passions they feel for various happenstance that occur.

*The work is not only useful, but necessary for painters and sculptors, as well as all others, who in this regard wish to acquire perfect judgment.*

# Contents

| | |
|---|---:|
| Dedication | 91 |
| Life of Albrecht Dürer | 97 |
| Preface to Readers | 105 |
| Book Five | 113 |
|   1. On the Utility of this Doctrine | 115 |
|   2. On the Differences of Humans with Respect to Countries, Sex, and Age | 117 |
|   3. On the Beauty of Human Bodies, Especially Women | 121 |
|   4. The Figure of a Strong Man | 127 |
|   5. How the Figure of a Timid Man Should Be Painted | 131 |
|   6. How One Should Paint a Furious and Angry Man | 134 |
|   7. The Figure of a Man, Who Is by Nature Cold and Wet, therefore, Meek and Humble, Feeble, Slow, Quiet, and Effeminate | 138 |
|   8. How an Ingenious Man Should Be Painted | 138 |
|   9. The Figure of an Uncouth Man Compared to One with Great Intelligence | 139 |
| 10. The Figure and Painting of an Effeminate Man, Soft by Nature and also through Incident | 140 |
| 11. How a Humble Man Should Be Painted, and One Who Is Shameful, either by Nature or Chance, and a Woman Again | 141 |
| 12. The Figure of an Insolent and Presumptuous Man | 143 |
| 13. The Figure of a Cheerful Man | 144 |
| 14. The Figure of a Melancholic and Grieved Man | 144 |
| 15. The Figure of a Cruel and Inhumane Man | 146 |
| 16. The Figure of a Flatterer | 146 |
| 17. The Figure of a Desperate Woman | 147 |
| 18. The Figure of a Man Full of Astonishment | 148 |
| 19. The Figure of Beastly or Savage Men | 149 |
| 20. The Figure of a Fraud | 149 |

21. The Figure of a Deceitful Man, and of a Mean, Miserable, and Cowardly Man — 150
22. The Figure of a Wicked Man, Who, in Speaking, Says Impertinent Things — 151
23. The Figure of an Insane Man Who Is, at the Same Time, Wicked — 151
24. The Figure of Big Eater, and of One of Great Memory — 152
25. The Figure of a Loquacious Man — 152
26. The Figure of a Drowsy Man — 152
27. The Figure of a Libidinous Man — 153
28. The Figure of an Envious Man — 153
29. The Figure of an Ugly Man and Woman — 154
30. On the Different Feet of Men, and Those Which Are Suitable — 155
31. On the Diversity of Heels or Ankles Compared to the Figure that [the Painter] Wishes to Represent — 156
32. On the Diversity of Legs with Respect to the Different Figures They Want to Make — 157
33. On the Diversity of Knees Appropriate to Different Figures — 157
34. Which Thighs and Buttocks are Appropriate for Which Figures — 158
35. Which Limbs and Stomachs Belong to Which Figures — 158
36. Which Back and Ribs Suit Which Figures — 159
37. Different Measures of the Stomach, Chest, and Belly that Suit Different Figures — 159
38. On Some Correspondences that Some Members Have between Them — 160
39. How the Chest and Shoulders Should Be Done in Several Different Figures — 160
40. On the Shoulders and Chest Most Appropriate to Different Figures — 161
41. On Arms and Hands Appropriate to Different Figures — 162
42. Which Fingernails Are Appropriate to Different Figures — 163
43. On the Diversity of Necks Appropriate to Different Figures — 163
44. Diverse Cheeks Appropriate to Different Figures — 165
45*. Diversity of Lips and Mouths Appropriate to Different Figures — 165
45*. The Way to Form the Chin in Different Figures — 167

| | | |
|---|---|---|
| 46. | On the Diversity of Noses Appropriate to Different Figures | 167 |
| 47. | On the Diversity of Faces Appropriate to Different Figures | 169 |
| 48. | On the Diversity of Eyes and Parts Nearby Appropriate to Different Figures | 170 |
| 49. | Which Face is Appropriate for Which Figure | 171 |
| 50. | On the Various Heads Appropriate to Different Figures | 172 |
| 51. | On the Diversity of Ears Appropriate to Different Figures | 173 |
| 52. | Which Hair Colors and Complexions Should Be Used for All Figures One Wants to Represent | 174 |
| 53. | On the Eye Colors Appropriate to Different Figures | 175 |
| 54. | On the Eye Movement Appropriate to Different Figures | 179 |
| 55. | On the Diversity of Hair Appropriate to Different Figures | 181 |
| 56. | On the Diversity of Stature Appropriate to Different Figures | 182 |
| 57. | In What Thing Beauty Consists, and Proportion of Bodies According to Marsilio Ficino and Painters | 183 |

# Dedication

TO THE HOLY MAJESTY OF MAXIMILIAN,[1] ELECT KING OF POLAND, AND ARCHDUKE OF AUSTRIA, DUKE OF BURGUNDY, Styria, Carinthia, Carniola, Wittenberg, and others.

### GRAND MASTER IN PRUSSIA

*of the Teutonic Order, and Master of the same for Germany and Italy, and the rest. Count of Habsburg and Tyrol, along with others.*

If it is true that good things are greater, and so much more divine, when they approach the goodness that God Almighty uses to universally communicate to all creatures, then it will also surely be true that the utility that comes from painting is more divine than would derive from any other art, mechanical or liberal. Therefore, if we make a comparison between this [art] and the others, we will clearly see that not only these, but all others are altogether far inferior. Is it not true that in all the other [arts], in all of their operations, they fail to aim or search for those conveniences continually sought by men for the benefit of their bodies? Likewise, others furnish the living, others clothing, others housing, and others ornaments of these things, while others the tools to be able to create these things that bring comfort to the senses, which will soon be lost. Painting is like a divine work for the eyes, which represents those divine lights in us that are immortal by nature, and, as windows to our soul while we remain locked in this prison, penetrates into the most secret parts, eliciting pain, joy, desire, and fear. Who is not moved to the contemplative life by the diversity of things that able painters represent through lines and colors, after having seen those Holy Fathers made by the hand of a talented living painter and wearing those things naturally

---

1   Maximilian III, Archduke of Austria (1558–1618).

produced in the Egyptian desert, where they nourished their souls with the contemplation of heavenly bread and, having nothing, found themselves content and full of all those goods that men can desire while living this mortal life? Who will not fear the punishment of God, seeing the desolation of the great city of Jerusalem, and mothers gnashing for need of bread, their sons roasted by His hand. Who will not hate sin once having seen the *Last Judgment* of Michelangelo in Rome, or elsewhere made by an expert hand? Who does not burn of the love of Christ, our Lord, having seen his life represented with such diligence, and in art in the many drawings of our Albrecht Dürer?

If I wanted to explain all of the passions that are generated in our souls and demonstrated by the expert hand of a pious and judicious painter, not only would a page not be enough, but so too would a book not explain even the smallest part. For the painter does not settle for merely advancing all of the mechanical arts, since with the soul the body has greater excellence, nor does it fall to part of the liberal arts. Indeed, if we were to investigate the truth, we would find it clearly between these. Therefore, even though the arts and sciences have their location in the soul, not all men are obliged to obtain from those the utility that they are wont to bring to the world. But painting so accommodates the taste and sense of everyone, and does so without any strength of effort and with much contentment to the body, that there is no man so well-learned or ignorant that he would not feel his soul touched and so swept away by beautiful paintings that almost with a certain suavity he feels himself violated and, in a certain way, feels many things carved into his intellect from which he immediately learns so many divine things that he could not have understood with long study and great effort.

Moreover, neither astrology, nor geometry, nor many other arts called liberal, can explain their concepts without using painting to make illustrations with lines, figures, and often even with colors, as can clearly be seen through their books.[2] Now for this divine faculty, Albrecht Dürer far surpassed all those who came before him (although they may be most celebrated in histories and verses), and left himself to posterity

---

2   As a prolific author in the field of astronomy, Gallucci himself used extensive illustrations to explain technical concepts and represent scientific instruments and constellations. See Giovanni Paolo Gallucci, *Theatrum mundi et temporis* (1588); *Speculum Uranicum* (1593); *De fabrica, et usu hemisphaerii uranici* (1596); *Nova fabricandi horaria mobilis* (1596).

in his writings and paintings on the idea of true painting and sculpture, seen clearly in the drawings for this book *On the Symmetry of Human Bodies*. Here he left out no particle[3] of our external bodies (considering the painter and sculptor are concerned with that which can be seen)[4] from his measuring and explaining with divine genius and such subtlety that he astonishes anyone who is a student or expert of art. Hence it happened, having written this work in the German language for the benefit of its painters, it was then translated into the Latin language by a man of great virtue, whose effort will be such appreciated by the world, and even though it was printed twice, one cannot find a copy anymore, except with someone whose kept them as dear as oriental pearls, and in the most honored places of their studies. Now, so as to ensure that this valuable work will not remain dead, and to allow every painter to take advantage of it (given that only a few prefer the Latin language), I have translated it to our Italian language. This I did, of course, after great effort due to the many mistakes that were in the Latin edition, and because the material itself is difficult to explain, as the author himself affirms.[5] But, I was not satisfied with this and found it very necessary to add a fifth book for students of this faculty, which is taught through the authority of philosophers and poets, who, along with those colors and lines, can explain both the natural and the incidental passions of the souls of men. This is known only to a few painters. Now, having brought this book back to its perfection, I felt compelled to dedicate it to Your Majesty for two reasons. First, the work of Dürer is of the most fortunate house of Austria, having been written while the author benefitted from the most honored salaries, initially from Maximilian I, and then from the most fortunate Charles V, who ruled both when [Dürer] lived and at

---

3  The so-called "particle" (*Trümlein*) used by Dürer was equal to less than a millimeter, which, Panofsky argues, went beyond artistic usefulness. Erwin Panofsky, "The History of the Theory of Human Proportions as a Reflection of the History of Styles," in *Meaning in the Visual Arts* (Garden City, New York: Doubleday, 1955), 55–107, at 103–104.

4  The precept reiterates the Albertian dictum first published in his *Della pittura* of 1435, that "No one would deny that the painter has nothing to do with things that are not visible," Leon Battista Alberti, *On Painting*, transl. John R. Spencer (New Haven; London: Yale University Press, 1966), 43.

5  Giovanni Paolo Gallucci, *Della simmetria dei corpi humani, libri quattro* (Venice: Roberto Meietti, 1594), 1: 1–2, https://archive.org/details/dialbertodurero00gallgoog/page/n4; Joseph Leo Koerner, *The Moment of Self-Portraiture in Renaissance Germany* (Chicago: University of Chicago Press, 1993), 161.

the time of his death. For this reason, I dedicate the book to you, because in doing so I do nothing other than return to you what is yours. If I did not, you could reasonably demand it so. The second reason is that knowledge of the good arts and sciences in Germany has been returned to the most fortunate house of Austria. Thus there is no prince that better satisfies the conditions set forth by the divine Plato, who wished for a good prince, such that the sciences, and all the liberal arts, shine in you so nothing other than that one most splendid sun beams among many stars.[6] Therefore, with the care that you take in your knowledge of all things that can adorn the soul, you are and will be in the future a mirror to all Christian princes, indeed to all of the world, which for many years, and even more now than ever, seek books, and the mathematical instruments, and men most expert in every field, who delight in your most honored court will not want neither for Platos, nor Aristotles, nor Euclids, nor Ptolemies, nor Archimedes, nor Apelles, nor Lysippi, nor others most famous in ancient times but until now buried in darkness for many centuries because they did not have strong states like that of Alexander [the Great], or patrons who kept them alive, as does Your Majesty now. This is deservedly true. Moreover, the persecution of Julian the Apostate[7] against the Church of God was the most perilous of all that came before, where an innumerable multitude of martyrs had to die, because I do not think he attempted to kill the bodies of the Christians, as had others before him, but to kill the souls and keep them locked in the dark burial of the bodies in this world, and keep the other in eternal darkness; wanting no Christian to attend to the letters, he threatened the cruelest punishment. On the contrary, Your Majesty, wishing not only to preserve the Christian religion, but also to expand it with your forces, embraces the letters and *literati*, and so inspires all your subjects with your example (as with the old proverb, such as are the citizens, so are their princes) that there can be no doubt that similar principles are true and that the Church of God flourishes and makes fruits worthy of

---

6   In the Introduction to *The Republic*, Plato argues that an ideal state must be ruled by philosopher kings, as all philosophers aim to discover the ideal polis.

7   Julian the Apostate (r. 355–363) was the last non-Christian ruler of the Roman Empire. His anti-Christian sentiment and promotion of Neoplatonic paganism caused him to be remembered as Julian the Apostate by the Church. Edward Gibbon, *The History of the Decline and Fall of the Roman Empire* (London: Penguin, 2001), chapter 23; Adrian Murdoch, *The Last Pagan: Julian the Apostate* (Stroud: Sutton Publishing, 2008).

eternal life. Deservedly then, I have wanted to dedicate these my vigils to Your Majesty, as a sign of my devotion in verse, as long as I am still able (God providing me with life and strength) to demonstrate it with more steadfast arguments. Preserve me, Your Majesty, and deign to consider me among the small number of your most faithful servants as I pray to our Lord God for your wealth and happiness.

Venice, January 20, 1591.<br>
Your Majesty's<br>
Most humble servant<br>
Gio. Paolo Gallucci.

# Life of Albrecht Dürer

We know that our Albrecht has ancient origins and that his ancestors came to live in Germany from Hungary. We will not spend a long time speaking of his origins, nor about his ancestors, because even though they were esteemed and honorable, they, nevertheless, received more glory from him than they had bequeathed to him. Nature gave him such an admirable body for its proportions and stature, which perfectly accommodated the beautiful soul harbored in him, so that his righteousness could not be forgotten. All this was famously discussed by Hippocrates, who noted that the soul of the ridiculous monkey is given an equally ridiculous body; likewise, singular minds are given equally appropriate bodies.[1] He had a sharp head, resplendent eyes, and a honest nose, which the Greeks called Τετράγονον ("four-angled"), as well as a very long neck, broad chest, moderate stomach, vascular thighs, stable legs, and fingers such that you could not see a more beautiful thing.[2] He had so much suavity and grace in speaking that listeners never wanted to see the end. He did not learn from letters, but rather studied the natural sciences and mathematics, which he learned together with the former, and because he understood these fundamental principles, he was able to explain their effects and clarify them with words. His writings in *The Four Books of Human Proportion*, wanting for

---

1   Hippocrates, *On Regimen in Acute Diseases* (Whitefish, MT: Kessinger Publishing, LLC, 2010), 1: 25.1–2; A similar quote found its way into innumerable Renaissance commentaries from Juvenal: "Mens sana in corpore sano" ("a healthy mind in a healthy body"). Juvenal, *Satires*, ed. Richard George (St. Albans: Baikal, 2012), 10.356; For a discussion on the Renaissance discourse on apes and "aping," see John Jefferies Martin, *The Renaissance World* (New York; London: Routledge, 2007), 416.
2   Euclid, *Elements*, transl. Thomas L. Heath (Sante Fe, NM: Green Lion Press, 2002), Book 4; The physiognomic reading here can be understood to communicate the strength of Dürer's character for those "that have well-jointed, sinewy and strong legs, are strong in character..." (Pseudo-Aristotle, *Physiognomics*, 6.1–30; Aristotle, *Minor Works*, transl. Hett, 110–112).

nothing that he left out of his writing, provide full testimony to this. He had such an adoration for the honest life and lived with such excellent habits that he was deservedly reputed to have an irreproachable life. Moreover, he was not overly severe or hateful, and, although he was old, he never really despised those things belonging to suavity and cheerfulness, such as exercising the body or enjoying music, nor was he ever distant from what was right or honest. But above all other things, Nature made him for painting. Thus, he put all his effort in that study, and he principally labored to see and learn about the famous painters who lived in every place, to understand the reasons behind their works, and to imitate the works he considered worthy. He acquired the favor and generosity of kings and princes: in particular that of Maximilian and his grandson Charles Augustus, obtaining from them a respectable salary.[3] As his skills developed with maturity, his sublime genius would be known from his own works, together with his great love for the virtues of life. Therefore, he made only great things of praiseworthy subjects. There are the *Encomia* of Maximilian and the immortal works of the *History of Astronomy*, from which one can conclude that, without mentioning other things, there is no praise or work by the ancient painters or from our age that would not desire to be called his.[4] It is certain that no sign whatsoever in nature is more certain or truer than the works made by his art. Now these [works] are of two types which exceed all others in this way, and that almost seem to come from the workshop of nature herself. These are the ones who imitate the appearance of things either with their hands or through speech. This first one, [which uses speech,] has the name of Poetry; the other has no proper universal name; it is divided into four parts, statues, painting, sculpture, and architecture.[5] Now as the focus of our research we shall speak of painting, which some call

---

3 Holy Roman Emperors Maximilian I (1459–1519) and Charles V (1500–1558).
4 Written by Johannes Michael Nagonius, the Italian poet had been called to glorify other European rulers. Here he argues for Maximilian's elevation to emperor in three books of panegyric poems. Francis Wormald, "An Italian Poet at the Court of Henry VII," *Journal of Warburg and Courtauld Institutes*, 14 (1951), 118–119, https://doi.org/10.2307/750355; Matthias Ringmann, *Cosmographiae Introductio* (1507) and Sebastian Münster, *Cosmographia* (1544).
5 Antiquity held four categories of the visual arts, which included sculpture (e.g. relief and three-dimensional), painting (e.g. murals, tempera), statues (e.g. portrait busts), and architecture.

Greek poetry that does not speak,⁶ and the place it holds within these most highly regarded four. We will judge that whatever is true for painters and their works is also true for poets and their writings, which is to say that Polygnotus painted that which was best and Pausias the worst.⁷ Who does not know from this that one was a high-minded genius, while the other a humble fool? Martial says that if he had had Maecenas, then he would have been as famous as Marsus but never Virgil, but let him be the judge of that.⁸ This has thus never been wished by anyone who has read his singular verses not only in that genre of the *Epigrams* but also in that other where not only abilities are weak before greater things, but also where everything is alien from them, and some things appear also ugly and dishonest. For that I cannot help but remember, with a smile on my face, the sentence of Catullus which states that the pious poet must be chaste, but not his verses.⁹ In fact, he did not intend that what was shamed in words

---

6    Though most famously cited from Horace's *Ars Poetica*, the oft-repeated Renaissance axiom "Poema pictura loquens, pictura poema silens" ("poetry is a speaking picture, painting a silent [mute] poetry") is first recorded by Plutarch. Plutarch, *De gloria Atheniensium*, ed. C. J. Thiolier (Paris: Presses de l'Université de Paris-Sorbonne, 1985), 3.347a. See Rensselaer Lee, *Ut Pictura Poesis: The Humanistic Theory of Painting* (New York: W. W. Norton, 1967).

7    Pausanias, *Description of Greece*, transl. W. H. S. Jones (Cambridge, MA: Harvard University Press; London: William Heinemann, 1918), 10.25–31.

8    "Give me leisure, and leisure such as once Maecenas provided for Flaccus and his own Virgil; then would I essay to build up works that should live throughout ages, and to rescue my name from the fire. Into unfruitful fields steers care not to bear the yoke; a fat soil wearies, but the very labour delights." Martial, *Epigrams*, ed. and transl. Gideon Nisbet (Oxford: Oxford University Press, 2017), 1.107.

9    "I'll fuck the pair of you as you prefer it,
Oral Aurelius, anal Furius,
Who read my verses but misread their author:
You think that I'm effeminate, since they are!
Purity's proper in the godly poet,
But it's unnecessary in his verses,
Which really should be saucy & seductive,
Even salacious in a girlish manner
And capable of generating passion
Not just in boys, but in old men who've noticed
Getting a hard-on has been getting harder!
But you, because my poems beg for kisses,
Thousands of kisses, you think I'm a fairy!
I'll fuck the pair of you as you prefer it."

Gaius Valerius Catullus, *The Poems of Catullus*, transl. Charles Martin (Baltimore, MD: John's Hopkins University Press, 1990), 16.

would be foreign from verse. Now, we leave the poets. How many poets have there been, or better still, among all painters how many have there been who do not show their own nature in their works? I will not speak of the ancients and instead provide examples from our own times. Who does not know that many have sought to achieve the praise and admiration of the masses by painting strange things, people who printed on plates or paper those things that cannot be created honestly, but cannot be concealed either, indeed, that cannot be made secretly without wickedness and defamation? We have also seen some very well painted works where the painter's ingenuity and diligence is perceived, yet where all art is lacking. In this place we will, therefore, reasonably admire Albrecht Dürer, most diligent guardian of piety and shame, who attended to the greatness of paintings knowing very well how much his own efforts would be valued, for not even in his lesser works is there anything to be denigrated. One cannot find a single line drawn without a reason, either of his own volition or external suggestion. What should I say about the firmness and certainty of his hand: everyone would swear that the lines he made with paintbrush or pen would have been traced using the ruler, or triangle, or compass. But because they were made without any help, they gave great astonishment to those who saw them. What can I say about those figures that he often drew with pen on paper to give shape to those things that frequently came in his mind? In this case, his viewers must have seen as a marvel his creative force, by which he made parts of stories and bodies so distant so developed and connected together that nothing more accommodating or appropriate could be found. This is because the mind of a singular creator, adorned with every cognition and an understanding of truth, and enjoying consensus between the parts moderated, rewards what is wanted by the hand, which is trusted without any other support. He had the same agility in holding the paintbrush, with which he painted the most minuscule things on canvas and panel without having first made sketches beforehand. Those works were, nevertheless, made in such a way that they could not be condemned for that, but they were deserving of praise. Many times this seemed deserving of great praise and astonished painters worthy of great honors who would, nevertheless, have found themselves lacking however much they toiled at it. Here, I cannot help but relate what happened between him and Giovanni Bellini. Giovanni Bellini was a famous painter in Venice and the whole of Italy when Albrecht arrived, and, having become familiar with him, as usually happens, the two showed multiple works to each other. Albrecht admired and sincerely praised all of the works by Giovanni Bellini; in the same fashion, Bellini ingenuously praised all of the other things, but especially the sharpness of the hair seen in the works of Albrecht. Once, as the two were finishing speaking about art, Bellini said: "Would you be such a good friend to do a favor for a friend of yours?" [Dürer replied] "If you ask me something that I can, dear Bellini, I will honor it." "I would like to have as a gift from you," said Bellini, "one of these paintbrushes, with which you usually paint hair." Then Albrecht, without hesitation, got out many paintbrushes, the same as those Bellini had been using, and told him to choose the one that he wished to have, if he did not want to take them all. Bellini then, thinking he was being cheated, said: "I was not talking about these, but those that you usually use to make many strands of hair with a single stripe, or many strands that need to be scattered and rather far apart, because, otherwise, it would not be possible to conserve such equivalence in the bend or distance." Then Albrecht responded: "I use no others but these, and I will show you this with an example." At once he picked up one of those paintbrushes and made very long and wavy [locks of] hair, as in particular can be seen in depictions of women, in such a steadfast manner that Bellini became so astonished, that he later told many people he would have never believed the story told by any man had he not seen it with his own eyes. The same praises were given by Andrea Mantegna himself, a man of singular genius, who had been raised in Mantua, and developed painting with a certain degree of severity and rule. He was certainly the first who deserved this praise, providing the art of statuary as an example that he had obtained even though these were scattered in many places or destroyed. Surely, his works are hard and rigid, since he does not have a hand accustomed to obeying the intelligence and alacrity of the soul. Regardless, it is held that art cannot find anything better than what he made. [Andrea], therefore, finding himself based in Mantua and hearing that Albrecht found himself in Italy, used every talent to get him there so that he could impart his security and the certainty of his art with his cognition and with the same art technique. He had, in fact, often complained in his own private conversations that he did not have Albrecht's talent nor his knowledge of science. Without wasting any time, after this was told to him, Albrecht immediately started traveling, but Andrea died before he was able to reach Mantua. The event was so maddening that he used to say that nothing that had ever happened to him in his entire life bothered him as much. Therefore, although Albrecht was held in highest esteem, and despite his great and noble soul, he always wished to be something better. We were amazed to see an image of man made by him on canvas made directly with the paintbrush, as we said, without any line made beforehand on the ground; the strands of the beard are almost as long as an arm and are drawn so exquisitely, and with such liveliness and such proportional distance between them that the more some people knew of art, the more astounded they were and the more incredible it seemed to them knowing that he did not trace them with the help of anything but his hands. In addition, nothing in his works is dirty or ugly, the thoughts of his innocent soul ridding all of such things. Oh, creator, worthy of such success! How mimetic, infallible, and truthful, were the portraits of living people he made? This was due to the fact that he would draw from the experience of art and intellect, which was not yet understood by painters, especially not by those of our time. Accordingly, who is among these who believes the reason his work receives great praise is due to random chance rather than science? But our Albrecht had all of these things set and ready, because he had brought precepts to painting and the reason for the doctrine, without which, as Cicero warns, something good made with however much help from doctrine, nevertheless cannot always be ready if made by chance.[10] These are the things in which he trained, and in order to have the most liberal and sincere nature, he explained in writing to the most illustrious and cultured man, Willibald Pirckheimer, to whom he dedicated a most sincere letter that we did not wish to translate into Latin, knowing our weakness in translating it from its natural purity.[11] But before he could accomplish everything,

---

10 Cicero, *De Officiis libri tre*, ed. Paolo Fideli (Florence: A. Mondadori, 1973), 1.2–3; Cicero, *De re publica*, ed. Günter Laser (Stuttgart: Reclam, 2014), 1.1.1–2.2.

11 Willibald Pirkheimer (1470–1530) was a German humanist and friend of Albrecht Dürer who is generally credited with bolstering the artist's Classical shortcomings. Corine Schleif, "Albrecht Dürer between Agnes Frey and Willibald Pirckheimer," *The*

and leave them in the correct light, he died a peaceful and desirable death; but, in my opinion, this was somehow bittersweet. In this man was infinite diligence; if we want to see in him something wicked, he did not inquire the same of others. Death took him from us when he had begun to print this work, which, nevertheless, his friends completed in the way he had imposed.[12]

---

*Essential Dürer*, ed. Larry Silver and Jeffrey Chipps Smith (Philadelphia: University of Pennsylvania Press, 2010), 85–205; Giulia Bartrum, ed., *Albrecht Dürer and His Legacy: The Graphic Work of a Renaissance Artist* (Princeton: Princeton University Press, 2002).

12  The artist had died before publication of his *Four Books* could be completed in 1528: Albrecht Dürer, *Vier Bücher von menschlicher Proportion* (Nuremberg: Hieronymous Andreae, 1528).

# Preface to Readers

## By M[onsignor] Giovanni Paolo Gallucci

*which shows the similarity painting has with poetry, what the painter and the sculptor can learn from these books, and proof that painting is an art.*

Painting is notably similar to poetry, and vice versa. This has not been overlooked by men, who have generously left in writing that painting is a poem that is silent, and poetry is a painting that speaks.[1] Therefore, we can say about these two most excellent faculties that which the philosopher[2] of Logic and Rhetoric already wrote, that they live together in balance, because both of these arts imitate natural and artificial things — one represents things to the ears of mortals with words, while the other the eyes with colors.[3] In addition, since the poet cannot imitate well with words that man whose actions he does not fully know, thus the painter cannot imitate well that body whose parts are not entirely visible.

Therefore, should a poet wish to represent a Hercules, or a man of virtue similar to Hercules, he needs to know all of the achievements of that valorous captain. He also needs to know what action is appropriate for whatever virtue. In order to imitate the actions that come from a strong and fearless soul, for instance, he does not imitate the effects of liberality or temperance. Likewise, if the painter wants to imitate a strong man, he should neither make the members of a shy or generous man, nor of another vice or virtue.

---

1  Plutarch, *De gloria Atheniensium*, ed. C. J. Thiolier (Paris: Presses de l'Université de Paris-Sorbonne, 1985), 3: 347a.
2  Among the many ancient authors Gallucci calls upon to bolster his arguments throughout his discourse, Aristotle is held up as the most authoritative philosophical source, specifically his *Rhetoric* and *Poetics*.
3  Aristotle, *Poetics*, transl. Stephen Halliwell (Cambridge, MA: Harvard University Press, 1995), 1: 2.

Because nature is most wise in every operation, and the most faithful minister of God Almighty, she does not want in necessary things, nor does she lavish on those who are excessive, but makes all things in agreement to her end. Wherefore in wanting to make the sky, which continuously spreads out, here He formed an orbital shape, and wanting the air and the water ready for all animals and plants, He made them fluctuating by nature. The land became heavy and stable to be able to support the plants and animals. He made the plants with their roots in the ground so that they may be nourished from it and imbued almost all the animals with motion so that they may procure food wherever they will be.[4] Lions, who were given the strongest soul, were made with strong front limbs suited to resist other's impulses, and were armed with claws and teeth in order to attack the others. Because He made hare and deer timid and defenseless, He gave them long legs made for running.[5] I would never find an end if I wanted to discuss all of the created things and their parts to prove the wisdom of nature in forming proportionate bodies appropriate to their purposes—all of these things must be imitated by poets and painters, and again by sculptors. But, because out of all things created the human creature is, after angels, the most excellent due to its form, according to the testimony of the prophet,[6] it seems that it is mainly in this that the poet and painter, together with the sculptor, toil and sweat. In finally imitating that form, they consume days, months, years, and their whole lives and are happy and blessed when rejoicing at having reached such perfection that with the satisfaction and praise of viewers, they represent this divine animal. The praise is deservedly merited, for is man anything other than a compendium of all visible and invisible things? This was known to those wise Greeks who named it the Microcosm, the smaller world, because in him are all those things that there are in this entire universe.[7] In writing on this topic, the pens

---

4   Genesis 1: 6–25.
5   The summary provided here is drawn from Pseudo-Aristotle's *Physiognomica*, 5: 809b.18–40; Aristotle, Minor Works, transl. W. S. Hett (London: William Heinemann, 1936), 109; and Aristotle's *The History of Animals*, transl. D'Arcy Wentworth Thompson (Oxford: Clarendon Press, 1910), 30: 2.9–10.
6   All of God's created work culminated in his fashioning of man in his own image and places the earth under his dominion. Genesis 1: 26–28; Psalm 8: 4–8.
7   See Allen G. Debus, *The Chemical Philosophy: Paracelsian Science and Medicine* (New York: Science History Publications, 1977); Walter Pagel, *Paracelsus: An Introduction to Philosophical Medicine in the Era of the Renaissance* (Basel: S. Karger, 1958).

of many writers, both profane and ecclesiastic, were drained.[8] Therefore, much has been said about this noble creature, and much more is left to say, because He included in him an infinity of things and wanted him to possess endless endurance. Individual men, moreover, possess different bodies between them so that it is not possible to find two men who are so similar in the face or in all the other members, [or who] are not in some part dissimilar. This fact again demonstrates the diversity of natural inclinations. For instance, the man who has some similarities with the members of the lion is robust and strong, as seen from experience, but if he has legs similar to that of the deer, he is shy. This is also said of other members and correspondences where the diversity of the members was prudently placed in men towards endless operations. But because it is not possible for everyone to be given strength, nor for time to make up for all things, it was necessary that one was waiting for one thing and another something else. This is why some members are more appropriate to one thing than to another: it was necessary that the members of men be quite different from each other, which is expected in all men. It is certainly true that if a man has long legs, running in a race will be more convenient; if he has short legs, and robust body, he will easily carry any load possible with human strength; and if he is between them of medium stature and soft flesh, then he will be suited to contemplation and command. Porphyry has already written about those beautiful bodies worthy of empire.[9] Thus we can conclude that the duty of the painter is to imitate all natural things, and principally man, because he includes within him all that is necessary and holds the complete knowledge of all sorts of bodies and their members, which mainly consists of large, small and medium, straight and bent, back

---

8   See Leonard Barkan, *Nature's Work of Art: The Human Body as Image of the World* (New Haven: Yale University Press, 1975).

9   Pupil of Neoplatonic philosopher Plotinus, Porphyry of Tyre (ca.234–ca.305) edited and published *The Enneads*, a collection of his mentor's work. In his *Life of Pythagoras*, Porphyry records the training of the Samian athlete Eurymenes, "who though he was of small stature, conquered at Olympia through his surpassing knowledge of Pythagoras' wisdom." Porphyry, "The Life of Pythagoras," *The Pythagorean Sourcebook*, transl. Louis H. Feldman and Meyer Reinhold (London: Soncino, 1935), 15. At the same time, Porphyry's *De Sole* influenced the imperial propaganda and portraiture of Gallienus based on his descriptions. The emperor, like Constantine after him, sought to associate him with the god Sol and early "good" emperors from the Augustan and Hadrianic traditions. Lukas de Blois, *The Policy of Emperor Gallienus* (Leiden: Brill, 1976), 168–171.

and front, or right and left. All of these things are quite difficult and cannot be learned from one who does not have a well sculpted soul or well-designed body, and whose members may be called mediocre or proportionate. This, being a definite measure, allows us to know which bodies are long and which are short, which are too thick and which are too thin compared to the proportionate body. The same should be said also about each member. Therefore, those without full knowledge of well-proportioned bodies cannot know [what is appropriate] (as I said). It then seems that students of painting should first struggle with these bodies, rather than others, so that through comparison they will turn away from these in order to have their paintings accommodate bodies proportionate to the people that they want to represent. This recommendation is prudent for painters as it is certainly necessary for them to have a complete knowledge of those natural inclinations that produce the diversity of members in each man so as to represent every type of person. In their figures, they want to introduce proportionate bodies, so it seems to me that the part of the painting most pertinent to explaining human nature mainly consists in the knowledge of two things: one is in knowing how to suitably form all kinds of bodies; the other in knowing the type of person for which each of those is appropriate. From here one sees the perversion of this once illustrious and noble art in our own time.[10]

For without a precept that would guide students with certainty, they instead propose their own or copy the drawings of others. They thus reduce this whole profession, which actually marries science and practice, to practice alone, and, to thus satisfy the ignorant and vulgar, like so many amputees limping and blind people groping about, they deprive their histories of the variety of many colors, as many as were

---

10  The decline of the visual arts was foretold in biological model Vasari established in his *Le vite de' più eccellenti pittori scultori e architettori: nelle redazioni del 1550 e 1568* (1550/1568). Deviation from the five established regole resulted in increasingly attenuated and complex forms with mannerism. In the last decades of the century, recognition of this crisis can be seen in the works of Bruno, Armenini, Lomazzo, and others. The evaluation was carried on in the following century when Bellori would open his own series of artist's lives with the deplorable state of the field prior to its revival by Annibale Carracci. Vasari, *Le vite...*, ed. Rosanna Bettarini and Paola Barocchi, 6 vols (Florence: Sansoni, 1966–1987), II: 96; Giovanni Battista Armenini, *Dei veri precetti della pittura*, ed. S. Ticozzi (Pisa: N. Capuro, 1823), Proem, 1; Giordano Bruno, *De umbris idearum* (1580); see Frances Yates, *The Art of Memory* (Chicago: University of Chicago Press, 1966), 1–5, 28.

in the earliest chaos, which they [wanted] to be the source of all things; they make figures that perform many strained actions and in their members is seen no proportion, which is identified with reverence in the [great artists], who are certainly few in our time, and for that reason we can rightly mourn the loss of this noble art that once was, when those painters so greatly celebrated by Pliny, Vitruvius, and, in recent times, Ariosto, were living and especially when our Albrecht Dürer was living, for he gave so much light to this most noble faculty and art.[11] But because I know there are many who do not want painting to be considered an art, arguing that it is only a practice of making or imitating what is seen, I would like them to tell me if among all painters there are not a few who paint better than others, and some adequately, while others completely poorly.[12] Tell me that this is true. Now, if among all of these painters one could be found who could advise others on their process in all things, who would he be? This man would be considered better than any other painter because he would have distilled unquestionable precepts; one would say that he had found the art of painting, if it had not been there before. Likewise, the philosopher [Aristotle] stipulates that the art is a habit of making something with reason, and for Cicero, it consists in things known and fully represented, purposeful and silent, which will be conditional concerns observed by our painter.[13] For example, providing precepts to form a proportionate foot from a

---

11  Pliny lauds the accomplishments and Canon of the ancient sculptor Polykleitos; Vitruvius cites Leochares, Bryaxis, Scopas, Praxiteles, and Timotheus as noteworthy practitioners of the visual arts; and Ariosto Zeuxis for his creation of the portrait of Helen. Pliny the Elder, *Natural History*, transl. John F. Healy (London: Penguin Books, 1991), 34: 55, 58, 65; Vitruvius, *The Ten Books on Architecture*, transl. Morgan (New York: Dover, 1960), Book VII; Ludovico Ariosto, *Orlando Furioso*, transl. Guido Waldman (Oxford: Oxford University Press, 2008), 11: 71.

12  The argument ultimately derives from Plato, whose writings were rediscovered, translated and popularized by Marsilio Ficino a century earlier. Elaborated on in his *Republic*, Plato excludes artists from his just city-state for they deceive the ignorant by imitating appearance. On the other hand, truth is discoverable only through contemplation of true divine forms. Plato, *The Republic*, transl. R. E. Allen (New Haven: Yale University Press, 2006), 13: 598b–c.

13  Art is a certain "habit" of "making" governed by true reason; the absence of art, the "habit" of "making" governed by false reason. Aristotle, *Nicomachean Ethics*, transl. Willliam Heinemann (Cambridge, MA: Harvard University Press, 1962), 6: 4; Cicero, on the other hand, compares the art of rhetoric with that of the visual and concludes that the Romans were superior with regards to the spoken, while the Greeks the silence of statues. Cicero, *Brutus*, ed. Centre Traditio Litterarum Occidentalium (Turnhout: Brepols Publishers, 2010), 67–71.

well-proportioned standard will always serve those precepts, and the foot will come out proportioned. The same should be understood for everything else that painters wish to create. Here then students of painting, sculpture and proportion will benefit from the true precepts of the human body, which will always aide and never fail, as certain and reliable guides to the perfection of this art and as roads leading safely to the most secret seclusions of painting. These are the precepts for practicing students, or patrons of that art, which were described by the prince of Peripatetics [Aristotle] as habit made with reason, from which then the actions of figures will never be random, but rather lively and purposeful.[14] In this way the prudent painter has not only considered the details in paint and all of the beautiful parts of particular bodies to reduce them to precepts, he has also led all of this back to perfection, such that one cannot improve on it in anyway, as has been written by Pliny, Vitruvius and others, on which we have reflected.[15] Thus, he not only gave the precepts of well-proportioned bodies, but established rules and taught those precepts, and found proportions even in bodies that were entirely disproportionate. Rightly he knew very well that that painter (as we said above), having to unfold in painting every sort of person, and form every idea of natural inclinations in all different bodies that proportionally corresponds to their nature, again needed to form multiple precepts that would give order to all bodies and their parts, as though searching for what each person needed in order to represent them in a particular way. Moreover, whosoever deviates greatly from the true proportion found in perfect bodies will lose all of the human form and will make something completely monstrous and ridiculous. Nature also suffers from similar aberrations, which sometimes occur due to a dearth or surplus of matter. In this instance, the painter must be the imitator of nature, and yet diligent, not an ape of men who only imitates actions that are ridiculous, vile or awful. Because of this, I will not deny that the painter could create a monster, but he should make

---

14    The appropriate action for each figure illustrates the equilibrium of their soul and desire for virtue. Aristotle, *Rhetoric*, ed. and transl. Edward Meredith Cope and John Edwin Sandys (Cambridge, UK: Cambridge University Press, 2010), 1097b, 24–1098a, 1114b, 23–4.

15    Pliny, *Natural History*, transl. Healy, 34: 55, 58, 65. Vitruvius, *De architectura*, Book VII; Ludovico Ariosto, *Orlando Furioso*, transl. Guido Waldman (Oxford: Oxford University Press, 2008), 11: 71.

him as a monster and monstrous according to his fantasy. In ordinary bodies of common men and women, moreover, any monstrous part must not be made, nor any part not correspond to the whole body. To avoid all these craggy cliffs, diligent painters and sculptors must steer the boat of their talents towards the rivers of these precepts. Without any doubt they will surely arrive at that port where there is the glory of sailors, where there is their certain profit, and where they are adorned with immortal crowns, and through fame will remain forever alive on earth, and useful to the world as their beautiful works remain in churches, exciting some to piety and penance for their sins, others to martyrdom, others to patience, humility and chastity, and, finally, to the love of God, whose every thing returns to his great benefit and to the profit of his soul, to which belong all the good and evil made by his reason both before and after they departed from this life.

# Book Five

## By M[onsignor] Giovanni Paolo Gallucci Salodiano

---

*This book teaches the way painters can express the passions of the body and soul in the figures of men and women with lines and colors, whether they be natural or incidental, according to the opinion of philosophers and poets.*

Now published for the first time.

# 1. On the Utility of this Doctrine[1]

Even though in the Preface at the beginning of these books we alluded to the necessity of this fifth book, we, nevertheless, are determined to explain it more thoroughly so that with such knowledge those that study painting can pay closer attention by taking part in this most noble art. For this reason, it must be noted that all figures painters make can be reduced to three principle categories.[2] Some of these come from nature, like portraits. Others from histories have a certain general usefulness, like those of Sts Peter and Paul, and other such figures. Alternatively, the painter may want to create his own history or fable and fill it with many figures, variously extracted from the Idea his soul has shaped after having considered and painted many different forms.[3] The Idea needs only the diligence of the skilled painter who does not omit any detail that is in the truth, including all in the portrait with his lines and colors, and should not portray anything he did not intend. Moreover, the second [portrait type] requires knowledge of the art that we are going to set forth in this book. Because even if it is customary, for example, to paint St Peter with a squared beard and St Paul with a long one, the first as a brawny man and the second as praying, it is nonetheless possible to do this so ungracefully, since it is left to chance, that instead of representing the constancy of faith, the sanctity, and the other virtues proper to these columns of the Holy Church, they represent them as squalid and wicked men. Nor it is far from truth that one who has never learned the way to Rome, might while traveling depart from the right way, like one who

---

1   Though often reserved for principles of religion, I have kept the translation of *dottrina* as "Doctrine" to highlight the author's belief that the stratagem he elaborates is supported by and found in biblical examples, as well as philosophical and poetical.
2   Gallucci divides physiognomic types used in painting to those derived from nature (*dal naturale*), idealized types for history painting (*dalle historie*), and those drawn from the imagination (*nell'animo scolpita*).
3   Vasari's conception of *disegno* considers the way in which the "Idea" of the artist can be transcribed via the intellective faculty through an artist's dexterity, after innumerable studies drawn from nature. Vasari, *Le vite de' più eccellenti pittori scultori e architettori: nelle redazioni del 1550 e 1568*, ed. Rosanna Bettarini and Paola Barocchi, 6 vols (Florence: Sansoni, 1966–1987), I: Technical Introduction. Michelangelo also used the analogy of "carving" images from an Idea in his sonnets, reiterated by his biographers. James M. Saslow, *The Poetry of Michelangelo* (New Haven; London: Yale University Press, 1991), 305; William Wallace, "Michelangelo, Tiberio Calcagni, and the Florentine 'Pietà'," *Artibus et Historiae*, 21.42 (2000), 81–99, at 87, https://doi.org/10.2307/1483625

does not know the difference between all the grains should select barley instead of wheat, or this instead of that. Amended with a knowledge of custom and history, this art can then direct the painter's hand and his judgment appropriate to all the images; painters have a certain universal cognition of the shapes of these images. The pictures or figures that painters do not know perfectly, because they have never existed (or, if so, existed a long time ago), are of two varieties: some of them are open to interpretation by the judicious painter, while specific features define others. The figures of history paintings are open to interpretation if they are not the principle [ones] while such freedom of interpretation is not possible in the figures of the gods from antiquity or in the embodiment of virtues and other such stations of men that are collected in histories. Moreover, having this universal knowledge of the various kinds of figures will be very useful. This affords familiarity with the various kinds of pictures and the variety of the shapes of the human body, the colors that correspond to those features, as well as the coloration of the head.[4] Homer demonstrates this stratagem well when he paints[5] his enraged Achilles with eyes that look like fire together with a hairy chest and swift feet.[6] How useful then is this contribution to the creation of the figures of the gods, and the concepts of virtues and vices, so well-known that it needs no further evidence, since we do not seek to explain the nature of these here.[7] Instead, we attempt to teach the methods by which painters can represent the disposition of human bodies, virtues and temperaments through the emotions of those bodies. Students of painting should thus note how useful what is explained in this book can be, should these things taught be carefully studied, including the features and colors that are appropriate to all human figures he wishes to represent. Therefore, the valuable commentary on the figures that the

---

4   Gallucci uses *lineamenti* to refer to both the appropriate complexion of different forms and the contours of the form of various figures. Likewise, the *colori del capo* is elaborated on in later chapters as including the complexion of the skin, color of the hair, lips, eyes, etc.
5   Building on his Preface where painting and poetry are discussed as "sister arts," Gallucci often uses *dipingere* as opposed to *dire* in order to reinforce the manner in which poets "paint" with words and painters "speak" with their images.
6   See "6. How One Should Paint a Furious and Angry Man," below. Homer, *Iliad*, transl. Barry Powell (Oxford: Oxford University Press, 2014), 1: 1–4, 85; 19: 349–353.
7   The temperaments (*vitij*) that he refers to are presented as self-evident, and based on everyday observation.

painter wishes to show his audience is of a singular benefit. Possessing this knowledge will continuously bring him a fame that makes him immortal and a property that produces pious fruits, a property that, as we mentioned in the beginning, leads to an understanding of the soul that will last as long as the world. For if while we are reading the lives of the glorious martyrs, we are moved in the least and feel some spark or desire for martyrdom, what stronger a reaction would we then have should we see them with our own eyes, almost sprinting to their martyrdom? So it is said about those Holy Fathers who used to live in the hermitage, and others, who are examples of Christian living.[8] In those, I would like to see the Christian painter describe the piety that writers attribute to them. But, because my aim in this book is not to cover doctrine in a verbose fashion, nor burden readers with its length, these few things will suffice to inflame the souls of students to embrace these precepts, lessening their labors with the hope of a reward both temporal and eternal.

## 2. On the Differences of Humans with Respect to Countries, Sex, and Age

Be this the universal precept for painters, who must primarily imitate the natural things, that those living in the northern hemisphere have a lighter skin color and tougher hair than those who live in the southern part: Germans, Flemish, English, and other nationalities situated towards the pole, have lighter-complected flesh than the people who live in the kingdom of Crete, Sicily, Spain, Berber Coast,[9] Egypt, or other places in the south. Furthermore, the bodies of peoples in the north are larger than those from the south. Tasso speaks of this when describing Arabs in Book 17 of his *Gerusalemme Liberata*,

---

[8] The most widely read treatment on martyrdom as a model for Christian living from the medieval and Renaissance eras survives in multiple editions and translations. Written in 1260, *The Golden Legend* by Jacobus de Varagine would be challenged in Gallucci's own time due to its apocryphal content, but remained highly influential, regardless. Jacobus de Varagine, *The Golden Legend: Readings on the Saints*, transl. W. G. Ryan, 2 vols (Princeton: Princeton University Press, 1993).

[9] The Barbary Coast includes the Berber coastal regions and cities throughout the middle and western coastal regions of North Africa — now Morocco, Algeria, Tunisia, and Libya.

> They have women's voices, bodies short and thin,
> and long, black locks of hair, and swarthy skin.[10]

Still others from the areas between these two extremes have a moderate complexion, such as the very noble city of Venice (and all of Italy), France, and other such places.[11] Although this middle region, said to be temperate, is inclined to be different in that it not only participates in universal qualities of extremes, [its peoples] are also so different in skin tone and in the stature of all of their bodies that some look like Germans, some Africans, and still some [look like] others. For instance, when Japanese ambassadors came to Venice, they said they were surprised by nothing more than the differences they saw among the Italians. Therefore, they are all olive-colored with small bodies and have faces that are almost shaped the same. I need to advise painters here that in all countries, and in all varieties, women have smaller heads, smaller and narrower faces, slender necks, more delicate chests, fewer ribs, while their waists and hips are fleshier than that of men; their calves are also different, and their knees are thinner. In general, they are softer, lighter and slenderer, and the shape of their entire body more delightful, light, noble, and generous. In addition, their bodies must be (as Dürer said)[12] smaller and less defined than that of men; Aristotle represents this fact with the figure of the lion for men and leopard for women,[13] given that (as he says) [the lion] has a downward-shaped mouth with a nose that is broad and large, rather than thin and narrow; the eyes are varied, often concave and not actually spherical, no less eminent, and

---

10   Torquato Tasso, *The Liberation of Jerusalem*, transl. Max Wickert (Oxford: Oxford University Press, 2009), 17: 21. The description of the peoples of the Levant includes the myriad of nationalities participating in the epic war, from Egyptians, Arabs, Turks, Ethiopians, etc.
11   The Mediterranean region.
12   Giovanni Paolo Gallucci, *Della simmetria dei corpi humani, libri quattro* (Venice: Roberto Meietti, 1594), 1: 1–2, 5, 21–22, https://archive.org/details/dialbertodurero00gallgoog/page/n4
13   The seminal ancient treatise on physiognomy, originally attributed to Aristotle and now considered pseudo-Aristotelian, forms the armature on which Gallucci builds his character assessments. In anthropomorphizing animal taxonomy, pseudo-Aristotle writes: "This being so, the lion of all animals seems to have the most perfect share of the male type"; "Among the animals reputed to be brave the panther is more female in appearance except in the legs..." Pseudo-Aristotle, *Physiognomics*, 5: 809b.15, 5: 810a.1; Aristotle, *Minor Works*, transl. Hett, 110–111. See also Aristotle, *The History of Animals*, transl. D'Arcy Wentworth Thompson (Oxford: Clarendon Press, 1910), 9: 1.

well-proportioned; the eyebrows are big and the forehead squared; and in the middle of this concave shape, between the nose and the eyebrows, we see a certain seriousness that could terrify whosoever looks at it, which is made of fearsome hairs that fall over the forehead to the eyes in order to protect them. Proportionate to other parts of the body is the head, resting on a large, long neck, just as well-proportioned as the rest of the body. The color of his hair is a dark blond with dark brown and yellow with red in the middle; some highlighted strands appear as thinly layered gold and appear both hard and soft, between curly and straight, midway at the nape of the neck. The robust shoulders and the hale chest mean that it is in full strength, and as he is curled up his massive back displays the animal's many ribs, along with noticeable hips and thighs that are not fleshy, but instead taut and full with strong muscles and veins. In the same fashion, he has strong, large and regal legs that show him to be elegant and brave while walking. In general, he is neither too moist, nor too dry, but with these qualities glides with long, deliberate steps, and, while in a pacing gait, shakes and flails his shoulders.[14] These qualities of the body correspond to the passions of the soul: therefore, he is polite, generous, cautiously magnanimous, truthful, a great lover of victory, and, finally, caring towards his benefactors and relatives. This figure of a lion is used by Aristotle to describe the universal figure of man, just as he uses leopards to characterize women.[15] In considering the qualities of all animals, leopards are not endowed with virtue or strength; the qualities of the shape of their bodies can be considered more appropriate for women than men. Though their rear legs appear to be capable of achieving something, we are only able to see some signs of strength in their speed among small animals and in their ability to catch small prey and tear them apart. Usually they have a small face with small, white, concave eyes set deep in the head, almost hidden, which they are able to shift quickly. Their foreheads are disproportionate in length and the area near the ears is more circular than flat; their neck is quite long and thin with few ribs in their chest and an apparent long back; and their hips and thighs are quite ample and plump. They have soft and supple

---

14   Although not cited as such, the description is an almost exact quotation of that found in: Pseudo-Aristotle, *Physiognomica*, 5: 809b.15–35; Aristotle, *Minor Works*, transl. Hett, 110–112.

15   Pseudo-Aristotle, *Physiognomica*, 5: 809b.15, 5: 810a.1; Aristotle, *Minor Works*, transl. Hett, 110–113.

sides (same as their belly) with hair that is uniform in color; their form is not well proportioned, with neither the different parts nor muscles defined. Leopards' bodies are the same as their souls, which is cowardly; and since they are little thieves, it is true to say of their nature that they are full of frauds and deceits. Therefore, painters must, even more than is possible, represent men with the limbs of a lion, while that of a leopard is appropriate for women and effeminate men, as Homer testifies in the third chapter of the *Iliad* when discussing the Trojan prince Paris:

> When, advancing together, the two armies
> came near, Alexandros, like a god, appeared wearing
> a panther skin on his shoulders, and his curved bow...[16]

The way in which this is discussed is appropriate for poets. Virgil, for instance, says of Aeneas (to whom great strength had been imparted, and who wanted to rescue his elderly father from the fire of Troy) that he wore a lion skin on his shoulders, which stirred in his soul the strength of the animal and its limbs.[17] The conceit is universal among poets [describing heroes]. Because it is possible that an individual man may be found that deviates from the universal, painters must be familiar with all types and variations. For instance, an individual man could be found that is fatter, paler and softer than any woman; or who is sickly and thin due to fatigue, hunger or illness; or made black by the sun; or a young man who is more delicate than an old woman; or a person who lives in the city and is always engaged in commercial activity in the shade; or, finally, a peasant who is continuously fatigued working in the hot sun. Besides these examples, there are many differences caused by the age of a person. Younger people are plumper, softer and paler than older people. Painters must be careful to ensure that everything is appropriate and not go against nature. I must also advise that in painting a small English or Flemish child, or one from another northern country, one must ensure that they are lighter than one from Egypt or the Barbary Coast, because all of these nations are (as we already said) more lightly complected than those.

---

16  Homer, *Iliad*, transl. Powell, 3: 13–16.
17  "I stooped and slipped over my neck and broad shoulders a tawny/ Lion's skin for a cloak; then I raise up my burden." Virgil, *Aeneid*, transl. Frederick Ahl (Oxford: Oxford University Press, 2007), 2: 722.

## 3. On the Beauty of Human Bodies, Especially Women

Even though the painter is obliged to imitate nature, he, nevertheless, strains himself in attempting to surpass it by choosing only the most beautiful parts. These are not the same for men and women, nor is there ever a man or a woman who is perfect in all parts. Perfection is also rarely found in nature, as Petrarch says in these eight lines:

> This fragile and fallen good of ours,
> this wind and shadow, Beauty by name,
> was never, at least not in our age, complete
> except in one body, and that was to my pain:
> since Nature does not wish, nor is it fitting,
> to make one rich, by impoverishing others:
> yet all its wealth was everywhere in here
> (pardon me you who are lovely, or think so).[18]

Zeuxis did this at Croton when he wanted to paint Helen the Greek, the most beautiful of all women. In order to capture her renowned beauty, he selected the five best most beautiful virgins of that city and, in copying the best part of each one, he created the most beautiful figure of Helen.[19] Now, in order for this immortal painter to demonstrate such excellence in his art, he possessed two things, as all artists should: a perfect understanding of the beautiful and ugly parts [in nature], and an expert

---

18  The portrait of Laura, model for the ideal beauty and woman as precious object, becomes formalized early on in Petrarchan sonnets as a topos. "There was never such beauty, ancient or modern,/ nor will be, I believe: but so concealed/ the world in error hardly noticed it./ She left us soon: and I am glad to lose that little glimpse of her that heaven gave me,/ only to take more pleasure in her sacred light." Petrarch, "Canzone 350," *The Complete Canzoniere*, transl. A. S. Kline ([n.p.]: Poetry in Translation, 2001), 487.

19  The legend dates from the fourth century BCE and was recorded in succeeding centuries by Cicero and Pliny in slightly modified forms. In his De Inventione (84 BCE), Cicero noted an early version in which Zeuxis, in order "to embody the surpassing beauty of womanhood" in painting Helen for the temple of Juno in the city of Croton, chose five of the most beautiful girls of the city, "because he did not think that all the qualities he sought to combine in a portrayal of beauty could be found in one person, because in no single case has Nature made anything perfect and finished in every part." Marcus Tullius Cicero, *De Inventione*, transl. H. M. Hubbell (Cambridge, MA: Harvard University Press, 1952), 168–169; "Inspexerit virgins eorum nudas et quinque elegerit, ut quod in quaequae laudatissimum esset pictura redderet." Pliny, *Natural History*, transl. Healy, 64, 308–309.

hand able to reveal what the soul could understand. This second ability could be obtained with the application of the first, I believe, like other things that could be learned through the classes of those who know better in these matters. Here I want to talk about beauty as it pertains to the artist, something that can be found described differently by various painters and writers, as well as in different ages. The wise painter should make a diligent effort to understand and consider what is written about beauty here and then take into account the general consensus of his time. If he considers only what seems wise and beautiful himself, disregarding everyone else's judgment, then he will be called mad, like one who judges something beautiful that everyone else in that era or city considers ugly. For example, if he would wish to paint a woman here in Venice with black hair, as the Greek poet Anacreon wanted, as a painter would his lover, many would consider it of low class and the painter would be considered foolish or ignorant for his choice, being that the general agreement is that the beauty of a woman is primarily due to her blonde hair, and the meaning of its golden color, as modern poets contend.[20] Keep, therefore, this universal rule of the painter and always consider the accepted conventions of the time or place where he wants to make a woman or a man or another beautiful thing. Regardless of period, moreover, we know that in all places and in all times a well-proportioned body has always been praised, though the same colors were not seen as appropriate for the body in the same fashion. Another accepted piece of advice that I should like to impart to the painter is that there is a huge difference between the beauty of men and women. What is laudable in women is of chief blame in men, as Homer has Hector rebuke his brother Paris in this manner, as if he were speaking Italian,

"Little Paris, nice to look at, mad for women, seducer boy."[21]

And again he says, a little later [of Paris],

> "...just because he was good-looking, while in his heart there was no strength or power."[22]

---

20 "First paint for me her locks, both soft and black." Anacreon, "Ode 28: On His Mistress," *The First Twenty-Eight Odes of Anacreon in Greek and English*, ed. John Broderick (London: Sherwood, Gilbert and Piper, 1827; repr. 2011), 197.
21 Homer, *Iliad*, transl. Powell, 3: 35–37.
22 Ibid., 3: 37–45.

He had a beauty that appropriately adorns women, not men. Speaking of this in his *Rhetoric*, Aristotle says that there are two types of beauty for men: that of the young, and another of middle-aged and old men. Therefore, he says, the beauty of a young man consists of having a strong body that can handle fatigue, and be pleasing to those that look upon it. Moreover, given their endowments, the young should willingly dance, jump, and joust in the presence of his lover in order to be reputed handsome; these things could not be easily accomplished if not with a well-proportioned body that possesses healthy coloring which makes anyone who looks upon him grateful.[23] But, [Luis de] Granada said in the fifth part of his *Symbolum* that the most beautiful things to see are likewise the most useful to life;[24] that concept is verified not only in men and others animals, but in all natural or artificial things that are used by the men. The beauty of a middle-aged man, [Aristotle] says, consists of a body that is adapted to and accommodates the toils of war, and who by nature strikes terror into onlookers.[25] This is what Anacreon wants, that a painter gives him the eyes of a warrior in his poem *Bathyllus*, dark and threatening like that of Mars, but still clear as Venus to ensure that others would be fearful in looking upon them, yet see through to the hope of his soul.[26] The old man is wished to have a body that performs

---

23 Gallucci returns to this section of the *Rhetoric* throughout his Book Five in order to reinforce points of different aspects of masculine beauty. As Aristotle opens the section: "Beauty varies with each age. In a young man, it consists in possessing a body capable of enduring all efforts, either of the racecourse or of bodily strength, while he himself is pleasant to look upon and a sheer delight. This is why the athletes in the pentathlum are most beautiful, because they are naturally adapted for bodily exertion and for swiftness of foot." Aristotle, *Rhetoric*, transl. John Henry Freese (Cambridge, MA: Harvard University Press, 1960), 1: 5.10–14; 55.

24 In the late 1580s, Gallucci translated into Latin the *Catechismus* of the Spanish Dominican Luis de Granada (1505–1588). Luis de Granada, *Catechismus in symbolum fidei*, transl. Giovanni Paolo Gallucci (Venice: Damiani Zenari, 1586). In the Platonic dialogue, Socrates debates the definition of beauty with Hippias and rotorts: "whatever is useful is beautiful." Plato, *Hippia Maior*, 295; David Sider, "Plato's Early Aesthetics: 'The Hippias Major'," *Journal of Aesthetics & Art Criticism*, 35.4 (1977), 465–470, at 465, https://doi.org/10.2307/430612

25 "In a man who has reached his prime, beauty consists in being naturally adapted for the toils of war, in being pleasant to look upon and at the same time awe-inspiring." Aristotle, *Rhetoric*, transl. Freese, 1: 5.10–14; 55.

26 A dancer and performer of pantomimes in Augustan Rome, Bathyllus was born in Alexandria and was the favorite comedic performer of Maecenas. Anacreon writes of his visage: "Power that awes, and love that trances;/ Steal from Venus bland desire,/ Steal from Mars the look of fire,/ Blend them in such expression here,/ That

the labors necessary for his age, and that in the same way they know that they were born with good coloring in their cheeks that was appropriate for their age and in this age we again seek a proportionate body as described by Dürer in his first book. Now let's see how Ariosto depicts the beauty of a woman in Angelica:

> The brutal, ruthless savages left the exquisitely beautiful damsel exposed on the shore to the cruel monster, and as naked as when Nature first fashioned her; not even a veil did she have to cover the lily-white, the rose-red, unfading in December as in July, which coloured her lustrous limbs.
>
> Ruggiero would have taken her for a statue fashioned in alabaster or some lambent marble, and tethered thus to the rock by some diligent sculptor's artifice, were it not that he distinctly saw tears coursing down her rose-fresh, lily-white cheeks and bedewing her unripe apple-breasts, and her golden tresses flowing in the wind.[27]

In such a way the painter could be clearer in the manner he represents the beauty of a woman, whom others look upon with astonishment. There is also no reason to omit how Tasso writes about the idea of beauty in [the figure of] Armida in these verses:

> Never did Argos, Cyprus, Delos see
> form of such fair deportment and address.
> Like gold her hair one moment gleams, lovely
> through veils, then unveiled glitters from each tress.
> So, when the sky is clearing, glad and free,
> now through a radiant cloud the sun shines less,
> now bursts that cloud and spreads its piercing ray
> more brightly and redoubles all the day.
>
> The breeze new-curls some errant tresses' maze,
> the rest by nature curl like waves of light.
> But inward-gathered is her close-kept gaze
> and hides love's treasures and her own from sight.

---

we by turns may hope and fear!" Anacreon, "Ode 22," *The Odes of Anacreon*, transl. Thomas Moore (London: John, Camden Hotten, 1871, https://www.gutenberg.org/files/38230/38230-h/38230-h.htm; repr. 2011), 112; Tacitus, *Annals*, transl. Ronald Mellor (Oxford: Oxford University Press, 2011), 1: 54.

27  Ariosto, "Canto 10," *Orlando Furioso*, transl. Waldman, 95–96; 103.

> A tint of roses in her fair face plays,
> sprinkled on ivory, mingling with the white;
> but on her mouth, warm with love's breath, there glows
> alone in simple ruddiness the rose.
>
> Her beauteous breast displays its naked snows
> that feed love's flame that they themselves have brought.
> Partly her budding unsucked bosom shows...[28]

As we have said, the Greek poet Anacreon speaks to a painter in a famous lyrical verse of one of his songs, asking him to paint his wife with soft, black, and perfumed hair;[29] the colors should appropriately represent the forehead, paired with proper oil, eyebrows that are arched, but do not touch each other. The tips of her hair should look as though they are even and make contact, and must be black in color. Then he wants the eyes to be greenish in color, as the poets describe Minerva's, or as we see with cats, lions and owls, and that they are as sultry as those of Venus, or like those of some soft, effeminate young man's, or, so to speak, consecrated with lasciviousness and love. Furthermore, he asks that the painter make the cheeks and the nose the color of roses mixed with milk; the lips should be persuasive, in other words, small and pursed in order to move quickly while speaking, and that the neck and the chin be smooth and polished. Finally, she must be clothed in a scarlet dress that reveals her naked limbs.

I would be amiss in neglecting to relate what Petrarch says of the beauty of his woman [Laura] in these few lines:

> Her hair pure gold, and hot snow her face,
> her eyebrows ebony, her eyes twin stars,
> from which Love never bent his vow in vain:
> pearls and crimson roses, where grief received
> the form of an ardent lovely voice:
> flames her sighs, and her tears were crystal.[30]

---

28  The Syrian sorceress sent to seduce the Christian camp uses her "sex's gifts" to request ten champions of the Franks. Tasso, *The Liberation of Jerusalem*, transl. Wickert, 4: 29–31.
29  Anacreon, *Odes of Anacreon*, transl. Moore, 17.
30  "Quel sempre acerbo et honorato giorno." Petrarch, "Canzone 251," *The Complete Canzoniere*, transl. Kline, 251.

Ariosto, also speaking of hair, says:

> They could tell by her golden curls and by the delicate beauty of her face.[31]

And of [Angelica's] lips, he says elsewhere:

> ...she took the ring which had saved her from more than one scrape and closed her rosy lips over it.[32]

But because we are going to address human limbs elsewhere in order to demonstrate which ones are better for each kind of person, this will suffice for now.

This beauty is universal and can be found in both men and women (as we said before) when each part of their body is appropriate and functional. Such a judgment derives from the Greeks who would find a woman ugly should she have buttocks that are small and flat. For having been made with these two little features is contrary to the function of her body in order to support it without injury. Knowing that it is the nature of women to stay home and remain seated for long periods, it would be more convenient if they had buttocks that were softer and fuller in order to sit more comfortably. Catullus also finds the most beautiful parts of a woman corresponding to her fair complexion, and proportion of the body relating to the rule of proportion, as he writes of Lesbia [in comparison with other women],

> Many find Quintia beautiful. For me she's fair-complexioned, tall, of good carriage. These few points I concede. But overall beauty — no.[33]

Seneca also speaks of a woman's beauty. He argues that it is, in fact, not the beauty of the arms or legs that should be praised, but instead a woman with a beautiful face who will receive all admiration, over

---

31 The description occurs after Ruggiero witnesses Marfisa in battle. Ariosto, "Canto 26," *Orlando Furioso*, transl. Waldman, 23–31; 310.

32 The episode comments on the magical quality of women's lips as the excised passage finds Angelica using the ring to cloak herself in invisibility from her pursuing suitors. Ariosto, "Canto 12," *Orlando Furioso*, transl. Waldman, 34; 120.

33 Catullus completes the stanza with a reminder that beauty resides in the totality of the parts: "It's Lesbia who's beautiful, and, being wholly lovely, has stolen from all of the others their every charm." Gaius Valerius Catullus, *Poems of Catullus*, transl. Peter Green (Berkeley, CA: University of California Press, 2007), 86: 1–6; 193.

the other parts of the body.³⁴ It is sufficient to relate the suggestion of Anacreon to painters in his bucolic poem *Bathyllus* that when attempting to capture the universal beauty of human bodies, he should form the idea of beauty in his mind, the figure of a young man.³⁵

He asked that the painter make the roots of his hair black and golden at the ends; the hair should be curly and remain free to sweep over the forehead. The forehead must be soft and rosy adorned with black eyebrows. The eyes, black in color, are terrifying, with the likeness of those of Mars, yet calm and dewy like those of Venus, so that the fear instilled in those who look upon them would become hopeful. The cheeks are rosy, as is seen in apples or young children when they feel ashamed; the lips are tender and full of persuasion, appearing as though he is speaking even when remaining silent; the face has to be quite large with a neck of ivory like Adonis, a chest and hands like that of Mercury, the legs of Pollux, and, finally, the stomach of Bacchus.

## 4. The Figure of a Strong Man

Although every man is capable of being strong, given strength is a habit carried by the soul, not every man and every body type is able to express all works of virtue. Erminia expresses such a belief in Book 6 of Tasso's *Gerusalemme* in these lines:

> "Ah! why did Nature and the heavens fail
> my limbs and heart as stoutly to inspire..."³⁶

The sentiment is supported by Cicero, who says the same when speaking of Africans, which is why Paulus could not emulate his father's studies

---

34 "A woman is not beautiful when her ankle or arm wins compliments, but when her total appearance diverts admiration from the individual parts of her body." Seneca, *Letters from a Stoic*, transl. Robin Campbell (London: Penguin Classics, 2004), 33: 6.

35 "And now with all thy pencil's truth,/ Portray Bathyllus, lovely youth!... Oh! let this pictured god be mine,/ And keep the boy for Samos' shrine;/ Phœbus shall then Bathyllus be,/ Bathyllus then the deity!" Anacreon, *The Odes of Anacreon*, transl. Moore, 17; Tacitus, *Annals*, transl. Mellor, 1: 54.

36 The pagan princess of Antioch, bent on helping her unrequited love Tancred, spies armor and laments the strength that she has been denied being a woman. Tasso, *The Liberation of Jerusalem*, transl. Wickert, 6:83.

relating to strength.[37] Here then I should describe only that body which possesses the habit of strength. When this habit is absent, we refer to the body as brawny, meaning nothing other than the possession of the strength of brute animals, such as lions and others of the same kind. The proper body, which possesses the quality of strength, must be straight in shape from the legs to the hips; all parts of the body must be strong and firm, with the bones clearly visible beneath the skin in all parts. Ariosto painted his characters Astolfo and Samsonet in this fashion in these four verses:

> Seeing Astolfo and Samsonet advancing, fully armed, and realizing at a glance that they must be no mean warriors — they were both of them tall and solidly built.[38]

The sentiment is confusing when Ariosto has Olympia say the same thing to Orlando in this manner:

> "But if your mighty, Herculean aspect is a true image of your valour…"[39]

This is not to say that the figure should have a menacing gaze in a strong body, a misconception some painters have, leading them to make Hercules look like a bear with his limbs drawn in on themselves so that it is impossible to see his hands, feet or any other part of the body. The hair ought to be somewhat rugged and disheveled. The stomach should be wide and concave, not bloated, as in the figures of Bacchus or cherubs, for in this fleshy type there is no room for strength. Accordingly, his shoulders should be broad and large, along with the neck and everything up to the head. Homer attributed such qualities to Ajax in his description of the great warrior. Standing atop a tower in order to see the field of battle with the Greek Helen, king Priam asked her Ajax's name, describing him in this manner:

> "Who is this other Achaean,
> brazen and tall, standing out among the Argives
> both for his height and his broad shoulders?"[40]

---

37 Marcus Tullius Cicero, *Dream of Scipio*, transl. Andre Chaves (Pasadena: The Clinker Press, 2012), 6.
38 The warrior-virgin Marfisa admires the warriors as she approaches to challenge them. Ariosto, "Canto 18," *Orlando Furioso*, transl. Waldman, 100; 205.
39 Ariosto, "Canto 9," *Orlando Furioso*, transl. Waldman, 56; 88.
40 Homer, *Iliad*, transl. Powell, 3: 222–225.

Tasso, likewise, wrote in a canto of his *Gerusalemme*:

> See, Guelf rides with him, who in deeds of fame
> rivals him, as in blood and high degree:
> Well do I know him by his square-cut frame,
> huge shoulders, deep chest.[41]

The nape of the neck still must be robust and proportionate to his other parts and compliment the broad chest and strong, robust legs like two incredibly strong columns able to support the large base of the fortress [that is, the body]. However, these limbs should not merely be big and strong, but also firm, just as large and tall columns are not in themselves sufficient to support large palaces. The material must also be of good quality, such as quality marble, porphyry or serpentine. This must be said for the legs again. The feet must be distinct in every single part, so that all of the bones can be seen beneath the skin, but they do not need to be emaciated, and should be appropriately fleshy. The color of the skin should be dark and ruddy, unlike the complexion appropriate for women and young boys. The eyes should vary in color or be dark blue and also be well-positioned in the skull, not too set in the eye sockets, nor too protruding, but of average proportion in size and location. Within the eyes, there should appear little flames that are used to frighten onlookers, as Ariosto describes Orlando when he sang about him in this manner:

> The approach of Count Orlando, a man unmatched for valour, a man of so lofty a countenance, so imposing a demeanour that the very god of battle seemed but his second, attracted the notice of Alzirdo, who was fascinated by his remarkable build, his fierce eye, his wrathful countenance; he reckoned he must be a most mighty champion, but could not restrain himself from challenging him.[42]

This stanza verifies not only what we have said about the eyes, which should frighten others, but also that the combination of different limbs should not be confused and disproportioned. The same thing is said by Virgil when speaking to Dante in these verses:

---

41   Erminia surveys knights arriving with Godfrey, leader of the crusader army. Tasso, *The Liberation of Jerusalem*, transl. Wickert, 3:63.
42   The youthful arrogance of Alzirdo leads to his undoing, for in challenging the Prince of Anglant, he was "run through the heart." Ariosto, "Canto 12," *Orlando Furioso*, transl. Waldman, 74; 124–125.

> "Instantly, Dares sticks up his face and his muscular, virile
> Vastness, and raises himself to a rumbling roar from the menfolk.
> This was the lone soul who'd often solicit a contest with
> Paris; He was the one, who, right on the tomb of Hector the Mighty,
> Battered Bebrycian Butes, from Amycus' blood, so he boasted,
> Massive in stature, a champion. But Dares gave him a thrashing,
> Left him sprawled on the tan-coloured sand and slowly expiring.
> Such, then, was Dares, his head raised high for the start of the/ contest,
> Flexing the breadth of his shoulders and stretching one arm, then
> the other,
> Out as he pummelled and slashed at the air with a series of punches...."[43]

In addition to this, we should add that his eyebrows need not be delicate and sculpted into clear contours like a woman's, but should instead be broad and unkempt, growing towards each other over the forehead, though not necessarily growing together. The forehead has to be broad, but not too high. We can add to the description the expression and sounds involved in acts of straining, such as screaming aloud, which are made during bloody battles and other such violent occasions where it is common for men to show their valor. Moreover, as our description entails a broad, strong chest, he would also have a loud and frightening voice. And with such an agreement of appearance, virtue and expression, he would demonstrate constancy in all of his actions.

The following derives from Seneca, and it could act as a summary of this chapter, where we find Virgil describing a strong man, while he deals with a noble horse in these verses:[44]

---

[43] The description does not come from Dante's poet-prophet, but rather the Aeneid when Aeneas holds funerary games for his father and the first challenger for boxing described is the Trojan Dares. Virgil, *Aeneid*, transl. Ahl, 5: 367–378.

[44] Seneca, *Letters from a Stoic*, transl. Campbell, 25: 1–7.

From the first, a colt of the best lineage walks in the fields with a higher step and brings his feet down lightly. He dares to go first on the path, to test raging rivers and commit himself to unfamiliar bridges, nor does he bolt at untoward sounds. His neck is arched, his head graceful, his belly trim and back plumped out, and his proud chest abounds in muscle. The finest colors are chestnut and gray, the worst white and dun. Then, if he hears the faraway sound of clashing arms, he cannot stand still, his ears prick forward, his limbs quiver, and, whickering, he snorts the gathered fires from his nostrils.[45]

I would certainly not make a figure of a strong man any other way. Should more explanation be necessary, I cite the intrepid Cato, who, when moving towards the battle among the cries of the civil war at the military activities in the Alps, expresses himself with such comportment that I would not recommend another face for a warrior, nor another kind of habit.

## 5. How the Figure of a Timid Man Should Be Painted

Although from the things said above about the characteristics of the strong man, we can easily understand those of a shy man to be the opposite; nevertheless, in order to elevate the understanding of painters, we are compelled to explain more clearly how it is possible that they can represent to viewers the true image and true idea of shyness. The timid man pulls his limbs as tightly to his body as possible, as when all men are alarmed by a serious fear for any reason; this comportment makes it look as though they are shrinking into themselves, looking for a narrower place to hide. They look like they are running away and are pale overall. This passion of the spirit [*passione dell'animo*] has already been divinely described by Ariosto in this stanza:

> He came upon many of the terrified fugitives routed by Orlando. Some bewailed the loss of a son, others of a brother whom they had seen expire before their very eyes. Abject cowardice was still imprinted on their wan features; such was their terror, they were still dumbstruck, dazed, and pallid.[46]

---

45  Book three is dedicated to the breeding and selection of best horses for war and other endeavors. Virgil, *Georgics*, transl. Janet Lembke (New Haven: Yale University Press, 2005), 3: 75–80.
46  Ariosto, "Canto 13," *Orlando Furioso*, transl. Waldman, 35; 141.

And in another place, he concludes a stanza in this manner:

> …everyone was pale with fear for Rinaldo.[47]

And in another place he also says of this topic:

> But when he noticed the Imperial Eagle, the Golden Lilies, and the Leopards close by, he blanched like a man suddenly aware that his incautious foot has trodden upon a horrid poisonous snake which has been slumbering torpidly in the grass: he recoils in a fright and flees from the angry, venomous reptile…[48]

In the same way Homer speaks of Paris, who was overcome with fear:

> Just as when a man sees a snake in the wilds of the mountain and he jumps back and his limbs tremble and a whiteness suffuses his cheeks, even so did godlike Alexandros [Paris] slip into the crowd of lordly Trojans, fearing the son of Atreus [Menelaus].[49]

And elsewhere:

> Pale fear
> took hold of both sides.[50]

And Ariosto also says:

> Never did a timid shepherd-girl start back more violently from a horrid snake…[51]

Paleness and cowardly retreat are not the only symptoms of fear; the shivers, loss of voice, and hair raising are also common. Ovid speaks of such trembling when recounting the tale of Philomela.

> She shivered like a little frightened lamb.[52]

---

47 Ariosto, "Canto 31," *Orlando Furioso*, transl. Waldman, 107; 382.
48 Ariosto, "Canto 39," *Orlando Furioso*, transl. Waldman, 32; 469.
49 The cowardly retreat incurs Hector's curses. Homer, *Iliad*, transl. Powell, 3: 27–35.
50 As the Trojans and Greeks drank and banqueted, Zeus caused a thunderstorm and ensured that no celebration would be had until proper rituals be carried out. Homer, *Iliad*, transl. Powell, 7: 480–482.
51 Ariosto, "Canto 10," 95–96; 103.
52 "Tereus, Procne, and Philomela," Ovid, *Metamorphoses*, transl. A. D. Melville (Oxford: Oxford University Press, 2008),6: 501–532.

Virgil also speaks of Turnus:

> For the first time, shock at a sight disables his body,
> Loosens his limbs. Horror bristles his hair, chokes sound behind locked jaws.⁵³

Aeneas had the same reaction when Mercury ordered him to leave Africa for Italy by decree of Jupiter.

> Senses lost, hair bristling in shock, voice frozen in locked jaws.⁵⁴

In a similar fashion, Ariosto also said:

> When the phantom surged up out of the water, the Saracen's hair stood on end and he paled, and his voice died in his throat.⁵⁵

Tasso also wrote this in Book 13 of his *Gerusalemme*:

> At this the cheeks of all who heard grew pale,
> their fear by countless signs made manifest.⁵⁶

Furthermore, Ariosto speaks of trembling in this manner:

> Or too great an anxiety to kill the baron; or whether his heart, trembling like a leaf, caused his arm and hands to shake as well...⁵⁷

Because some men are more susceptible to this passion than others, painters need be aware of how to portray them. Those embodying this passion have soft hair and a long neck with faces as those described above: their eyes flicker with fright; their eyelids seem to flutter in perpetual motion, as is seen in those who are fearful, illustrated by the painter through careful description of wrinkles of the forehead or temples that move the eyelids under their long eyebrows. The chest is small and weak, having within it a cold heart, an important indicator of fearfulness. To portray a shy man, the hands must be long and the legs swollen and full. The prudent painter must not only take care,

---

53  Virgil, *Aeneid*, transl. Ahl, 12: 867–868.
54  Ibid., 4: 280.
55  Ariosto, "Canto 1," *Orlando Furioso*, transl. Waldman, 29; 4.
56  Tasso, *The Liberation of Jerusalem*, transl. Wickert, 13: 22.
57  Ariosto, "Canto 1," 76; 90.

knowing the true idea of fear, but also be aware and advised that in his paintings he cannot give heavy loads to shy men over strong men. Therefore, timid characters should not be shown with weapons of war or hunting, since they lack strength and loud voices (necessary to illustrate both hunters and warriors), attested to by many credible witnesses.[58]

## 6. How One Should Paint a Furious and Angry Man

Although it is necessary that the strong man be wrathful, unable to conquer anything without a measure of fury, as the philosopher [Aristotle] wants, he must, nevertheless, display moderation.[59] Otherwise, artists portraying them would represent a figure who looked perpetually angry, as opposed to strong. Discussing the representation of fury and those incidental qualities that might convey anger, Seneca, in the second [book] *On Anger*, says: "the very furious are ones who are by nature tawny and blonde-haired, and, since others define those who are angry in this way, we are going to describe them together here."[60] Ariosto describes Gradasso angry in this manner:

> Thus humiliated, he blushed, with shame and anger...[61]

Elsewhere, he again says:

> In the end Ruggiero, flushing with anger, drew his own sword.[62]

And Tasso in Book 6 of his *Gerusalemme* says:

---

58  "The signs of the coward are soft hair, a body of sedentary habit, not energetic; calves of the legs broad above; pallor about the face; eyes weak and blinking, the extremities of the body weak, small legs and long thing hands; thigh small and weak; the figure is constrained in movement; he is not eager but supine and nervous; the expression on his face is liable to rapid change and is cowed." Pseudo-Aristotle, *Physiognomics*, 3: 807b.5–10; Aristotle, *Minor Works*, transl. Hett, 98–99.

59  "Thus Temperance and Courage are destroyed by excess and deficiency, and preserved by the observance of the mean." Aristotle, *Nicomachean Ethics*, transl. William Heinemann (Cambridge, MA: Harvard University Press, 1962), 2:2.6–7; 77.

60  Lucius Anneaus Seneca, "De Ira," *Dialogues*, transl. A. Bourgery (Paris: Les Belles lettres, 2003).

61  Mandricard publicly strikes Gradasso, causing him to lose hold of Durindana. Ariosto, "Canto 27," *Orlando Furioso*, transl. Waldman, 64; 330.

62  In failing to calm Marfisa with words, the two come to blows in a duel. Ariosto, "Canto 36," *Orlando Furioso*, transl. Waldman, 53; 437.

> At this he halts, burning with rage and shame
> within and flushing red as flame without...[63]

As such, it is advisable to include the color of fire on the faces of angry and furious men, especially in the eyes, as Homer described the enraged Achilles:

> In their midst, godlike Achilles armed himself for battle. There was a gnashing of teeth, and his two eyes showed like the gleam of a fire. Into his heart an unbearable pain descended.
> And raging against the Trojans, he put on the gifts that the god Hephaistos had labored so to make...[64]

Tasso again wrote this in Book 7 of his *Gerusalemme*:

> Crimson with rage the prince's cheeks grow now,
> his eyes flash fire and, under veins that swell,
> his flaming glances issue, while beneath
> resounds the furious grinding of his teeth.[65]

Ariosto again locates fury mainly in the eyes when he says:

> The enchantress, then, presented herself to Ruggiero in Atlas' likeness, with Atlas' grave, venerable face which had always commanded his respect; on his face he wore the look of angry menace which Ruggiero had feared from early childhood.[66]

And elsewhere:

> ...now as she glowered and looked daggers...[67]

---

63 The Christian knight Tancred is shamed that he did not initially meet the taunts of Argant, allowing Otho to ride into battle first. Tasso, *The Liberation of Jerusalem*, transl. Wickert, 6: 31.
64 Homer, *Iliad*, transl. Powell, 19: 334–339, 457. The rage of Achilles is central to the extant books of the *Iliad*. The very opening of the epic begins: "The rage sing, O goddess, of Achilles, the son of Peleus,/ the destructive anger that brought ten-thousand pains to the/ Achaeans and sent many brave souls of fighting men to the house of Hades and made their bodies a feast for dogs/ and all kinds of birds." Homer, *Iliad*, transl. Powell, 1: 1–4.
65 Rambault, who was charmed by Armida to abandon Christianity, battles Tancred. Tasso, *The Liberation of Jerusalem*, transl. Wickert, 7: 42.
66 Ariosto, "Canto 7," *Orlando Furioso*, transl. Waldman, 56; 66–67.
67 Ariosto muses, "...you cannot insult a woman worse than by telling her she is old and ugly." Ariosto, "Canto 20," *Orlando Furioso*, transl. Waldman, 120; 243.

There he wrote about the speed at which such furious men are able to run, arising from the same heat which affects not only the complexion of the face, but almost all of the body, as bright and vermillion. As we have said, this is more so true in the face than elsewhere. Their hair must be very dark and thick, always complimenting their flesh, the color of fire; such characteristics are appropriate for one experiencing rage. This is seen in the color of their hair, which should be like that of a lion. Likewise, furious men should have full beards to complement their bushy mane, though without hair on their chests. These figures must be made so as to appear in motion; since it is not their nature to remain still, they will move their hands if they cannot do anything else. The extremities of their bodies must be big and strong, with unkempt and curly hair. The veins of the eyes appear quite large and red, while the arteries in the neck bulge greatly. As we have said above, the chest of the furious man must be hairless; nevertheless, some authors prefer it to be hairy, as seen when Homer describes Achilles:

> A pain like grief weighed on the son of Peleus [Achilles],
> and in his shaggy chest this way and that
> the passion of his heart ran.[68]

And he said these things when he described him as angrier than he had ever been. Again, it is appropriate for an angry man to bite his own lips, confirmed by Ariosto, who says in these verses:

> ...and Ravenna is sacked. "In his anguish the Pope chews his lip..."[69]

Tasso understood the same to be true and explained it in Book 7 of his poem in this manner:

> Biting his lips in rage, the wicked one,
> cursing, throws down his broken lance and draws.[70]

Virgil provides another characteristic feature of this passion when he describes the anger Dido felt towards Aeneas because of his departure from Africa. As he says:

---

68 Achilles contemplates killing Agamemnon for the insult of losing his war prize, Briseïs. Athena appears and persuades him otherwise. Homer, *Iliad*, transl. Powell, 1: 185; 17.
69 Ariosto, "Canto 33," *Orlando Furioso*, transl. Waldman, 41.
70 The Circassian warrior Argant engages the leader of the Gascon crusaders, count of Toulouse, in combat. Tasso, *The Liberation of Jerusalem*, transl. Wickert, 7: 87.

> For a while, she just watched him obliquely,
> Eyes flashing this way and that as he spoke, scrutinizing at random
> His whole being with silent looks.[71]

In fact, this makes her turn her back, and yet still continue to eye every single part of him that inspired her wrath. This passion, which inspires hateful glances, was used by Tasso to describe an angry man in these lines of Book 7 of his *Gerusalemme*:

> Behind his shield that foe comes, helmeted,
> his naked falchion poised to strike and slay.
> Fiercely the prince to meet his blows sets out,
> threats in his eyes and terror in his shout.[72]

And elsewhere:

> Only the fierce Circassian never rose,
> but with a terrible and scornful face
> sat silent, like a lion in repose,
> rolling his eyes and moving not one pace.[73]

Now, because Seneca divinely describes an angry man, I considered it prudent to put his seal of authority on this topic, of which he says the following:

> In order that one recognize people possessed by the passion of fury are not mentally healthy, we should now consider his gestures and actions. There are some gestures that are indicative of the insane, such as having a threatening face, sad forehead, vacant stare, quick pace, gesticulating hands, and an odd complexion. Finally, inhaling deeply and exhaling loudly are all signs of furious people. The eyes are fiery with a very flushed face due to the boiling blood deep in their hearts, causing the lips to tremble. His hair curls up and his spirit shrinks as he strides forward, limbs contorted, his moaning speech intermittent and unintelligible. He beats his hands and stomps the ground with his feet; his entire body provokes fear and greatly menaces those around. The face is frightening and ugly to see; it shall soon be known if it is more hateful or ugly.[74]

---

71  Virgil, *Aeneid*, transl. Ahl, 4: 361–365.
72  Tancred violently pursues the traitor Rambault. Tasso, *The Liberation of Jerusalem*, transl. Wickert, 7: 37.
73  Ibid., 10: 56.
74  Seneca, "De Ira," *Dialogues*, transl. Bourgery, 3: 1.

## 7. The Figure of a Man, Who Is by Nature Cold and Wet, therefore, Meek and Humble, Feeble, Slow, Quiet, and Effeminate

In many ways the angry man appears strong due to his warmth. Therefore, men who rarely burn from anger and have a cold heart appear shy and cowardly, lacking all virility. Though he is shaped as a man, he has the soul of a woman, which is slow by nature, and is thus different in appearance in many parts. These men must have a very light complexion with soft skin and a good stature with hair spiked upwards, as Aristotle recommends.[75] Others want such a man to be yellowish in complexion with eyes tending to be a little black and languid or set in; the extremities of the body must be small and weak with thin, long hands.[76] Because he feels easily ashamed, his shape must be made in accordance with one who is oppressed by such passion, about which we will speak more in the appropriate place. Suffice it to say here that his head and the eyes must be looking down towards the ground; and because these usually are idle and downward cast as women do, it is not appropriate for the painter to indicate a modicum of manhood in the face, which would be used to dignify the figure that he wishes to paint.

## 8. How an Ingenious Man Should Be Painted

The ingenious man was called Daedalus by the Greeks, which means varied, as if the excellence of the craftsman lies in the variety of things [he creates].[77] So if one wished to paint Daedalus — who made the

---

75  Because humors also determined skin color, "complexions" became an alternative term when discussing style and humoral balance. "But the excessively fair are also cowardly; witness women." Pseudo-Aristotle, *Physiognomica*, 6: 812a.15; Aristotle, *Minor Works*, transl. Hett, 126–127.

76  When Lomazzo became blind and abandoned painting for writing, he advised his fellow artists to mix their colors to make the skin of sanguine figures rosier, melancholics swarthier, cholerics yellower, and phlegmatics paler. Gian Paolo Lomazzo, *Scritti sulle arti*, ed. Roberto P. Ciardi, 2 vols (Florence: Centro Di, 1973–1974), II: 262–69.

77  The prolific inventor actually derives his name from the Greek term for "craftsman" or to "work artfully" (*Daidalos*). R. S. P. Beekes, *Etymological Dictionary of Greek* (Leiden: Brill, 2009), 296. The fame of Daedalus is importantly related through his

Labyrinth and escaped from it, making wings for himself and his son [Icarus] — this figure must be painted with the color white mixed with red, have hair of medium length and a slight wave, and have soft, damp flesh, though not necessarily plump, because corpulence would smother his ingenuity. Nor should he be made scrawny, but the areas around the shoulders, neck and face must be the leanest of all the areas of the body. The area around the shoulders ought to be drawn together, while the parts around the ribs should have the skin drawn taut over the bones. If possible, colors should be used to assure that the proper judgment can be conveyed when viewing the thinness of the skin. Finally, the eyes should appear as those of a cat or an owl, which Homer usually describes as belonging to Minerva.[78] We should acknowledge the debt to Aristotle's wisdom in these things, since I have not found any other source addressing this topic.[79]

## 9. The Figure of an Uncouth Man Compared to One with Great Intelligence

Therefore, from the figure of an ingenious man one can deduce how to paint a boor, who has no intelligence, since his opposite is unwavering. In order to clarify for scholars of painting, and because the philosopher [Aristotle] wrote on each topic separately, we, as well, will write on both of them again in separate entries. His complexion has to be painted completely white or black, and must be fleshy in all parts of the body, but especially the belly, which must hang from the weight of the fat. The legs should be long with girth and rounded near the heels, while all the other limbs are shorter and should almost look like they are tied in a bundle of flesh, and this should be seen mainly near the neck, which must be really short and supported by thin shoulders; the forehead is rounded and large, and the cheeks round and full; the eye is pale

---

    role as an innovator in many fields by later Roman authors. Pliny, *Natural History*, transl. Healy, 7: 198; Penelope Reed Doob, *The Idea of the Labyrinth: From Classical Antiquity through the Middle Ages* (Ithaca, NY: Cornell University Press, 1992), 36.

78  In a characteristic Homeric epithet, Athena is described as "The grey-eyed goddess." Homer, *Iliad*, transl. Powell, 1: 212.

79  Pseudo-Aristotle, *Physiognomica*; Aristotle, *De Sensu*, 45: 18–20; quoted in T. K. Johansen, *Aristotle on the Sense-Organs* (Cambridge: Cambridge University Press, 1997), esp. 98–100.

and motionless, seemingly unable to see; and the palms of the hands are round, and shoulders protruding, but all joints of the body hidden beneath the flesh, so that they cannot be seen.[80]

## 10. The Figure and Painting of an Effeminate Man, Soft by Nature and also through Incident

In general, a man who has nothing other than the distinction of sex making him masculine and is in every other respect similar to women in his customs, should be similar to women in both form and action with habits again similar to women. A painting of a man with this character should appear to be in motion with all of his limbs actively moving, but slowly. He has a curved neck with thick and voluminous eyebrows, and his eyes must be shown as though looking himself over, as women do before going out of their houses. The corners of his eyes should have many wrinkles or creases, and his head should lean more on the left shoulder than the right one, while some more so on the right side. Ariosto describes Ruggiero in this manner in Alcina's labyrinth:

> The delicious softness of his dress suggested sloth and sensuality; Alcina had woven the garment with her own hands in silk and gold, a subtle work.
> 
> A glittering, richly jeweled necklace fastened round his neck and hung to his chest, while his two arms, hitherto so virile, were now each clasped by a lustrous bangle. Each ear was pierced by a fine gold ring from which a fat pearl hung, such as no Arabian or Indian ever boasted.'
> 
> His curly locks were saturated in perfumes, the most precious and aromatic that exist. His every gesture was mincing, as though he were accustomed to waiting on ladies in Valencia. All about him was sickly, all but his name; the rest was but corruption and decay. Thus was Ruggiero discovered, thus changed from his true self by sorcery.[81]

Ovid divinely described this manner of looking around that women do in the tale of vanity in this way:

---

80 "These are the marks of the little-minded man. He is small limbed, small and round, dry, with small eyes and a small face, like a Corinthian or Leucadian"; "Bulging eyes mean stupidity; this is appropriate and applies to the ass..." Pseudo-Aristotle, *Physiognomica*, 3: 808a.30; 6:811b.22–25; Aristotle, *Minor Works*, transl. Hett, 105, 123–125.

81 Ariosto, "Canto 7," 53–55; 66.

The boy and seeing, saw her heart's desire.
Yet though her heart would haste she paused a while.
Till, dress inspected, all in order placed,
Charm in her eyes set shining, she deserved
To look so lovely, then began to speak.[82]

Virgil again has Numanus say to the Trojans that they are not men, but women, pointing primarily to their habits.

"You, with your needlework saffron and gleaming purpled apparel,
You take delight in inertia, indulging yourselves in your dances.
Tunics for you come with sleeves, and your bonnets have nice little ribbons.
Phrygian women, not Phrygian men…"[83]

## 11. How a Humble Man Should Be Painted, and One Who Is Shameful, either by Nature or Chance, and a Woman Again

Shame resides principally in the eyes, as the philosopher [Aristotle] describes in his *Rhetoric*, and for this reason the painter has to focus his attention here, making them not too bright, but at the same time showing a certain glee;[84] they should be black and shown as neither too open nor closed, as half-lidded as he does not have to move or close his eyelids. He must be slow in every movement and speech. These things cannot be easily communicated through colors; nevertheless, the painter who knows them could relay his figure with a certain vivacity since he has the strength to portray what he wants. But now we turn to how poets

---

82 Recounting the tale of 'Salamacis and Hermaphroditus,' Ovid warns of being overcome by avariciousness as in her raptured state Salamacis "entwined him, like a snake" and "both bodies merged." Ovid, *Metamorphoses*, transl. Melville, 4: 318–320; 83–84.
83 Virgil, *Aeneid*, transl. Ahl, 9:613–617.
84 "The eyes are the abode of shame. That is why they feel more ashamed before those who are likely to be always with them or who keep watch upon them, because in both cases they are under the eyes of others." Aristotle, *Rhetoric*, transl. Freese, 2: 6:1384a.13–19.

paint this passion in men and women, which is typical and useful for the preservation of their creation. This is how Ariosto spoke of Angelica:

> On hearing him speak she perforce became like white ivory sprinkled with carmine, seeing those parts of her exposed to view which, for all their beauty, modesty would conceal.
> She would have covered her face with her hands were they not tied to the hard rock. [85]

The same poet describes men taken by this passion in this manner:

> ...they were so stung with unwonted shame that their faces all blazed like fire. None dared look at another; they kept their eyes down, silent, and crestfallen. [86]

And elsewhere says this of Zerbin:

> At this, Zerbin felt so humiliated that his cheeks burned red-and it would have been small wonder had every piece of armour he wore blushed scarlet too. [87]

Ovid, likewise, describes the flushed face of Arachne shamed in this manner:

> ...Yet she
> blushed all the same; a sudden colour tinged
> her cheeks against her will, then disappeared...[88]

And elsewhere:

> It marked red the face of the boy.[89]

Tasso said this about Armida, illustrating her shame and scorn:

> Or else, her eyes in modesty kept low,
> she decks herself with chastity's pale scorn,
> and alters with a hint of frost or snow

---

85   The reaction of Angelica follows a description that compares her to a statue fashioned by a sculptor. Ariosto, "Canto 10," *Orlando Furioso*, transl. Waldman, 98–99;104.
86   Ariosto, "Canto 20," 99; 241.
87   Ibid., 130; 244.
88   Ovid, *Metamorphoses*, transl. Freese, 6: 27–58; 122.
89   Ibid.

> the roses that her lovely face adorn.
> Even as at first birth the new dawn will glow
> in the coolest hours of the earliest morn,
> so disdain's blush in her fresh blush of shame
> confounds itself and mingles with shame.[90]

Seneca also explains in the same fashion this passion in the first of his Letters. He describes that it is as with comedy-actors, who imitate suffering, fear and dread, will represent melancholy by mimicking the sign of shame. Therefore, they lower their heads and their voices, looking to the ground, but they cannot control the flush of their faces, since it is not possible to have it when we want or drive it away when it comes.[91]

This is enough concerning shame.

## 12. The Figure of an Insolent and Presumptuous Man

The insolent and presumptuous man is the opposite of the shameful, who lowers his eyes as he goes while hanging his head low. Instead, he walks with his head held high, and upon careful inspection appears to be walking on his tiptoes; they seem to walk about like preening cocks. As such, diligent painters should focus on the following: the eyes should be prominent and bright, and they should appear to be in constant motion; the eyebrows are straight and thick; the nose is big, concerning the look they must be made lascivious; the eyelids must be big, and full of blood; the eye that appears to focus on the person or people to whom he speaks must be made so that it looks unmovable; the shoulders somewhat protruding, but not in the manner look alike to those who walked with crutches, as all of the form must be sufficiently bent towards the ground, although appearing as though raising their heads proudly; the face must be circular, and the chest lifted up; and the color of all the body must be red, which tends to the color of blood.

---

90   Tasso, *The Liberation of Jerusalem*, transl. Wickert, 4: 94.
91   Seneca, "On the Blush of Modesty," *Letters from a Stoic*, transl. Campbell, 11: 7.

## 13. The Figure of a Cheerful Man

The figure principally consists of the appearance of the forehead and eyes, agreed upon by all ancient writers, who, in their writings, demonstrate this passion through its opposite when the brow cringes, showing pain and severity. Plautus, for instance, said that his head should stick out a little when speaking.[92] And Horace speaks to Maecenas, inviting him for dinner in such a fashion:

> Often a change is pleasant to the rich,
> and a simple meal beneath the poor man's humble roof,
> without tapestries and purple, has smoothed
> the wrinkles on the care-worn brow.[93]

Additionally, Ariosto describes that sudden joy makes the face become suddenly pale in these four verses:

> So it was that the damsel looked her beloved in the face and turned pale with sudden joy; then, as a flower drenched from heavy rain revives when the sun comes out, she revived.[94]

The same are described again in the face in the following undersigned effects:

> So strange a sight smoothed Jocondo's brow and cleared his eyes. He became more jocund, as his name implied, and his glumness turned to gaiety. He became happy again, filled out, took on colour, looked once more like a cherub from paradise — a transformation which astonished his brother and the king and the entire household.[95]

## 14. The Figure of a Melancholic and Grieved Man

The grieved man, or one who is melancholic by nature, should be painted in an opposite fashion as the cheerful passion just described. Therefore, the forehead must be wrinkled like a newly plowed field

---

92  Plautus, *Pseudolus*, transl. David Christenson (Indianapolis: Hackett Publishing Company, Inc., 2013), 174.
93  Horace, *Odes and Epodes*, transl. C. E. Bennett (Cambridge, MA: Harvard University Press, 1968), 3: 28; 273.
94  Ariosto, "Canto 23," *Orlando Furioso*, transl. Waldman, 67; 274.
95  Ariosto, "Canto 28," *Orlando Furioso*, transl. Waldman, 39; 343–344.

with relaxed eyebrows that appear to quiver, but with fixed and solid eyelids. In all aspects he should appear troubled, having discomfort in everything. The Ariosto divinely paints a man grieved in the person of Jocondo in this manner:

> His brother assumed that he was dejected at having left his wife all alone- while on the contrary he was fretting and fuming that he had left her all too well cared for. With knitted brow and pouting lips the poor man gazed down at the ground. His brother tried every way to console him but to little effect, not realizing the matter.
>
> He kept applying the wrong salve to the wound, increasing the pain where he should have removed it, widening the gash where he should have closed it- all this by talking to him of his wife. Jocondo had no rest day or night; sleep and appetite shunned him past recalling, and his face, once so handsome, changed beyond recognition.
>
> His eyes seemed to have sunk into his head, his nose seemed bigger on his gaunt face; so little remained of his good looks that there was no further point in matching him with others.[96]

Elsewhere in the same source, Rinaldo is described as thinking in this manner:

> As Rinaldo thus brooded, head bowed, he was closely observed by one of the boatmen who sat facing him.[97]

Moreover, common are those who by nature are melancholic, such as those who are grieving due to some misfortune, going about with head bowed, described in the same way by Ariosto in this case:

> But on approaching, he recognized among the prisoners the King of the Nasamons, Baliverzo, Agricalt, Farurant, Manilard, Clarindo, and Rimedon, all weeping with bowed heads.[98]

And elsewhere he describes a pensive man in this manner:

> The knight sat down on the bank of the stream and rested his cheek on his arm; so deeply did he lapse into thought that he might have been turned to unfeeling stone.[99]

---

96  Ibid., 25–27; 342.
97  Arioso, "Canto 43," *Orlando Furioso*, transl. Waldman, 67; 516.
98  Arioso, "Canto 40," *Orlando Furioso*, transl. Waldman, 73; 484.
99  Arioso, "Canto 1," 39; 5.

## 15. The Figure of a Cruel and Inhumane Man

It is quite clear that beastly spirits have been found in human form, living almost as a man, not finding every day this inhumanity. But the painter should know how he should portray these strong, human beasts, naming them as such in front of other men, and creating a figure that is the most truthful as possible. This must be visible in the face, which appears to threaten everyone, pale in color with dry eyes, a wrinkled face, black hair that is stiff and long, and having little facial hair. The appearance must be in accord with the proverb by which everyone knows him: little hair, and light in color, no worse than anyone under the heavens. The hands of the man must be made as if pummeling something or himself; if appropriate, he should be represented barefoot and quite wrinkled. In this way, Suetonius describes the Emperor Caligula, a wild beast in human form:

> He was tall, of a pale complexion, ill-shaped, his neck and legs very slender, his eyes and temples hollow, his brows broad and knit, his hair thin, and the crown of the head bald. The other parts of his body were much covered with hair.[100]

In the face, he was all frightful by nature and experience.[101] In the second satire of Martial, he says of those who are very hairy:

> As it is, your shanks are shaggy with hair and your chest is with bristles: but it is your mind, Pannychus, that is depilated.[102]

## 16. The Figure of a Flatterer

The flatterer is the ape of his friend. Therefore, because the ape only imitates human actions that are ridiculous, so too do flatterers copy only those parts of their friends that are not essential for friendship. It is commonly known that the courts are crowded with these sorts of men as they aim only to satisfy their limitless desires, which they

---

[100] C. Suetonius Tranquillus, *The Lives of the Twelve Caesars*, transl. Alexander Thomson ([n.p.]: Simon and Brown, 2013), 50: 285.
[101] Suetonius relates that he purposefully cultivated such an figure: "His countenance, which was naturally hideous and frightful, he purposely rendered more so, forming it before a mirror into the most horrible contortions." Ibid.
[102] Martial, *Epigrams*, transl. Nisbet, 2: 36; 131.

cannot do without taking money from the wealthy by pretending to love them. In wanting to make one of these ravens, so called by the Greeks, the painter must give them large and fat jowls; the corners of the eyes near the jaws must be crinkled and wrinkled. The whole person must be polished and appear as though moving with grace and almost with the timing of the people who dance the pavane, in which movement should not be affected by gravity, which would be appropriate for the moderate man.[103] This will be accomplished by making the figure appear as though he is an early riser with a face like one who has just awoken.

## 17. The Figure of a Desperate Woman

In the figures painted by Virgil of Queen Dido and Amata, wife of King Latinus, and in the figure of Olympia, narrated by Ariosto, we are going to describe how the painter should depict the desperation of a woman. [Virgil writes:]

> Dido, fearful yet crazed at the ghastly extent of her planning,
> Frantically glances about her with bloodshot gaze, and impending
> Death now discolours her quivering cheeks with its pallor and blotches.[104]

And [Virgil] speaks of Amata in this manner:

> And the viperous venom of fury
> Now seeps deep in her entrails, courses the whole of her being.
> All fulfillment denied, driven wild by the monsters within her,
> She's now a force of fury herself unleashed through the city's Vastness...[105]

---

103 This majestic processional dance was popular among the aristocracy, commonly opening ceremonial balls and was used as a display of elegant dress.
104 Virgil, *Aeneid*, transl. Ahl, 4:890.
105 The Fury Allecto sends a serpent to drive Amata, wife of King Latinus, mad. Virgil, *Aeneid*, transl. Ahl, 7: 375–380.

And what follows from this madness [sent by Allecto]? Now there is what Ariosto says about Olympia:

> No longer did she snuggle warmly in her bereaved bed; she leapt up and was outside in a twinkling, and ran down to the sea, tearing her cheeks, full of forebodings, indeed past all doubt. She tore her hair and beat her breasts and strained her eyes, the moon still being up, to see whether anything could be made out beyond the shore- but she could see nothing, only the shore. She called "Bireno," and at his name the sympathetic caves echoed "Bireno."[106]

Tasso wrote this about Armida in the same way:

> ...with hair blown loose, eyes blazing, face aflame.[107]

## 18. The Figure of a Man Full of Astonishment

It is certainly impossible for a man not entirely wise to hide in his face the passions of his soul. Should more of the same wisdom shine in the face of the one who possesses it, his face will slowly change. Ariosto describes Leo in this manner:

> ...Leo was so aghast that he was struck motionless as a statue: dumb, rooted, unblinking, he looked less like a man than like a statue donated to a shrine by a votary.[108]

Elsewhere he again describes the change seen in the face of a man when astonished in this manner:

> "Well, I shall tell you — see if you don't compress your lips and arch your brows in disbelief!"[109]

Such a passion was described by Tasso in this manner:

> The knight, dumbfounded, lifts his eyebrows and
> wrinkles his forehead, and with transfixed eyes
> sees cloud and chariot hurtling overland
> so rapidly, it seems to him he flies.[110]

---

106 Ariosto, "Canto 10," 20–21; 95.
107 Tasso, *The Liberation of Jerusalem*, transl. Wickert, 16: 67.
108 Ariosto, "Canto 46," *Orlando Furioso*, transl. Waldman, 38; 561.
109 Ariosto, "Canto 10," 4; 93.
110 Tasso, *The Liberation of Jerusalem*, transl. Wickert, 10:17.

## 19. The Figure of Beastly or Savage Men

By beastly men, I intend to describe not those who allow themselves to be overcome by rage or pleasure or other such passion, but rather those who care not for their body, civil life or dress. These are similar to wild beasts and are depicted in this manner by Ariosto:

> They have come out from their forests and lairs, and they number sixteenth thousand, or nearly. They are as hairy as beasts- their faces, chests, flanks, and backs, their arms and legs are covered in hair.[111]

Virgil confirms the same when describing Cacus, that he was not only beastly, but the very idea of a thief. Sannazaro explains that his name means thief,[112] and so Virgil describes him:

> People stare at his terrible eyes, at this half-beast's
> Facial expressions and thick-bristled chest, at this jaws' now extinguished
> Flames.[113]

## 20. The Figure of a Fraud

Fraud is continuously found among men, and they practice it gladly; our plazas, circles, and houses are always rife with it. Should the painter wish to imitate the truth, it is necessary that he know fraud again, and fraudulent men, and he should become accustomed to painting it. Here we find scholars of painting describing the idea of fraud, as in the case of the divine Ariosto:

> Fraud was pleasant-looking, soberly dressed; her eyes were meek, her bearing dignified, and she was so benign and simple in her speech she might have been the angel of the Annunciation. For the rest, she was ugly and mis-shapen, though she contrived to conceal her deformities

---

111 Ariosto, "Canto 10," 89; 103.
112 In his description, the Italian poet Jacopo Sannazaro cites Ovid: "Cacco, qui è detto per antonomasia e per disprezzo Ovidio nel Lib. i. de' Fasti, ove narra come questo mostro fu ucciso da Ercole, così lo descrive: Cacus Aventinae timor, atque infamia silvae, Non leve finitimis, hospitibusque malum. Dira viro facies; vires prò corpore; corpus Grande: pater monstri Mu.la.ber hujus erat." Jacopo Sannazaro, *Arcadia* (Roma: Carocci editore, 2013), 129.
113 Hercules, who pulls him into the light from his cave to be seen in all his beastly form, dispatches the cattle thief. Virgil, *Aeneid*, transl. Ahl, 8: 265–267.

beneath a long and ample robe- which always concealed, in addition, a poisoned dagger.[114]

With Brunello, again, he painted, I think, a fraudulent man in this manner:

> He is of medium build; his hair is black and curly; his skin is dark, but his face is pale and his beard most shaggy, as also his eyebrows. His eyes protrude and have a shifty look; his nose is flattened. To complete his picture, his dress is like that of a messenger, short and close-fitting.[115]

If judiciously treated, the painter can make use of this idea in men and women, diligently regarding the nature of the other figures, with what he wants to put together, because the fraudulent makes himself accommodating with many colors, as well with his habit and words. For this reason, Ariosto paints the fraud with long clothes, in general, but among soldiers he paints them with short clothes, being the proper habit of soldiers.

## 21. The Figure of a Deceitful Man, and of a Mean, Miserable, and Cowardly Man

The sum of explaining with colors a deceitful man primarily resides in the eyes, which ought to be such that they appear languid and weak. The whole figure must, nevertheless, be appropriately proportioned and should appear as though constantly moving. The miser, moreover, must be made smaller in all of his parts just as he is in his soul, with a small face, and small in all of the other parts. In this, he must mainly differ from all of the others, as he has little hands. The eyes must be equally small, darting and shining, and those parts should be disproportionate because of the smallness; its color should be dull and dark, with a little bit of vermillion, but he must have long hair, that it looks as though he put effort into brushing it; the beard should be grown out and very thick around the lips; the shoulders should be rather curved, and the whole face like the one of a man who usually drinks a lot. The whole figure must be made to look as though he pairs many words, speaking quickly, and should be very skinny.

---

114 Ariosto, "Canto 14," *Orlando Furioso*, transl. Waldman, 87; 147.
115 Ariosto, "Canto 3," *Orlando Furioso*, transl. Waldman, 72; 29.

## 22. The Figure of a Wicked Man, Who, in Speaking, Says Impertinent Things

The head of a wicked man, who speaks impertinently, must be rigid and oblique, and the color of his flesh should lean towards green, and look like a man who has just awoken from sleep, or rather a man who stands up from the table full of food. This figure must have very large ears with flat hair and a thin and languid neck, weak forehead, and hard and sour eyes that appear dark, small, dry and sunken. When moving, he appears unmovable and straight with cheeks and chin that are narrow and long, almost as though the mouth is open and divided into two parts. The face should be made rather long, and his stature bent with a large belly and legs. The articles of the hands and feet must be rather long and open.

## 23. The Figure of an Insane Man Who Is, at the Same Time, Wicked

In wishing to represent an insane man, who is at the same time said to be wicked, the painter must portray him with black hair on a small, narrow head, as did our Dürer.[116] The ears should be disproportionate in size and almost detached; the neck must be in all aspects circular; the eyes must be dry, dark and small, sunken in the head; and proportionate with the head, the cheeks are long and thin with a protruding mouth that appears to speak incessantly. The whole of the body should appear somewhat curved with a large stomach and legs, and, when possible, the colors should be made to appear hard with flesh greenish in complexion. The face below his eyes should be made to appear puffy, as though just awoken in the manner in which Ariosto in his Orlando depicts an image in these verses of the insane man:

> His eyes were almost hidden in his face, which was lean and wizened; his hair was a matted, bristling mass, his bushy beard looked appalling and hideous.[117]

Sallust also describes Catiline in this manner, since he was nagged by his own conscience having poisoned his future stepson; his soul was stained

---
116 Gallucci, *Della simmetria*, 3: 80–85.
117 Ariosto, "Canto 29," *Orlando Furioso*, transl. Waldman, 60; 358.

with sins in the eyes of the gods, and hateful to men. He could not find respite in the day or night. So afflicted was his conscience and troubled was his mind that his color was bloodless, his eyes dark. He would come and go early and late with the imprint of insanity on his face.

## 24. The Figure of Big Eater, and of One of Great Memory

If the painter wishes to show, through his lines and colors, one who eats a lot, he should make the mouth large, especially the part that receives food. In doing so, that part of the body from the navel to the chest will also be made larger, along with the area from the chest to the neck, because the area that receives food needs to be able to accommodate a great quantity.[118]

If one wants to portray a man that has a great memory, ensure that his face is wide at the bottom and tapers towards the top of his head, which are, nevertheless, proportionate to each other, in the way that Dürer teaches in the Third Book. The body will still need to be fleshy and beautiful, because his likeness is still of a man who sleeps little.

## 25. The Figure of a Loquacious Man

The talkative man must have a larger upper body in order to make what is taught by Dürer in the Third Book. He must be good looking with a hairy stomach. In addition to this, he must have some lines along the bridge of the nose between the eyebrows that stretch down towards the nose.

## 26. The Figure of a Drowsy Man

The drowsy man must be painted in this manner: make the upper body parts larger than the lower, but the most important aspect of this task involves the eyes. Whenever there are men who are this way by nature,

---

[118] "Those who are longer from the navel to the chest than from the chest to the neck have good appetites." Pseudo-Aristotle, *Physiognomica*, 3: 808b.4–5; Aristotle, *Minor Works*, transl. Hett, 104–105.

I would want their figure to be as such. Nevertheless, if one makes the eyes sleepy then all of the other figures would also look drowsy, and one will deprive them of their own vigor. This figure must also have a hairy stomach.

## 27. The Figure of a Libidinous Man

If one wants to portray the figure of a prurient man, which is often necessary for a painter, one will need to include many white hairs around the lips with thick, straight black hair receding at the forehead. The eyes are imploring, though watery and fat; the legs are thin, nervous and hairy, but the belly is fat.[119] His beard is withdrawn from the nose and chin, and the veins in his arms protrude in a noticeable fashion; mainly on the thighs, there are thick, horrible hairs, [and he has] curved feet like that of a bear. In general, the upper body is larger than the lower, such that the skinny legs convey that he is a lustful man, as Suetonius wishes to describe Nero.[120]

## 28. The Figure of an Envious Man

Called upon to know how to unfold all things that fall under his sight, by choice and by accident, the painter should not be ignorant of the figure of an envious man, the plague of which, however common, still has something peculiar to itself. Therefore, his figure should see the left side of the body larger than the right; the eyebrows should continue down to the cheeks, his color livid, and thinness that is manifested in the face, as Virgil sang in his epigram on envy.[121]

---

119 "He has pale skin and is covered with straight, thick, black hair; his temples are also covered with black, straight hair. He has a bright and appetive eye." Pseudo-Aristotle, *Physiognomica*, 3: 808b.5–10; Aristotle, *Minor Works*, transl. Hett, 104–105.

120 "In stature he was a little below the common height; his skin was foul and spotted; his hair inclined to yellow; his features were agreeable, rather than handsome; his eyes grey and dull, his neck was thick, his belly prominent, his legs very slender, his constitution sound..." Suetonius, *The Lives of the Twelve Caesars*, transl. Thomson, 51: 379.

121 "Dire Envy will fear the Furies and the grave stream of Cocytus and the twisted serpents of Ixion and the huge wheel and the rock that cannot be overcome." Virgil, *Georgics*, transl. Lembke, 3: 37–39; Virgil, *Aeneid*, transl. Ahl, 1: 294–296.

## 29. The Figure of an Ugly Man and Woman

We had described at the beginning[122] that which makes a woman and a man beautiful; now, at the end, we are going to describe that which makes them ugly, though this can be understood from their contraries. There is only one verse in his satires where Horace describes an ugly woman in a contrary fashion to what we have mentioned above:

> This girl has no buttocks, a long nose,
> a short body and big feet.[123]

The same thing is confirmed by Catullus, again in this sense:

> Hi there, girl with a nose by no means tiny,
> non-dark eyes and two most undainty ankles,
> not-long fingers and undry lips...[124]

Ariosto describes again the ugliness of Alcina in this manner:

> ...he was astonished to find that in place of the beauty he had just parted from, he was confronted with a woman so hideous that her equal for sheer ugliness and decrepitude could be found nowhere on earth.
> She was whey-faced, wrinkled, and hollow-cheeked; her hair was white and sparse; she was not four feet high; the last tooth had dropped out of her jaw...[125]

Homer describes an ugly man in this manner:

> Thersites, a blabbing soldier,
> who had an impudent way with officers,
> thinking himself amusing to the troops —
> the most obnoxious rogue who went to Troy.
> Bowlegged, with one limping leg, and shoulders
> rounded above his chest, he had a skull
> quite conical, and mangy fuzz like mold.[126]

---

122 See "Chapter 3: On the Beauty of Human Bodies, Especially Women."
123 The grotesque description is based on alternates of proportion of over-small and over-large features. Horace, *Satires and Epistles*, transl. Smith Palmer Bovie (Chicago: University of Chicago Press, 2002), 1: 2:93.
124 Catullus, *The Poems of Catullus*, transl. Peter Green (Berkeley, CA: Univeristy of California Press, 2005), 43: 1–4; 91.
125 Ariosto, "Canto 7," 72–73; 68–69.
126 Homer, *Iliad*, transl. Powell, 2: 247.

I speak of the Phrygian in the same fashion. Although he possessed a very excellent soul, he was the most deformed of his time, as Maximus Planudes wrote in his life. Therefore, he had a small head with pressed nostrils, a short neck, and lips that protruded greatly. He was black, which is how he got his name Aesop, meaning the same in Ethiopian.[127] He had a large stomach and was bent with legs folded outward. Such was his ugliness that it exceeded the Homeric Thersites.[128] From this, painters will easily be able to make an ugly man and woman, for we discussed the ugliness of women and men. This is not the case for those painters who make their paintings ugly because they cannot make them beautiful; not knowing, they would make them in this manner and it would be said that they are beautiful paintings. Otherwise, the painter would force himself to represent a handsome man or a beautiful woman.

## 30. On the Different Feet of Men, and Those Which Are Suitable

It seemed to me that I should now treat all of the parts separately in imitation of the master of color, so that painters could select material of all members from this great forest of diversity to make their works overall beautiful, and from expert praise. First we will discuss the principle of feet, which will be made big, but not disproportionately so, and well made, as our Dürer teaches; they should be muscular with veins seen through the skin, apparent that they will be very appropriate to a Hercules, a Milo of Croton, a Hector, an Orlando, and, in general, a brave and bold man. These feet are to be used in the case of man, but not woman, because her feet should be made small, slender, fleshy, and tender, without defined muscles; when viewed [these feet appear] unshaped rather than strong, suitable instead to those men that we wish to dress in costumes similar to women; those are effeminate, soft, with a weak and helpless body. Should the painter wish to represent a

---

127 The thirteenth-century Byzantine scholar had been the first to write a biography of Aesop based on *The Aesop Romance* suggesting that he was Ethiopian based on his name. Maximus Planudes, *Aesopi Phrygis Fabulae* (Lyon: Jean de Tournes, 1570), 9; Frank M. Snowden, Jr., *Blacks in Antiquity: Ethiopians in the Greco-Roman Experience* (Cambridge, MA: Belknap Press, 1971), 264.

128 The only man in Homer's *Iliad* to be described as ugly. He opposes the war and is promptly beaten and scapegoated.

fair nature with great weakness, he ought to make the feet short and wide; if one makes the feet longer than that, every proportion will be violated, and one will know that a man full of fraud, deceit and betrayal is represented. This follows those figures where we wish to represent a man whose soul is fragmented into different parts. On the other hand, should one wish to create the figure of a wicked man, these need to be even smaller than those; said appropriate measurements will represent a man who is evil of mind. Wishing to represent an evil man, one will still make the feet curved above and concave below; the same [man] again should be made with the soles of his feet very large and even, with ankles very close to the ground, from which one can see that all ends are considerable, and [represent] the golden mean, as Horace sang.[129] If then one will make the nails and the feet curved, like those of birds of prey, the ferocious man, who is brash without shame will be portrayed, which of all these characteristics are believed appropriate. When one wishes to portray a shy and timid man, one should make the toes webbed, almost joined together, which is found in quails, therefore, they are very shy animals.[130] With this, enough has been said about feet if we also add what Aulus Gellius says about the way to determine the size of Hercules' [feet] from the size of a stadium in Pisa, where running at the Jupiter Olympics was held, which was measured at six hundred feet by Hercules. And since the other stadium in Greece, likewise, was six hundred feet, and because when speaking about Hercules we know he was larger than the other men, and the stadium measured by his foot would then also be larger than that measured by the feet of other men.[131]

## 31. On the Diversity of Heels or Ankles Compared to the Figure that [the Painter] Wishes to Represent

Wanting to make a strong man, we must give him strong ankles and make those parts surrounding them sinewy and muscular. Yet if on the contrary one should wish to form a figure of a weak man, who is

---

[129] Horace, *Odes and Epodes*, transl. Bennett, 2: 10.
[130] Pseudo-Aristotle, *Physiognomica*, 6: 810a.20–25; Aristotle, *Minor Works*, transl. Hett, 114–15.
[131] From this comes the proverb *Ex pede Herculem* — "you may know Hercules by his foot." Aulus Gellius, *The Attic Nights*, transl. John Carew Rolfe (Cambridge, MA: Harvard University Press, 2015), 1: 1.

effeminate and shy with very little spirit, these parts should be made very soft, fleshy and without any appearance of veins or muscles. If the ankles are made very thin, this will represent a timid and intemperate man. Some want the ankles to be thin, with fleshy feet and sharp heels, stubby fingers and thick legs; these are mostly the members of a man that goes mad and raves.

## 32. On the Diversity of Legs with Respect to the Different Figures They Want to Make

When one wants to form a robust, strong and brave man, the legs need to be sinewy, muscular, and strong, and those legs are universally appropriate for men. The legs of women are effeminate, tender, timid, and of little spirit, smooth with no evidence of veins or muscles. Should one portray them muscled and sinewy yet thin, one forms the legs of figures that convey timid and luxurious men. Therefore, these are the legs of the birds, that all of these are of this nature. If it will be necessary to make the figure of an odious, immoderate and abominable man, one will have to make his legs much larger, appearing as though they are about to crack. These [are the legs] of insolent men, who do not respect anyone, nor do they feel ashamed of anything. Therefore, those who are modest and temperate are well-proportioned in all the parts of their body, and every disproportionate element is an evident sign of a part of a soul which is equally disproportionate.

## 33. On the Diversity of Knees Appropriate to Different Figures

The knees of the arrogant man must be equally made proportionately flabby and soft, meaning big and fat, and full of flesh over the necessary measures, which will still show that they are not accustomed to any hard strain, and are full of vanity. Therefore, most of the time this occurs with men who are not good with facts and who therefore try to assert themselves instead using words, in which there are many lies. On the other hand, wanting to make the figure of a strong, bold, fearless and modest man, his knees must be proportionate and skinny, and those are again discreet and tough.

## 34. Which Thighs and Buttocks are Appropriate for Which Figures

The figure of a man of valor with much spirit and courage [should be given] thighs that are full of bones, veins and muscles, which is proper to men, just as the contrary is appropriate for women where [the thighs] are lascivious and full of feminine effects, having them full of flesh without the appearance of bones, though they may be bony, or sinew, or muscle; likewise, buttocks tight around bones that stick out must be made for the strong, brawny, and brave, like in the opposite way they must be made fat and full for timid, lascivious and effeminate men. Nevertheless, I advise that in wanting to make the buttocks of a strong man, do not make them too thin, and make them similar to those of apes, because those convey men of bad habits, those who are evil, scoundrels and wicked men, the worst of all.

## 35. Which Limbs and Stomachs Belong to Which Figures

To portray the strong man, his limbs must be made well and large, but not disproportionately so, only large and sinewy, which one must do with hunters, where we find that the lions, dogs, and cats that are also delighted by hunting are like this. The opposite [limbs] should be used in creating those of women, and also of men who wear similar costumes to women, being small, full and soft. The stomach then, which is proper to the men who are brave, strong, magnanimous, and ingenious is the one which is large and partly full in the manner that in all parts it is pronounced or inflated; cowards, pushovers and boors of little intelligence should have stomachs that are very short and shallow. To an immoderate man who drinks and eats a lot, his belly has to be made big, full, marked, and soft, which should be equally applied to lechers. If to the contrary one forms a figure with the belly that looks hard and irregular with a great deal of flesh all compacted, this will illustrate overt vileness and an insatiable appetite. If one should want to make the figure of a brave, gentle, smart, or talkative man, then the stomach must be made hairy.

## 36. Which Back and Ribs Suit Which Figures

Men should be made with broad, large and robust backs, especially the courageous who have much spirit and courage. Otherwise, the backs of women, effeminate men and the weak and timid, who possess no or little courage, should be made small, narrow and feeble. Again, the ribs of those with much spirit should be painted according to the ornament of fortitude, large and protruding; otherwise, those of women and effeminate men should be made small, almost completely hidden, but I should warn you, however, that if, together with these big things, there is an excessive swelling made, the figure represents a mumbling man, who imprudently says whatever is in his soul with his mouth, and he does not do anything more unwillingly than be silent, which is understood from the frogs that are the same in body and voice. These parts also accompany greedy men and gluttons, the rough and senseless, and those who possess very little judgment. In sum, they are like children in action and in bodily appearance.

## 37. Different Measures of the Stomach, Chest, and Belly that Suit Different Figures

In wanting to create the figure which suits a most gluttonous man, who eats much because he is stupid and senseless, and lacking any judgment, the part that goes from the navel to below the chest can be made much larger than from there to the throat. Because this is the area that contains the organs that receive food, and because he eats a lot, the area needs to be large. Moreover, since a generous amount of food fattens, and fat hinders cleverness, these men are rough and senseless, as they do not set aside room for judgment. Yet if, on the contrary, one wants to make those same parts to represent a wise and prudent man, the chest should be larger than the area between the stomach and the chest, because prudent men are content with food that is enough provided by nature. Should, on the other hand, one make that space from the stomach bigger than the space from the chest, a man that is always sick and short-lived will be formed.

## 38. On Some Correspondences that Some Members Have between Them

It is not without benefit to tell students of this noble art that some relationship exists between members not only with respect to size, but also to flesh. For experience teaches us this truth, that if we meet a man who is fat in the face and corpulent, he will also have a stomach that is fat and rotund; if his face is gaunt, so too will the stomach correspond to him; and if the painter should make a figure with short arms, the legs should also be made short. The same correspondence should also [be found in] the feet, hands, necks and legs, which should be noticed also in certain signs, such as the veins that are seen in some, both in the face and in the other parts of the body. Therefore, if the painter makes one of these veins at the top of the forehead, and if the figure is nude, he should make one similar in the penis; if in the eyebrows, another one [should be painted] in the chest; if in the eyelids, he should make another one under the stomach in the belly; and if he makes one in the nose, he should make another similar one in the genitals, or rather in the middle of the chest, or rather around the organs of generation, the signs that are on the cheeks are shown the same as the others in the genitals; if [veins are found in] the lips, he will also make [them in] the arm, between the shoulder and the elbow; [and, finally,] if in the hands, they should be in the penis, and in the genitals again. And in the throat, they should also be made in the straight band of the chest. Those things, although seemingly minute, lend gracefulness to the figures and make them appear natural, and make the painter immortal.

## 39. How the Chest and Shoulders Should Be Done in Several Different Figures

The big and broad chest, endowed conspicuously with muscle, must be used to create strong men of great daring, as we said above of the figure of the horse, or strong man of Virgil;[132] on the contrary then, the shy, weak and cowardly must be made small and narrow, and with no evidence of muscles or veins. The bestial and cruel, who are without humanity or

---

132  Virgil, *Aeneid*, transl. Ahl, 2:168; 4:10.

compassion, must be made with abundant flesh. For a lascivious man, who is of the habit of drinking much, his parts must be made equally full with the breasts very swollen and corpulent; the shoulders, moreover, must be made equally broad and muscular as with the strong and valorous, which are proper to men and women, as one reads in Plato. Effeminate and shy men, on the other hand, must be made small, with no muscles or veins.[133] For a fool, they must be made narrow; the senseless, full of flesh; a magnanimous, prudent, and lovely man, large and rather rounded; and the crazy, envious and immoral, curved so that the shoulders cover the parts in front. On the contrary then, the vain, lascivious, and [those] full of feminine desires, must be made not curved, but concave.

## 40. On the Shoulders and Chest Most Appropriate to Different Figures

The shoulders of the strong in spirit and body must be made vascular, muscular, or firm, while those appropriate to women, effeminate men and the weak, given their languid nature, have no apparent veins or muscles. These again are appropriate to the insane, vain, avaricious, and worthless, unlike their superiors, prudent and reasonable men, [who are] equally liberal and courteous. Lascivious men must be painted tall, thin and evil. Stupid men must be made separately, as they have a depression in the middle [of their chests]. If one paints a figure of that part of the chest with an equally sunken throat, a place for intelligence and the vivacity of the senses is shown. In this, therefore, is the large path through which the spirits go from the heart to the brain, for which one portrays the senses. Otherwise, the painter will portray a senseless man. If one depicts this part of the chest disconnected and near in a picture, the same should be accorded to all of the stupid fools and the ineffectual; the sum of this matter consists to form the fork or the key that is found in that part [of the chest]. Therefore, if one makes it too large, that figure will represent lasciviousness and habits of feminine rashness and foolishness.

---

133 Along with Philo of Alexandria, Plato described the chest as the location of the soul. The amount of fat around the chest was associated with temperament of an individual. Plato, *Timaeus*, transl. Benjamin Jowett (New York: Dover Publications, 1985), 70c-d.

## 41. On Arms and Hands Appropriate to Different Figures

As Dürer taught in the First and Second Books, arms made with due proportion are appropriate for a figure in which one wishes to show readiness in working, strength, goodness, and courage. On the other hand, making them shorter than this proportion (in the way that Dürer teaches in the Third Book) will produce a figure that represents envy, malevolence, and one who delights in harming others. If one paints them as gaunt and thin, then some tenderness of soul and body is shown. If instead, one wishes to show a rough and stupid [figure], make the arms thick and fleshy with hands, likewise, proportionate to his body and arms. Therefore, ingenious and valorous men must be made proportionate (as in the relationships Dürer taught) with tender and soft flesh, in contrast to a strong man. The dim-witted must be made rugged and larger than the appropriate proportion; then men, who are astute, absorbed, weak, and with little goodness, must be made shorter than the appropriate size. Those figures where one wants to represent a glutton, a garrulous man, or the figure of a miserly and rapacious thief must be made thin and distorted; they must be made short and narrow, which is appropriate to represent a Judas.

The insane must be made very short; lunatics and scoundrels are both short and large. If one makes both the hands and fingers very short, then with them one will represent perfectly a traitor, a deceitful thief, and a trickster. Yet if one makes these fingers quite short and also pudgy, one will achieve the appearance of vices, namely lust, pride, wrath, and envy.

Moreover, if one wants to form a vain and foolish man, one must make him small with thin fingers, which compliment his mind, always full of tantrums and unfounded hearsay. For a man who is crude, immoral and also vulgar, one must make the fingers crooked, uneven and contracted, which is also appropriate for the greedy.

Furthermore, it is noteworthy that Homer describes Juno, Nausicaä (daughter of King Alcinous), and the two bridesmaids as having white arms, which are beautiful.[134]

---

134 Hera (Juno) is referred to as "white-armed." Homer, *Iliad*, transl. Powell, 1: 59; Nausicaa "...Nausicaa of the white arms led them in their song." Homer, *Odyssey*, transl. E. V. Rieu (Harmondsworth: Penguin, 1966), 6: 57; 104.

## 42. Which Fingernails Are Appropriate to Different Figures

As everyone knows, there is no small difference between the fingernails of men, but even in this the good painter must use diligence. Therefore, the fingernails of the prudent who are of good intelligence, singular goodness, and great wisdom should be made thin, clear, long, vermilion, even, broad, soft, glossy, and shining. The nails of the arrogant, shameless and rapacious should be curved like birds of prey, [specifically] hook-shaped; and if painters make the same with long and narrow nails like animals have, they will show in those figures that there is no wit or prudence, nor any positive virtue of the body, being instead continuously tormented by beastly appetites. Finally, the fingernails of the vile, full of every wicked act, must be made truly ugly, as in the figure of a lustful man who must have circular nails; [likewise] if the painter will make the nails pale, black and without any splendor, he aspires to create a figure without any sign of a balanced spirit, little inclined to virtue.

## 43. On the Diversity of Necks Appropriate to Different Figures

Although the master painter should use diligence in explaining all of the parts of the body, nevertheless, he must be quite diligent around the head, especially in the face. Plutarch wrote of this already in his *Life of Alexander the Great*, noting that [the face] clearly signals the habits of the soul [*costumi dell'animo*].[135] In order to do this better, we will speak of each part separately. In figures where the painter wishes to represent strength and valor, one must make the neck moderately large; and to make a weak and shy [man], the neck should be appropriately thin, which is explained divinely by Juvenal in his third Satire in the same manner:

---

[135] "Therefore as portrait-painters are more exact in the lines and features of the face, in which the character is seen, than in the other parts of the body, so I must be allowed to give my more particular attention to the marks and indications of the souls of men, and while I endeavour by these to portray their lives, may be free to leave more weighty matters and great battles to be treated of by others." Plutarch, *Life of Alexander the Great*, transl. John Dryden (New York: Modern Library, 2004), 1.

> And aren't they the people most adept at flattery, praising
> The illiterate speech of a friend, praising his ugly face,
> Likening a weak, scrawny neck to that of brave Hercules.[136]

What is more, if the neck will be made large, long and burly, one will form the figure of a man that is similar to a bull: choleric, bold and boastful, ready and expedient in his actions. The beautiful proportion of the neck consists of a certain likeness to the neck of a lion: mid-length, nicely toned and vascular. This is appropriate for magnanimous men, and others who are naturally inclined to discipline and are of cheerful wit. But [necks that are] long and thin, such as those of deer, should be used to make figures where one wishes to show those who embody timidity, weakness and cowardice of spirit. Fitly then, the presumptuous, traitorous, fallacious, and mockers will have a very short and squat neck. These, moreover, hate the light and love the darkness for their activities, as thieves are always a danger to the simple ones, the lambs. Additionally, figures of coarse and insane men, who, like those who are unintelligent, have a neck that always seems to be stiff and straight.

Those who lack intellect and are lewd and offensive must have necks oriented as though they were astrologers, wishing to contemplate the stars. Again, with the insane who never stress about accumulating wealth, [the neck] must be oriented downward so as to hide all before it. The prudent, adorned with beautiful costumes and manners appropriate to gentlemen, must have the neck bent towards the right side, since a leftward orientation conveys lustfulness, such as with Sardanapalus, according to men of good advice.[137] If the painter wishes to form a figure that appears to have a neck which seems to be oriented to one side and then another, he would make an unstable and frivolous man. An evil and wicked man should have a limp and languid neck that seems deflated and without bones. On the contrary, both the rude and those who are ignorant of letters should be shown with stiff and short [necks], the backs of which being rough, which will make the part facing out represent fickleness, talkativeness and presumption, and

---

136 Juvenal, *Satires*, ed. Richard George (St. Albans: Baikal, 2012), 3: 58–125.
137 According to the Greek writer Ctesias of Cnidus, Sardanapalus was the last king of Assyria. Later Diodorus compiled the lost works of Ctesias. Dressing in women's clothes and wearing make-up, Sardanapalus was said to have exceeded all previous kings in sloth and luxury, ending his life in a self-destructive orgy.

laziness in his actions. Those then who will be made in this manner, but tall and eminent in his own way, will again be appropriate to show pensive, miserable and disdainful men.

## 44. Diverse Cheeks Appropriate to Different Figures

The painter must use diligence to confirm that all of the parts of the body accurately represent the figure of man, which was formed first in the soul. Moreover, more diligence must be paid when forming the face and head, as in some manner those parts contain all of man. Those parts are where observers first direct their eyes and form their first opinion of the author of that [figure] and have a greater power for those who seek to represent the affections of the soul that are held locked within. I must warn, therefore, that cheeks, which are longer than due proportion demands, should only be used to make those figures that represent prurient vanity, and whose many words are rife with lies. The cruel, weak, fraudulent, and cowardly should be made smaller on the right and rounded. Those of a lazy man, who adores Bacchus as his god, should be painted full and pudgy. On the contrary, those of a vicious man, who relishes when he injures and ridicules, should be made thin and skinny. A jealous man, who always frets for his soul due to the success of others, should have cheeks and a jaw that are proportionally large and protruding, so that others can see them.

## 45*. Diversity of Lips and Mouths Appropriate to Different Figures[138]

We will speak here of great certainty and grace that is sighted in beautiful lips, whence it is that in thousands of ways they are celebrated by the poets. Those of magnanimous and strong men should be made similar to the lips of a lion, thin and soft, especially in the corners of the mouth, and the upper one much bigger than the lower one; in other words, it should rather stick out in the way that the mouth

---

138   The numbering of the chapters as printed in the original edition contains a misprint. Chapter 45 is used twice in both *Diversita' di labbri, & bocca conveniente a diverse figure* and *Modo di formare il mento a diverse immagini*. The incorrect order has been retained to correspond to the original for reference.

has the right proportion, which was taught by our Dürer in his well-proportioned figures.¹³⁹ If those lips are made in a rather small mouth, they will well accommodate a woman and effeminate men. If one makes a painting in order to illustrate an unpleasant, annoying, perfidious, and presumptuous man, who is generally insolent, one must make the mouth and lips larger than the correct proportion should be. A lustful man must have lips that are hard and thin, and really protruding next to the canine teeth, and those parts also show the same with the poorly created chatter who willingly does outrage and who, when he talks, does so loudly and, finally, with the mouth and habits of a pig. For a rude man, and those of poor judgment, one must know that the lips are to be made full with the lower one sticking out more than the upper one; these are similar in mouth and related costumes.

A very large and open mouth [is appropriate for] the faces of the greedy and gluttonous, who are never sated, and have (as the sacred letters explain) their stomach as their god;¹⁴⁰ together they produce [a figure that is] unpleasant, cruel and has a large torso full of madness. Yet scoundrels, murderers and traitors must be made with small and protruding mouths that stick out. Likewise, the mouth that is made large with rounded lips that excessively juts out will be best adapted to those men who represent a pig in their physique. In those that truly have fickle habits, the mouth is then curved inward and full, like those who are angry, and is also applicable to those figures where one wants to represent evil, immodesty, envy, timidity, and deception. Lastly, a dry mouth befits a beautiful woman as Catullus wrote after the *Argonautica* [of Apollonius Rhodes], calling dry lips beautiful. In mocking the mistress of Formianus, he says that she is ugly since she does not have a dry mouth [i.e. drooling].¹⁴¹

---

139 "Those who have thin lips and slack parts at the joining of the lips, so that the upper lip overhangs the lower at the join, are magnanimous; witness the lion." Pseudo-Aristotle, *Physiognomica*, 6: 811a.18–20; Aristotle, *Minor Works*, transl. Hett, 120–21.

140 Philippians 3: 19: "Their destiny is destruction, their god is their stomach, and their glory is in their shame. Their mind is set on earthly things."

141 The denigration of a woman's beauty was earlier tied to the dryness of her mouth and lips. Should a figure have an overly wet mouth (i.e. drooling), they lack refinement. As the poet writes, "Hail, girl, with not over-much of a nose, with no pretty foot, nor black eyes, nor long fingers, nor dry mouth, nor particularly pleasing tongue, hail, spendthrift Formianus' mistress!" Catullus, "Poem 43: The Mistress of Formianus," *The Poems of Catullus*, transl. Green 63: 315; 43: 1–4;

## 45*. The Way to Form the Chin in Different Figures

The well-formed chin, along with a beautiful body of more than a little grace, draws the eyes of observers due to its diversity and elicits different feelings in their souls. And for this reason, painters need to be aware of which chin suits which figure. For the man who is well proportioned in body and soul, and because of this is good, loyal and brave, the chin should be made pointed; while women, as well as lustful and effeminate men, should be made long and round, as is appropriate when one wants to show vanity, glibness, imprudence, and other things unworthy of such men. The [chin] on the face of such men who are cruel, deceitful, wicked, and, in short, have many serpents in their souls, should be made short and squat as their chins are similar [i.e. to a serpent]. The square chin then suits those figures where one primarily wants to represent fortitude. Painters who wish to include a dimple found mainly on the chin should be especially diligent here. For if he makes one that is very large, he represents fraud, deceit and wickedness; if he makes it small, he will make the figure loving, graceful and full of merriment.

## 46. On the Diversity of Noses Appropriate to Different Figures

We cannot say with words what is understood by all, for there is no part of our body that most increases beauty or ugliness than the beautiful or misshapen nose, and for this [reason] Virgil calls a disfigured nose the dishonorable wound.[142] Hence, great diligence must be used in this to ensure that it is proportionate to figures, since one wants to make paintings significant for the diversity of their members. Therefore, the extremely broad nose that oxen have indicates slowness and laziness in that figure. The nose of a rude and stupid [man] must be made

---

91. Another poem by Catullus was also carefully crafted and meant to be read alongside the *Argonautica*. R. Clare, "Catullus 64 and the *Argonautica* of Apollonius Rhodius: Allusion and Exemplarity," *Proceedings of the Cambridge Philological Society*, 42 (1997), 60–88, https://doi.org/10.1017/s0068673500002042

142 Virgil relates that disfigurement was a common punishment for criminals: "Here he sees Priam's son, every part of whose body is mangled:/ This is Deiphobus, all of whose face is completely disfigured,/ Face, yes, and both of his hands: ears ripped from dehumanized/ temples,/ Nose lopped off as a common criminal's mark of dishonor." Virgil, *Aeneid*, transl. Ahl, 6.494–97.

bulging in the middle; if one makes it slim and thin on the top, then that figure relay great anger and resentment. For a magnanimous man, who is bold, brave and talks much (and is somewhat boastful) the nose must then be made like those of lions, rather hard and rounded everywhere, and very broad on the top. If one makes it round, but sharp at the end, one will represent lax morals in human form, which is to say a man who is slightly unstable, talkative, inconstant, and libidinous. A virile and prudent man shall be made proportionate to the face in the manner which Dürer has taught us, and, as such, to a foolish, effeminate and soft man, it must be made without any proportion.[143]

Furthermore, it is appropriate for virtuous men for the [nose] to be very large, while one can make, especially, vicious thieves, swindlers and fraudulent men smaller than the true proportion. For one who speaks little, it is appropriate to make [the nose] straight, appearing as though drawn with a line; for brash men, the nose must be curved where it rises between the eyes, and then in the rest straight. This [design] befits scoundrels and evil men, who are similar to ravens that eat each other's meat. If one paints a figure with an aquiline nose that is broad at the top and hooked towards the end, one will portray a man of great spirit, magnificent and noble. Suetonius writes of this in [the lives of] both Emperors Augustus and Galba, who were fierce and eager to possess other's empires and authority.[144] To a bold hedonist, who is like a rooster, must be given a nose similar to that animal, which is crushed in the middle, while the extreme parts are eminent and curved, especially in the upper part. If one forms it depressed at the top, as with goats and deer, this befits those men who are lustful and shy. Dishonesty and wickedness will be represented by the nose that is shaped large and flat at the top. If the nostrils are made flared, this will be a sign of much anger and scorn, and of a robust and luxurious body; on the other hand, if one

---

143 Gallucci, *Della simmetria*, 3: 80–85.
144 Suetonius describes Augustus: "His eye-brows met; his ears were small, and he had an aquiline nose." Later he writes of Galba: "In person he was of a good size, bald before, with blue eyes, and an aquiline nose..." Suetonius, *The Lives of the Twelve Caesars*, transl. Thomson, 79: 130; 21: 414; Physiognomic tracts reiterated this association as referenced in the *Physiognomica*. See Jennifer Montagu, *The Expression of the Passions: The Origin and Influence of Charles Le Brun's Conférence sur l'expression générale et particulière* (New Haven: Yale University Press, 1994).

makes them narrow and curved, then one will represent [a man suffering from] madness who threatens to drown someone. Strong appetites are thus represented with noses that are twisted in every which way.

## 47. On the Diversity of Faces Appropriate to Different Figures

Moreover, since we have talked about the nose, mouth and cheeks, we will now consider the diversity of faces appropriate to the different figures and passions we want to represent. A painter wanting to make a joyful and cheerful man, who is lustful but remembers little, must make the face large, plump, moist, and quite fleshy. Such a face also represents timidity, envy, or impudence, and sometimes the frenzies of Bacchus. If, on the contrary, the painter should want to make a diligent, prudent and attentive man, or a vicious and stingy thief, he must give him the head of an ape, or a female cat, that is narrow, thin, gaunt, and dry. And again these represent mainly the habits of a female cat, who with deceit during the night perpetrates robberies and evil deeds. A virtuous man, who is moderate and good, must be adorned with one of those well-proportioned faces that Dürer described in the first two books; those made larger represent men who are sluggish, lazy, drunken, who speak jealously and are not clever, while those that are smaller are appropriate for tough and greedy men, [who are] rapacious for other's goods and accompanied by many insanities.[145] Now the painter must be warned that even if all of the extremities are depraved, the face, nevertheless, can be made large, flat and fleshy if we want to [make a man who] has much love, faith and civility, and who is patient in the face of adversity which arises in this life. One must then make the face of a man who is a liar, who is scandalous, envious and full of vanity, similar to that of the birds, which are narrow and sharp. The face of murderous thieves and wicked men must be made concave in the middle in the manner Dürer teaches in the Third Book. A crazy person must be made with a face that looks insane and cheeks that seem to tremble, but if one makes him trembling with a cheerful face, one will represent a lustful man.

---

145 Gallucci, *Della simmetria*, 3: 80–85.

## 48. On the Diversity of Eyes and Parts Nearby Appropriate to Different Figures

The eyes are certainly the principle part of the human face, and, because of this, the most loved by men. Hence it follows that the painter also must strain as much as possible to make [eyes] in the manner that searches the figure that he wants to represent. Therefore, the neighboring parts under the eyes, properly called cheeks, must be made large, and eminent; in those parts we represent a weak man, who is feebleminded and easily intoxicated. A man who is burdened by sleep (as one would make the three disciples who accompanied Christ our Lord in the garden) must be made with eyelids, which is the cartilage that covers the eyes; when they are closed, [they] are also swollen, demonstrating in that shape a great desire for sleep. Along with sleeplessness, should people by some accident want to portray these passions, the shapes are also appropriate for representing intoxication.[146] Diligent painters represent intoxicated figures with heavy lids below the eyes, while those who have slept a lot [show heaviness] in the upper part. Eyes that are larger than those of regular, well-proportioned figures ought to be used when the painter wants to represent the laziness and idleness of oxen, who likewise have eyes of this sort. It is true that this together will form a certain Idea of compassion, pleasantness, and meekness. The painter will then make the eyes of a timid and cowardly man smaller than the true proportion; if painters want to represent in a figure the malice of apes, they must make the eyes of apes, which are concave, as Suetonius describes Emperor Caligula.[147] If astonishment, boorishness, and lethargy of a dimwit [are to be represented], the eyes must be equally and greatly protruding from the head. Moreover, with concave eyes, one portrays shrewdness of dress, as well as fraud, envy, pitfalls, abrupt betrayals, and infidelity, which will be shown if we make them weak; and if they appear as though they are falling, one will show the frauds and deception, while if with those we associate moisture, that will represent madness. If then a figure has prominent eyes, but in such a manner that they are also surrounded by a tight and deep pit, or rather by such a crease of missing flesh, this represents

---

146 Matthew 26: 36–46
147 Suetonius, *The Lives of the Twelve Caesars*, transl. Thomson, 50: 285.

the eyes of frauds, swindlers, and the wicked; however, if one makes the eyes the same but filled with blood, then one will show that he is very brash in these lascivious things delighted in before this, such as drinking and overeating. If this is what one wants to portray, which is at the same time right and imprudent, they ought to be white in color with heavy eyelids over them giving more of an indication of madness. A prudent man, who is fair and clever, must certainly then be made pronounced, but misty, and like flashing stars, quite large and pure. Murders, sorcerers, poison makers, and other such scoundrels, must be made plain, small, dry, and full of darkness. If then they are made very prominent, small, and gloomy, the creator will represent a figure that is well prepared in hand and in language. Well-proportioned eyes, therefore, ought to be between these extremes of large, small on the outside and medium [on the] inside, and these accommodate that shape in which we want to show the group of all virtues, and the best dispositions of body and soul.

## 49. Which Face is Appropriate for Which Figure

Men who are abrasive and ignorant must be made with their foreheads narrow and taut as seen in boars; on the other hand, if one wants to make a figure that represents laziness and sloth, then the shapes should be larger than the proper proportion demands, as Suetonius writes is the case with Emperor Caligula and adds that [his forehead] was also bowed.[148] Fickle men, and equally those who are frail, must be made with small [foreheads]; choleric and haughty men, rounded; and the dim-witted, and those who lack any kind of judgment, spherical but unequal and mountainous. Effeminate and weak men must be made with a very narrow one. Imprudent men must be made with a high and very rounded one, while malicious and dishonest men [must be made] furrowed with a broad surface. The forehead appropriate to insane and furious men is again long and broad, such as is seen in lions. The appropriate forehead for ingenious men, who easily understand any doctrine or artifice and are believed to be knowledgeable teachers, is described by Petrarch and Plato. As we read in his life, this forehead is

---

148  Ibid.

appropriate for magnanimous, enlightened and courtly men, as well as persistent and steadfast men.[149] The forehead appropriate for liars and philanderers, the strict and confidant, and the querulous and contentious has no wrinkles or creases between the eyebrows. On the contrary, many creases would represent again with that shape the pensive, afflicted and obstinate. As Juvenal says in his ninth Satire:

> I'd like to know why I so often see you looking gloomy,
> Naevolus, your brow all overcast, like Marsyas in defeat.[150]

And later he says:

> ...Where
> Are those fresh furrows from?[151]

## 50. On the Various Heads Appropriate to Different Figures

The head that is larger than any due proportion is appropriate for those human figures in which the painter wants to demonstrate villainy of spirit or a beastly soul with the greatest of cruelty. Furthermore, [this head represents] greedy avarice, carelessness and a soul that is completely rough. If, on the contrary, the painter makes the head smaller than the due proportion, he will make a figure that represents fraud, arrogance and wickedness. A bold and sensitive man must be made with a well-proportioned head, which is somewhat large, as Dürer teaches.[152] Should one add to that somewhat large head the upper part that reveals the beginnings of baldness, then one will represent in that figure the head and habits of a donkey. Brash people should be made with a forehead that is sharp at the top like pinecones; these are similar to ravens and crows. Courageous and daring men should have a head that is modest and turned downward, which is also suited to both proud and reckless men. If the painter wants to represent the fraudulent and duplicitous,

---

149  In fact, his later biographers reiterated that he may have received his name from the very breadth of his forehead. Diogenes Laertius, *Lives of the Eminent Philosophers*, transl. R. D. Hicks (Cambridge, MA: Harvard University Press, 2015), 3: 4.
150  Juvenal, *Satires*, ed. George, 9: 1–47.
151  Ibid.
152  Gallucci, *Della simmetria*, 3: 80–85.

he must make their heads concave at the temples; again, this figure will represent hatred, and a hurtful and bestial soul. The head that is then well-proportioned and rounded, without concave temples, but rather full, must be made for ingenious, rational, kind, merciful, and prudent men; in short, those adorned with every virtue.

## 51. On the Diversity of Ears Appropriate to Different Figures

Ears have the strength to demonstrate the quality of a person that the painter wants to represent in his lines and colors. Therefore, lustful and wicked men, thieves, and, finally, all of those whose habits are similar to apes must be made with smaller ears than proper measure demands; on the other hand, ears that are too large and exceed the size of due proportion taught by Dürer represent a donkey in ears and habits, which is to say a man who is rude, silly, foolish, and stupid. Formed in this figure, then, is a well-proportioned intellect, a singular talent, a happy docility, clemency, and compassion. The ears must be made proportionate in size, formed in a half circle, protruding little, [so] that they just rest on the side of the head, as though languid and falling, but that serve uniformity in all its parts. Of this sort were the ears of Caesar Augustus, as Suetonius writes in his life.[153] Therefore, every virtue relates to uniformity, and uniformity informs and directs the tools that painters are to acquire. If then one makes them protrude greatly from the head, that painting [will represent] many vanities and many words: two things that are always joined together. Envious men must be made with longer ears than are the due proportion. Portraits of men where the painter wants to represent a breathless anxiety, full of color, he must make the ears dry and thin. Those who are full of thoughts and are uncommunicative must be made straight and stretched; and if one includes many hairs in the ears, this makes ears that hear very well.

---

153 "His eye-brows met; his ears were small, and he had an aquiline nose." Suetonius, *The Lives of the Twelve Caesars*, transl. Thomson, 79: 130.

## 52. Which Hair Colors and Complexions Should Be Used for All Figures One Wants to Represent

For the figure of a lustful, timid, and cunning man, one will choose a very dreary color for his flesh and hair, which seems black, seen mostly with the Moors, which Africa is wont to send forth. White [flesh], then, is somewhat moist and bright with very black hairs; one must make the colors bold, ingenious, pleasant, and shifting. In such a complexion, the hairs will be made sparse and white, appropriate for women and effeminate men who are full of fear. The spirited, magnanimous, dignified, and proud, who are like lions, should be made with hairs that are the same color of the lion, not with black nor white, but from these [colors] a third one that is moderately composed and clearly open. Those that will be made with a red color, as is found with foxes, will represent again crafty habits, which are slyness and wickedness together. The fearful must be given that pallor which comes to those who fear and also to those who are in love, as Plato describes.[154] In a figure in which one wants to represent laziness, slowness, incontinence, fraud, betrayal, treachery, and impiety, one must make the color of ash or lead. The color of apples [must be used], then, to [represent those who are] slow in spirit and body, who feel at the same time afraid and garrulous, and also greedy. If one wants to form a figure that demonstrates truth, lies, and fear, one must likewise use a light green color with many hairs on the face; in such a figure one also represents a perpetual desire to eat. A jealous and unpleasant [man] must then be made with the color green on a fully dry face with very sparse, black hair, which will show mundane thoughts and virulent malevolence. A man who is nimble, mobile, lightweight, and fast in body and soul must be made with the color red on his skin and hair; the exact redness is determined by the extent to which the figures embody those qualities. If, however, one mixes a great amount of blood with flesh that is white, soft and radiant, one will form a man who is ready to learn and is good, kind, friendly, courteous, and quick to forgive. Nevertheless, if one makes the hair fiery like live coals,

---

154 Ficino quotes the poet Agathon, who is an interlocutor in Plato's *Symposium*: "Glowing because it influences the character of Man at the blooming and glowing age, and it desires blooming things." Marsilio Ficino, *Commentary on Plato's Symposium on Love*, transl. Sears Jayne (Dallas, TX: Spring 1985), 96.

but very hard and large, and one makes the flesh tough and dusky, but not damp, one will form the idea of fury, anger, outrage, malignancy, and extremely sad thoughts of frauds, deceits, betrayals, and infidelity. If the painter wants to represent a man who is gravely inflamed with anger, he will make the chest a flaming color along with building veins in the neck and very swollen temples, which will better record this fury. In fact, using just one of these signs is enough to represent a choleric figure, and this is to be formed in him still, who, due to some accident, is very angry. Where the painter will make a cheerful and joyous figure, he must make the face strewn with the color of roses, then the hair blonde, or vermilion, or any other cheerful color. Also in this figure can be seen a perfectly natural blush due to the slightest reason together with great modesty, and this seems to be very appropriate for women. Here the painter must be warned that the color should be spread well throughout the face. For if he painted only a very small area of the cheeks, modesty and virtuous shame would not be formed, but rather a rapacious desire to drink or one, who because of some circumstance, had been ashamed. Anyone wishing to form a wicked man in order to conjure the ugliest vices that can be conceived of and cannot be mentioned should show a man lost in drink, whose nose is so colored with blood that is almost black, or truly of the color which is seen to be the liver, and this figure, even more so than the spoken vices, will also represent slander, envy, pride, or rather bestiality, and cruelty.

## 53. On the Eye Colors Appropriate to Different Figures

The eyes, which are called the windows of the soul, have the profound power to move observers, so much so that in them seems to be the sum of this vocation of explaining the passions of the soul through those things that fall under the senses. Therefore, painters who aspire to immortality must be quite diligent in painting them in the manner that seeks out the figure that they wish to form. First of all, the painter must note that the eye is composed of three parts: the white, the pupil, and that small circle that contains the pupil [the iris], which is contained within the white. The first two parts are the same in all men and do not vary, while the [iris] is the only one that varies in color. Besides this, I must, likewise, warn that this same part changes in different ages;

therefore, the color of youth is different than that of old men or of children, while yet another is for decrepit men. This difference is so vast that I met a seller of glasses here in Venice, who, upon seeing the eyes of a man, could immediately find in his box of glasses one that suited that sight even though he had many boxes of very different [strengths] in his workshop. All of these warnings must, therefore, be noted by diligent painters, which they can more easily learn from these precepts, as had that glasses maker who learned after much experience; besides this, the painter must know that the pupil does not change despite the color no matter the size. For instance, small pupils, like those of foxes, snakes and apes, must be made to appear wicked, covetous, full of evil thoughts, and a little daring, as these animals' pupils are. If the painter makes the eyes white and olive, he will represent the same vices more clearly; and more so if he makes the eyes concave, dry and in a certain way full of darkness; [finally] he will further suggest malice should the eyes be made almost stained with various colors. If the pupils are made large, as with sheep and oxen, he will show in that figure a rough man, talented later in life [*ingegno tardo*], very patient and, finally, simple and coarse. A man of good taste and moderate in decorum must be made with the pupils between small and large, of moderate size; should the painter wish to make a figure of a man far removed from goodness and righteousness, and suffering with confused emotions, he must make the pupils both ornate and angular. These same passions are also demonstrated in those eyes that have one pupil larger than the other. A man who is very choleric, disdainful and proud must be made with veins full of blood in the whites of the eyes; the greater the amount [of blood] included, the more his fury is captured. On the other hand, should these veins be made together with eyes that are dewy rather than dry, the moisture will represent a Bacchus, while a prideful and serious [man], [who is] completely insane, has a certain pale blotchiness scattered throughout the eye; and if the eyes are shown moving together, then one wants to show a man who has a great memory and good judgment, as well as one who is thoroughly contemplative. A man who is jealous and spiteful must have blue eyes with some white rays around the pupil that are almost imperceptible. The eyes of dim-witted liars will be made green with gold rays radiating from the pupil. The lustful should be made, as they are called, changeable, or charming, according to the Greeks.[155] The greedy and intemperate must be made in the same way, but with these differences: the rays that emanate from the pupil are so thick that they cover all of the small circle located around the pupil, and these eyes are called black eyes; should one also add blood veins to the white area, rage is represented (as we said), and combined together with dryness, extreme anger will be represented with the said things. Should they be made misty, one will represent magnanimity, fortitude, and good judgment, which Suetonius says of Julius Caesar.[156] And these things signify those [characteristics], but with some sort of irascibility and lust. The painter must be warned that if he makes the eyes stained white, almost like spikes, that he will represent frauds, robbers, sagacity, and temerity; but if he includes these [spikes] in those eyes, which we called changeable or charming, he will represent a rude man with unpleasant habits; and if he makes red stains scattered in the blacks of the eyes, he will form a murderer, a lecher, a cheat, a crafty [man], or whatever he holds in his heart or his mouth. Pale and dry spots [in the eyes] represent a man desirous of impossible things, an investigator of the things created by nature to use in predictions for men, and a big trunk of fury. In sum, when the painter makes eyes that are stained, it always represents a soul cluttered by many vices. Now the painter should follow these universal precepts concerning the eyes: where the color is pale and clouded, it always means some kind of misfortune; and if these are also dry, it will more openly communicate treachery and infidelity; and, moreover, making them small, along with these characteristics, will more clearly indicate infidelity, fraud, betrayal, and deception. If the painter will make [the eyes] pale and of moderate size, they will be appropriate to attentive, clever and ingenious people, and others who are able to apprehend every difficult thing, and together in a certain way, moderately sparing. Shining eyes then, which can be seen in roosters, although very beautiful, should, nevertheless, only be used for the very lustful, as indeed can be seen with roosters. The eyes appropriate to men who are smart, ingenious and of great valor are described as attractive. These should be shown as shining and watery, as

---

155 Pseudo-Aristotle, *Physiognomica*, 6: 812b.1–13; Aristotle, *Minor Works*, transl. Hett, 127–29.
156 "It is said that he was tall, of a fair complexion, round limbed, rather full faced, with eyes black and piercing..." Suetonius, *The Lives of the Twelve Caesars*, transl. Thomson, 45: 30.

indeed can be seen in lions and eagles, and as Suetonius [describes] the eyes of Augustus.[157] Nevertheless, should those be larger than due proportion, gleaming and seeming to move, as in a man burning with anger, and should they have very large and open eyelids that are similar to the eyes of wolves or wild boars, then they will show cruelty, bestiality and thievery. Indeed, this is the nature of these animals as it was with the cruel Tiberius Caesar.[158] If these will be made smaller than due proportion demands through research, [the painter] illustrates the diseased and the fraudulent, while, likewise, robust and flashing eyes are appropriate to gluttons and fools. If the terms of proportion are not exceeded, either in greatness, smallness or splendor, but are moderated within these extremes, they will be appropriate to a great soul, a singular spirit, desirous of honor and glory; and if they occur together with arrogance, unbridled anger and a love for excessive drinking, and that fleeting disease will not be contrary, then one can make the worn-out eyes of Alexander the Great. In sum, all pulsating eyes should be made to [illustrate] scoundrels. Those eyes, then, which are only seen half-opened and looking down, should likewise represent those who can be called old foxes; and if those are also concave, they will be worse, and are appropriate to those men who are tarnished with some evil. If the painter could form in a figure those eyes which have been mentioned but with a smile on the lips and a certain tremor in the forehead, cheeks and eyebrows, he will represent a very wicked man, and even worse if he raises and lowers his eyebrows often while gazing around at bystanders; again one makes the eyes of this figure as though they seem to be keeping themselves open by nature. The aforementioned smile, along with teary eyes, are appropriate for a fool, while if the figure is made with the eyelids taut and the forehead weak, as well as the parts around the ears equally weak, here the painter represents a virtuous man. Thoughtful and ingenious men should have eyes that are somewhat swollen and dewy with a beastly and frightful appearance. If these [characteristics] are joined with dryness of the eyes, illness and desperation will be demonstrated; should next to them be a rugged forehead and fixed eyes with upturned eyelids, this will make him more proud and brash. The

---

157 "His eyes were bright and piercing; and he was willing it should be thought that there was something of a divine vigour in them...." Ibid., 49: 130.

158 Second Roman emperor of the Julio-Claudian line who was highly criticized by Roman historians such as Suetonius and Tacitus. Ibid., 51: 379.

eyes appropriate to a timid man are fixed, rigid, firm and watery; those of the insane are dry, while those of fools, pale. Wrathful, cruel and malicious men should be made with very long eyebrows, where one wishes to disappear [due to fear] for the eyes. In the jealous and lustful, the eyes should be made large and rigid with the color vermilion, while if to those eyes are added certain creases in the cheeks, shamelessness, injustice, instability, desperation, and unhappiness will be described. The eyes of the greedy should be made small and fixed, while adding a rugged forehead forms the figure of a fraud; moreover, making the entire figure slope will create the idea of thieves along with cholerics. The eyes of swindlers and the wicked should be made similar to olives, rigid and dark. The eyes appropriate to a young student are small and misty; the forehead should be without wrinkles with eyelids that appear as though they are moving themselves.

## 54. On the Eye Movement Appropriate to Different Figures

Although the painter cannot make eyes that move, as they remain fixed in the figure he has made, nevertheless, experts well know that, when they want, they seem to move. These few precepts will provide no little help to those [interested], which I will finish in a few words. So, in the face of a figure where the painter wants to represent the idea of carelessness, betrayal and confusion, the eyes should seem to move quickly. The eyes and eyelids should move together with the timid, while those who are bold and confident in peril have eyes that move with firm eyelids. The lazy and slow, who unable to begin anything, nor complete what was begun, should be made with eyes that move slowly. The insane and useless should have eyes that dart rapidly from one side to the other. Those who are drunk, greedy, dull, stupid, and foolish appropriately have large and trembling eyes. Eyes that are trembling, white and small are appropriate for the unjust, insolent and faithless. Those who waver and are lustful, but not wicked, dedicated to indecent behavior, along with those who are ambitious and envious often [appear] close to birds of prey; likewise, [the eyes] befit the ingenious and intelligent when they have some wetness. Those which are pale and trembling show a troublesome mind that is ingenious, but with a greatly discontented soul.

For the lustful and thoughtless, make the pupils of the eyes (as we have said elsewhere) turn upwards when opening and closing. If the painter does not make them turned upwards, but straight and fixed with eyes of proportional size, pleasant splendor, balanced moisture, and without wrinkles in the forehead, he will form in respect to this part, a religious man, cautious, eager to learn, kind and loving. But if, on the contrary, he will make these same [eyes] dry, [this is the] formula for an unjust, proud and bestial man; and should he join this dryness with wrinkles on the forehead, eyebrows that meet and with a hardness of the eyelids, he will make a bold, brash and bestial man that delights in many gifts. In order to make a singular genius, the eyes should be fixed, watery and splendid, opened so that all the circumference of the eye, or the circle located around the pupil [the iris], is visible, such that their stare is content. But if they are dry and dark, and, nevertheless, were intended to look content, they will be appropriate to the brazen and extremely bold. Now it must still be advised that the eyes are not straight in all men, or look straight ahead; there are some that seem to look to one side and often watch the other. Moreover, eyes that look to the side are appropriate for insane and careless people; those that look to the left are appropriate to the lustful; and those that look at the nose, or mustache, are useful for travelers, as Macrobius notes.[159] If one includes dryness in these eyes, and if they will always appear in all aspects fixed, they will be appropriate to those who are genuine, but through good judgment deceive men that are without shame and are overcome with sorrow, which will be even more appropriate if they will be made trembling along with the conditions above. If the painter then makes the eyes as though the right one stares ahead, while the left appear crooked, they are appropriate for both the insane and the lustful; moreover, the extent of the crookedness indicates one vice more than the other, depending upon the severity; and if the painter makes them completely crooked, he will represent a Bacchus, a lecher, and a figure of those who are seduced by evil. The painter will show this more clearly if he makes them look

---

159 In the Dream of Scipio, he travels through the planetary spheres and notes the light is "too bright for your eyes," and that "I was amazed at these wonders, but nevertheless I kept turning my eyes back to earth." William Harris Stahl, transl., *Commentary on the Dream of Scipio by Macrobius* (New York: Columbia University Press, 1990), 74; also see: Macrobius Ambrosius Theodosius, *Commentarii in Somnium Scipionis*, transl. James Willis (Berlin: De Gruyter, 2013), 1: 3.

as though they are trembling, but if he does not make them trembling, but pale, he will show a cruel and deadly figure. If he will make them large and red, this will be appropriate to the gamblers, the lustful, and the greedy; if he will make them cross-eyed and looking down with the eyelids almost closed, he will represent the same, as it was said of those whose eyes are completely crooked, and still demonstrate firmly those same emotions. If he makes them so that one looks up and the other looks down, while the eyes are closed and they appear to tremble, he will make a figure that seems fearful of a debilitating disease. Now the painter should be advised of those eyes that are called beautiful and well proportioned, not only to learn about the beauty in those and the right proportion, but also to know and learn about the diversity that we have narrated above. If the ends of the hair of the eyebrows draws a line to the last extremity of the hair of the eyelids, and it is found that this line is completely circular, then these will not be prominent nor narrow. When the eyebrows move beyond the eyelashes, they are said to protrude, and when they are shorter, they are said to be hollow. Therefore, the accord of the eyes consists in this: the eye should be in the middle where one cannot see more of one part of the whites than another, while ensuring that they remain fixed; this will occur when the outer part of the circle enclosing the pupil [the iris] is equally covered by the eyelids in the top as in the underside.

## 55. On the Diversity of Hair Appropriate to Different Figures

Although we have touched on the diversity of hair elsewhere, nevertheless, it seems appropriate to me here to speak more specifically about the treatment so that the painter will have a particular place to find these established precepts. The painter will make a timid and fraudulent [figure] with very curly hair, but those who are unpleasant, immoral, unwise, and irritating in manner should be made long and flowing. A beastly and violent man will have very thick hair all over, while the malicious and deceitful have little hair; soft hair [is appropriate for] women and effeminate men, but neither should have rigid hair, which is appropriate to the beastly and rough. Moreover, the just, temperate and of good wit should be made in the middle between these extremes:

this does not mean curly or straight, but rippling in a certain way, not too thin, neither too thick, not rigid, nor soft. Along the same lines, if the painter includes many hairs on the legs, he will form a fierce and rough man; if hair is only on the upper part and none below, there will be only fierceness. If, however, there are hairs only around the ankles, painters will represent bestial lust along with foolishness; he will show it most clearly if there will be much hair on the thighs, hips, and genitals. The frivolous, fickle and lascivious should have ample hair on the chest and stomach, while swindlers only [have hair] on the chest; if the shoulders and back are hairy, this will create a figure that represents a man who continually forms in his mind new fantasies. One should include much hair on the necks of the magnanimous and fearless, as is seen in lions. Similarly, those who, like a bear, will have the whole body covered in hair, as Suetonius says Caligula should be, who was, in fact, most beastly.[160] Those who are by nature grieved, melancholic, and altogether evil and envious, must be made with rigid, thick and tangled eyebrows. This figure is similar to a pig, which has thick and dense eyebrows that extend to the temples and bend somewhat towards the eyes. If then the eyebrows do not extend towards the temples, but are only somewhat bent in the front, he will represent a certain awkwardness and bashfulness. But if, to the contrary, they turn away from the nose and come very close to the temples, the painter will shape in that picture a liar, who is vapid and fraudulent; and if he bends them not to one side nor the other, but makes them straight and equidistant to either side, a fiery lust will be manifested in that figure. If then he will make the hair descending to the middle of the forehead, split into two parts, the painter will show in this and put before the eyes of observers a figure of courtesy, courage, and other similar virtues that benefit human society.

## 56. On the Diversity of Stature Appropriate to Different Figures

Should the painter wish to form a figure that is astute with a shrewd wit and quick in his actions, and then present it to the eyes of observers, he should be made small of stature, but well-proportioned. This was

---

160 "The other parts of his body were much covered with hair." Suetonius, *The Lives of the Twelve Caesars*, transl. Thomson, 50: 285.

the height of Augustus Caesar, whom Suetonius wrote in his life of the same was five feet and three-quarters tall.¹⁶¹ On the contrary, should one wish to show a figure representing slowness in wit and action, he must be made disproportionate in size. This is the sort of body that Tiberius Caesar had, who was full of many vices and especially cruel, as Suetonius notes.¹⁶² If then the painter makes a small figure with parched flesh and black or red hair, he will form a man unstable in all things who never finishes anything. On the other hand, making a man tall, fleshy, and with white hair, will form one who is entirely useless and indifferent to everything, because these [men] are simple, uncouth and lazy. If then he makes the picture of a short man with white [hair], he will make a prudent and rational man; this will be even more clear should the painter make a large man, who is lean, hairy, and with a dark complexion. And from all of these things, the painter, who, wishing to form a beautiful man adorned with genius, needs to form a well-proportioned body of moderate stature, musculature and hair, which does not show excessive moisture nor excessive heat, but a well-balanced nature.

## 57. In What Thing Beauty Consists, and Proportion of Bodies According to Marsilio Ficino and Painters

Although at the beginning of this book we named the thing in which the beauty of human bodies consists with the authority of Aristotle and of the poets, here we will speak of the beauty of the human bodies according to the doctrine of Plato explained by Marsilio Ficino over the banquet of the same, and together tell what measures modern painters use, in order to conclude our book with beauty, which should serve painters to reach their goal at their panels because students will not have to search elsewhere for these measurements which are commonly used. Now painters listen to what Ficino says:

> What thing consists of the beauty of the body? A certain liveliness of action, and a certain grace, that shines in the same beautiful thing for the influence of its own idea. This splendor does not descend into matter if the material is not properly prepared, that it is possible, now this

---

161 "In stature he was a little below the common height." Ibid., 51: 379.
162 "His cruel and sanguinary disposition was exhibited upon great as well as trifling occasions." Ibid., 34: 324.

preparation of the body that lives consists in three things: order, mode, and species;[163] the significant order being the intervals of the parts, the quantity the mode, the species of lines, and colors. In order that all parts of the body have their natural place, the ears, the eyes, the nose and the other parts must first be in their proper positions, the eyes at an equal distance from the nose and both ears equally spaced from the eyes. And this proportion of distances, which is part of the order, is still not enough if the mode of the parts is not added, attributing to each limb its proper length in accordance with the proportion of the whole body, so that three noses placed end to end will fill the length of one face, the semi-circles of both ears joined together will make the circle of the open mouth, and the joining of the eyebrows will also amount to the same; the length of the nose will match the length of the lip, and likewise of the ear. The twin circles of the eyes will equal the one opening of the mouth; eight heads will make the length of the body; this same length the spread of the arms to the side and likewise of the legs and feet will also measure.

Furthermore, we consider the form necessary so that a graceful disposition of the line and curves, and the splendor of the eyes, will adorn the order and mode of the parts. Although these three particulars are in the matter, they nonetheless may not be any part of the body.

The order of the members is not member, because the order is in all the members, and any member is located in all members. Moreover the other is nothing other than an appropriate interval of the parts, and the interval in nothing other than the distance of the parts, and the distance, or is anything, a useless vacuous, as it is some stretch of line. Now being without profundity, and without width, which are necessary to the body, as could we name them bodies? Equally the manner is not a quantity but a term of quantity, and the terms are surface, lines, and points, which missing profundity are not bodies.[164]

The species then assures a sweet agreement of lights, shadows and lines, which is not in the material. Of all these things that are manifest, that beauty in all distance of the material of the body, is never communicated the same to the body, if it is not to be disposed with these incorporeal preparations, which I have recounted.[165]

---

163 Alternatively translated by Jayne as "Arrangement, Proportion, and Aspect." Ficino, *Commentary on Plato's Symposium on Love*, transl. Jayne, 93.

164 Ibid., 88.

165 The section was cribbed almost verbatim by Nicholas Poussin for one of his longest aphorisms published in Bellori's *Lives*, "Della Idea della Bellezza." Anthony Blunt, *Nicolas Poussin* (London: Pallas Athene, 1967), 364. Giovan Pietro Bellori, *Le vite de pittori, scultori e architetti moderni*, ed. Evelina Borea and Giovanni Previtali (Turin: Einaudi, 1976), 461–2. Also see Bellori, *The Lives of the Modern Painters, Sculptors and Architects*, transl. Helmut Wohl and Alice Sedgwick Wohl (New York: Cambridge University Press, 2005), 339.

These things are from Ficino, from which students of painting will glean much, especially if they turn to their soul from which they will know that:

> Painting is nothing other, than an idea of the things in everything incorporeal, which although represents bodies, represented only the order, and mode, and species of things, that are in all incorporeal things.[166]

Now we shall speak of what modern painters say about the proportions of the human bodies, who, nevertheless, follow the ancients, as can be seen in Pliny[167] and many others, who divide the face from the root of the hair to the bottom of the chin into three equal parts, each as long as the nose, which is also as long as a thumb on the hand, slit of the mouth, and as much as all that area that contains the eyes — from where the nose is joined with the forehead, as well as where both eyes come together — that is as much as the space of two noses, or two thumbs; this area is also divided into three equal parts: two are given to both of the eyes and one is the space between them. Again, the space between the eyes and the beginning of the earlobe should be the length of a nose, which should also be the length of the ear. Now to measure the whole body, painters must take a measurement of three noses — the distance from the root of the hair to the bottom of the chin — and with this should measure all of the body in this manner. Then all of the body should be made as long as nine or ten of these measurements that is required from the head, though should the figure be made with nine heads, the following should be done. From the base of the throat to the end of the torso should measure three of these, and two from here to the knees, and another two to the neck, or top of the foot; another then divided into three parts should one be from the forehead or root of the hair to the top of the head, the second one until the neck, and the third from the sole of the foot to the top, called the mount of the foot. Then

---

166 Likewise in Poussin's aphorism on the descent of beauty we find that: "And thus we conclude that painting is nothing but an idea of incorporeal things even though it shows bodies, for it only represents the order and the mode of the species of things and it is more intent upon the idea of beauty than on another thing." Blunt, *Nicolas Poussin*, 364.

167 Ghiberti and earlier Renaissance writers reiterated the proportions of Polykleitos in his lost *Canon* as recorded by Pliny. Pliny, *Natural History*, transl. Healy, 34: 55, 58, 65.

from the base of the throat to the beginning of the arms makes one, and from here until the wrist makes three; furthermore, in a manner such that from the shoulder until the elbow there is one and two-thirds from here until the wrist will be one and one-third, and the hand is as equally long as the head. Whoever wishes to make a body of ten heads [should note that] the first head is from the top of the head to the base of the nose, while from here until the base of the throat is another; the third the middle of the chest, the fourth until the navel, the fifth until the genitals, two are along the thigh until the bone over the knee, and from here until the soles of the feet there ought to be three, which all joined together makes ten. Likewise, the transverse size should be measured in this manner, making the outstretched arms and hands together equal ten heads. And this is the universal measure that is used by modern painters, who have demonstrated their usefulness in highly selective examples from nature and ancient statues. Nevertheless, they can see that the measurements of our Dürer are more assured and indisputable as each particle is measured. Although small, these are the principal members, and, besides giving those measures to all sorts of bodies that can be found among men, should only be of nine or ten heads. Students should then not regret studying the measurements of Dürer, as these discourses, most assuredly, have the power to reveal the nature of men in order to imitate the best in nature as they should, and to bear that fruit that their labors deserve.

The end of the fifth and final book.

May the honor and the glory be given only to God.

# Bibliography

## The Works of Giovanni Paolo Gallucci

Gallucci, Giovanni Paolo, ed. and transl., *Ionnis Hasfurti…de cognoscendis et medendis morbis ex corporum coelestrium positione libri IIII cum argumentis et expositionibus Ioannis Paulli Gallucci Saloensis…quibus accesserunt in eandem sententiam auctores alii…* (Venice: ex officinal Damiani Zenarii, 1584).

— *De formis enthymetatum* (Venice: P. Marinelli, 1586).

— *Theatrum mundi et temporis…ubi astrologiae principia cernuntur…nunc primum in lucem editum* (Venice: J. B. Somascum, 1588), http://digital.onb.ac.at/OnbViewer/viewer.faces?doc=ABO_%2BZ186392402

— transl., *Della simmetria dei corpi humani, libri quattro* (Venice: Domenico Nicolini, 1591; repr. Roberto Meietti, 1594), https://archive.org/details/dialbertoduraro00gallgoog/page/n4

— *Della fabrica et uso del novo horologio universale* (Venice: Giovanni Battista Ciotti, 1592), https://books.google.co.uk/books?id=nB5aAAAAcAAJ&printsec=frontcover&hl=it#v=onepage&q&f=false

— *Speculum Uranicum in quo vera loca tum octavae sphaerae tum septem plaentarum… ad quodlibet datum tempus ex Prutenicarum ratione colliguntur, una cum regulis fabricandi duodecim coeli domici'ia ex Regiomontano et Alcabitio et dirigendi significatores* (Venice: Damiani Zenarii, 1593), https://www.e-rara.ch/zut/doi/10.3931/e-rara-49833.

— *I tre libri della perspettiva commune dell' illustriss* (Venice: G. Varisco, 1593).

— *Historia naturale e morale delle Indie* (Venice: B. Basa, 1596).

— *De fabrica, et usu hemisphaerii uranici* (Venice: Bernardo Basa, 1596).

— *Nova fabricandi horaria mobilia et permanentia, et permanentia, tam acu Magnetico, quam sine acu ad omnem latitudinem, ratio nuper excogiata* (Venice: Bernardum Basam 1596).

— *Della fabrica et uso di diversi stromenti di Astronomia e Cosmographia* (Venice: Ruberto Meietti, 1597).

— transl., *Margarita filosofica* (Venice: Barezzo Barezzi, 1599).

— *Coelestium corporum et rerum ab ipsis pendentium accurata explicatio per instrumenta, rotulas et figuras* (Venice: J. A. Somaschum, 1605).

— transl., *Specchio e disciplina militare* (Venice: Paolo Jordano Orsini, 1616).

## Primary Sources

Alberti, Leon Battista, *De re aedificatoria*, ed. Giovanni Orlandi and Paolo Portoghesi (Milan: Edizioni Il Polifilo, 1966).

— *Della Pittura*, transl. John R. Spencer (New Haven; London: Yale University Press, 1966).

— *Leon Battista Alberti on Painting and Sculpture: The Latin Texts of "De Pictura" and "De Statua,"* ed. Cecil Grayson (London: Phaidon Press, 1972).

Anacreon, *The First Twenty-Eight Odes of Anacreon in Greek and English*, ed. John Broderick (London: Sherwood, Gilbert and Piper, 1827).

— *The Odes of Anacreon*, transl. Thomas Moore (London: John, Camden Hotten, 1871, https://www.gutenberg.org/files/38230/38230-h/38230-h.htm; repr. 2011).

Ariosto, Ludovico, *Orlando Furioso*, transl. Guido Waldman (Oxford: Oxford University Press, 2008).

Aristotle, *The History of Animals*, transl. D'Arcy Wentworth Thompson (Oxford: Clarendon Press, 1910).

— *Rhetoric*, transl. John Henry Freese (Cambridge, MA: Harvard University Press, 1960).

— *Nicomachean Ethics*, transl. Willliam Heinemann (Cambridge, MA: Harvard University Press, 1962).

— *Minor Works*, transl. W. S. Hett (London: William Heinemann, 1936; repr. Cambridge, MA: Harvard University Press, 1963).

— *Politics*, transl. Carnes Lord (Chicago: University of Chicago Press, 1984).

— *The Complete Works of Aristotle*, ed. Jonathon Barnes, 2 vols (Princeton: Princeton University Press, 1984).

— *Poetics*, transl. Stephen Halliwell (Cambridge, MA: Harvard University Press, 1995).

— *Politics*, transl. C. D. C. Reeve (Indianapolis: Hackett Publishing, 1998).

— *Rhetoric*, ed. and transl. Edward Meredith Cope and John Edwin Sandys (Cambridge, UK: Cambridge University Press, 2010).

Armenini, Giovanni Battista, *Dei veri precetti della pittura*, ed. S. Ticozzi (Pisa: N. Capurro, 1823).

— *On the True Precepts of the Art of Painting*, transl. Robert Baldick (New York: Vintage Books, 1977).

Ashcroft, Jeffrey, *Albrecht Dürer: Documentary Biography*, 2 vols (New Haven: Yale University Press, 2017).

Ashmole, Elias, *Theatrum chemicum britannicum*, ed. A. G. Debus (New York: Johnson Reprint Corporation, 1967; facsimile of London, 1652).

— *Theatrum chemicum Britannicum* (Hildesheim: G. Olms, 1968).

Avicenna, *The Life of Ibn Sina*, ed. and transl. W. E. Gohlman (Albany, NY: State University of New York Press, 1974).

— *Remarks and Admonitions*, ed. S. Dunya (Cairo: Organisation Générales des Imprimeries Gouvernementales, 1960).

— *The Canon of Medicine*, ed. I. a-Qashsh (Cairo: [n.p.], 1987).

— "Essay on the Secret of Destiny," transl. G. Hourani, in *Reason and Tradition in Islamic Ethics* (Cambridge, UK: Cambridge University Press, 1985), 227–48.

— "The Book of Scientific Knowledge," ed. and transl. P. Morewedge, in *The Metaphysics of Avicenna* (London: Routledge, 2017), 11–109.

— *The Metaphysics of Healing*, transl. Michael Marmura (Provo, UT: Brigham Young University, 2005).

— *The Book of Salvation*, transl. F. Rahman (Oxford: Oxford University Press, 1952).

Baldinucci, Filippo, *Notizie de'professori del disegno*, ed. F. Ranalli and Paolo Barocchi, 7 vols (Florence: Eurografica S.p.A, 1974).

Bareggi, Filippo. *Il mestiere di scrivere. Lavoro intellettuale e mercato librario a Venezia nel Cinquecento*. Rome: Bulzoni, 1988.

Barocchi, Paola, ed., *Trattati d'arte del cinquecento, fra manierismo e controriforma*, Scrittori d'Italia 221, 3 vols (Bari: Laterza, 1961).

— *Scritti d'arte del cinquecento*, 3 vols (Milan: Riccardo Ricciardi, 1971–1977).

Bellori, Giovan Pietro, *Le vite de pittori, scultori e architetti moderni*, ed. Evelina Borea and Giovanni Previtali (Turin: Einaudi, 1976).

— *The Lives of the Modern Painters, Sculptors and Architects*, transl. Helmut Wohl and Alice Sedgwick Wohl (New York: Cambridge University Press, 2005).

Biralli, Simone, *Delle imprese scelte*, 2 vols (Venice: Giovanni Battista Ciotti Senese, 1600).

Borghini, Raffaello, *Il riposo* (Florence: Giorgio Marescotti, 1584).

Borromeo, Carlo, "Instructiones fabricate et supellectilis ecclesiasticae," in *Trattati d'arte del cinquecento, fra manierismo e controriforma*, ed. Paola Barocchi, Scrittori d'Italia 221, 3 vols (Bari: Laterza, 1961), III: 1–112.

Boselli, Orfeo, *Osservazioni della scoltura antica dai Manoscritti Corsini e Doria e altri scritti*, ed. Phoebe Dent Weil (Florence: S.P.E.S., 1978).

Brancaccio, Lelio, *Fucina di Marte: nella quale con mirabile industria e con finissima tempra d'instruzioni militari s'apprestano tutti gli ordini appartenenti à qual si voglia carico essercitabile in guerra* (Venice: Giunti, 1641), https://gallica.bnf.fr/ark:/12148/bpt6k51208j.image

Camillli, Camillo, *Imprese illustri di diuersi, coi discorsi di Camillo Camilli, et con le figure intagliate in rame di Girolamo Porro Padouano...*, 3 vols (Venice: Francesco Ziletti, 1586), https://archive.org/details/impreseillustrid04cami/page/n4/mode/2up

Camillo, Giulio, *L'idea del theatro* (Venice: Agostino Bindoni, 1550), https://archive.org/details/bub_gb_R59T2RFRhjkC/page/n10/mode/2up

Camillo, Giulio, *L' idea del theatro con "L'idea dell'eloquenza", il "De transmutatione" e altri testi inediti*, ed. Lina Bolzoni (Milan: Adelphi, 2015).

Carducho, Vincente, *Dialogos de la Pintura. Su defense, origen, esencia, definicion, modos y differencias*, ed. F. Calvo Serraller (Madrid: Ediciones Turner, 1979).

Catullus, Gaius Valerius, *The Poems of Catullus*, transl. Charles Martin (Baltimore: John's Hopkins University Press, 1990).

— *Poems of Catullus*, transl. Peter Green (Berkely: University of California Press, 2005).

Cherchi, Paolo, *Polimatia di riuso: mezzo secolo di plagio*. Rome: Bulzoni, 1998.

Cicero, Marcus Tullius, *De Inventione*, transl. H. M. Hubbell (Cambridge, MA: Harvard University Press, 1952).

— *De Officiis libri tres*, ed. Paolo Fideli (Florence: A. Mondadori, 1973).

— *Brutus*, ed. Centre Traditio Litterarum Occidentalium (Turnhout: Brepols Publishers, 2010).

— *De re publica*, ed. Günter Laser (Stuttgart: Reclam, 2014).

— *Dream of Scipio*, transl. Andre Chaves (Pasadena: The Clinker Press, 2012).

Condivi, Ascanio, *The Life of Michelangelo*, transl. Alice Sedgwick Wohl (University Park, PA: Pennsylvania State University Press, 1999).

Conway, William Martin, transl., *The Writings of Albrecht Dürer* (London: Owen, 1958).

Cozzando, Leonardo, *Della libraria bresciana* (Brescia: Gio. Maria Rizzardi, 1685).

Danti, Vincenzo, *Il primo libro del Trattato delle perfette proporzioni* (Perugia: Bartelli, 1830).

Della Porta, Giovanni Battista, *De humana physiognomonia, libri VI* (Vico Equense: Giuseppe Cacchi, 1586).

— *Della fisionomia dell'huomo* (Venice: Presso C. Tomasini, 1598).

Dürer, Albrecht, *Vier Bücher von menschlicher Proportion* (Nuremberg: Hieronymous Andreae, 1528).

— *Von der Malerei* (London: Ernst Heidrich, 1928).

— *Die Unterweisung der Messung mit dem Zirkel und Richtscheit*, ed. Alvin E. Jaeggli and Christine Papesch (Dietikon-Zuerich: J. Stocker-Schmid, 1966).

Euclid, *Elements*, transl. Thomas L. Heath (Sante Fe, NM: Green Lion Press, 2002).

Ferro, Giovanni, *Teatro d'imprese*, 2 vols (Venice: Sarzina, 1623).

Ficino, Marsilio, *Commentary on Plato's Symposium on Love*, transl. Sears Jayne (Dallas, TX: Spring, 1985).

— *Three Books on Life*, ed. and transl. Carol V. Kaske and John R. Clark, Medieval and Renaissance Texts and Studies 57 (Binghamton, NY: The Renaissance Society of America, 1989).

Galen, *Doctrines of Hippocrates and Plato*, transl. Phillip de Lacy, 2 vols (Berlin: Akademie-Verlag, 1980).

Gellius, Aulus, *The Attic Nights*, transl. John Carew Rolfe (Cambridge, MA: Harvard University Press, 2015).

Ghiberti, Lorenzo, *I commentarii*, ed. Ottavio Morisani (Naples: R. Ricciardi, 1947).

Granada, Luis de, *Catechismus in symbolum fidei*, transl. Giovanni Paolo Gallucci (Venice: Damiani Zenari, 1586).

Grattarolo, Bongianni, *Historia della Riviera di Salò* (Brescia: Vinc. Sabbio, 1599).

Heikamp, Detlef, ed., *Scritti d'Arte di Federico Zuccaro* (Florence: L. S. Olschki, 1961).

Hippocrates, *On Regimen in Acute Diseases* (Whitefish, MT: Kessinger Publishing, LLC, 2010).

Hippocrates, *On the Nature of Man*, transl. W. H. Jones (Cambridge, MA: Harvard University Press, 2014).

Hollanda, Francisco de, *Tractato de pintura antigua* (Porto: Edição de "Renascença Portuguesa," 1918).

— *De la pintura antigua por Francisco de Hollanda, versión castellana de Manuel Denis (1563)*, ed. E. Tormo (Madrid: Ratés, 1921).

Homer, *Oyssey*, transl. E. V. Rieu (Harmondsworth: Penguin, 1966).

— *Iliad*, transl. Barry Powell (Oxford: Oxford University Press, 2014).

Horace, *Odes and Epodes*, transl. C. E. Bennett (Cambridge, MA: Harvard University Press, 1968).

— *Satires and Epistles*, transl. Smith Palmer Bovie (Chicago: University of Chicago Press, 2002).

Juvenal, *Satires*, ed. Richard George (St. Albans: Baikal, 2012).

Laertius, Diogenes, *Lives of the Eminent Philosophers*, transl. R. D. Hicks (Cambridge, MA: Harvard University Press, 2015).

Leonardo da Vinci, *On Painting*, transl. Martin Kemp and Margaret Walker (New Haven; London: Yale University Press, 1989)

Lomazzo, Giovanni Paolo, *Trattato dell'arte della pittura, scultura ed architetta* (Milan: Paolo Gottardo Pontio, 1584).

— *Scritti sulle arti*, ed. Roberto P. Ciardi, 2 vols (Florence: Centro Di, 1973–1974).

— *Idea del tempio della pittura* (Milan: Paolo Gottardo Pontio 1590, https://archive.org/details/bub_gb_YC59KugXgdQC/page/n4/mode/2up; repr. ed. Robert Klein, Florence: Istituto Nazionale di Studi sul Rinascimento, 1974).

— *Idea of the Temple of Painting*, transl. Jean Julia Chai (University Park, PA: The Pennsylvania State University Press, 2013).

Lunze, Johann Gottlob, *Academia Veneta seu della Fama in disquisitionem vocata* (Leipzig: [n.p.], 1701).

Mancini, Giulio, *Considerazioni sulla pittura*, ed. Adriana Marucchi and Luigi Salerno, 2 vols (Rome: Accademia Nazionale dei Lincei, 1957).

Martial, *Epigrams*, ed. and transl. Gideon Nisbet (Oxford: Oxford University Press, 2017).

Ovid, *Metamorphoses*, transl. A.D. Melville (Oxford: Oxford University Press, 2008).

Pacioli, Luca, *Summa de arithmetica, geometrica, proportioni et proportionalita* (Venice: Paganini, 1494).

— *De viribus quantitatis* (Bologna: unpublished, 1500).

— *De divina proportione* (Venice: Paganini, 1509).

Pausanias, *Description of Greece*, transl. W. H. S. Jones (Cambridge, MA: Harvard University Press; London: William Heinemann, 1918).

Peroni, Vincenzo, *Biblioteca bresciana*, 3 vols (Brescia: Bettoni, 1818–1823).

Petrarch, *The Complete Canzoniere*, transl. A. S. Kline ([n.p.]: Poetry in Translation, 2001).

Planudes, Maximus, *Aesopi Phrygis Fabulae* (Lyon: Jean de Tournes, 1570).

Plato, *The Laws of Plato*, transl. Thomas L. Pangle (New York: Basic Books, 1980).

— *Timaeus*, transl. Benjamin Jowett (New York: Dover Publications, 1985).

— *Sophist*, transl. Nicholas P. White (Indianapolis: Hackett Publishing Company, 1993).

— *The Republic*, transl. Tom Griffith (Cambridge, UK: Cambridge University Press, 2000).

— *The Republic*, transl. R. E. Allen (New Haven: Yale University Press, 2006).

Plautus, *Pseudolus*, transl. David Christenson (Indianapolis: Hackett Publishing Company, 2013).

Pliny the Elder, *The Elder Pliny's Chapters on the History of Art*, transl. K. Jex-Blake (London: Macmillan, 1896).

— *Natural History*, transl. John F. Healy (London: Penguin Books, 1991).

Plutarch, *De gloria Atheniensium*, ed. J. C. Thiolier (Paris: Presses de l'Université de Paris-Sorbonne, 1985).

— *Life of Alexander the Great*, transl. John Dryden (New York: Modern Library, 2004).

Porphyry, "The Life of Pythagoras," *The Pythagorean Sourcebook*, transl. Louis H. Feldman and Meyer Reinhold (London: Soncino, 1935).

Roskill, Mark, *Dolce's "Aretino" and Venetian Art Theory of the Cinquecento* (New York: New York University Press, 1982).

Sannazaro, Jacopo, *Arcadia* (Rome: Carocci editore, 2013).

Saslow, James M. *The Poetry of Michelangelo* (New Haven; London: Yale University Press, 1991).

Schlosser, Julius von, *Jahrbuch der Kunstsammlungen des Allerhöchsten Kaiserhauses*, 26 (1903).

— *Lorenzo Ghilberti's Denkwürdigkeiten (I commentarii)*, 2 vols (Berlin: Bard, 1912).

— *Le Letturata artistica; manuale delle fonti della storia dell'arte moderna*, 3rd ed. (Florence: La Nuova Italia, 1964).

— *La Letteratura artistica*, ed. Otto Kurz (Florence: La Nuova Italia, 1977).

Scribani, Charles, *Amphitheatrum Honoris in quo Caluinistarum in Societatem Iesu criminationes iugulatae* (Palaeopoli Aduaticorum: Apud Alexandrum Verheyden, 1606).

Seneca, Lucius Annaeus, *Dialogues*, transl. A. Bourgery (Paris: Les Belles lettres, 2003).

— *Letters from a Stoic*, transl. Robin Campbell (London: Penguin Books, 2004).

Tacitus, *Annals*, transl. Ronald Mellor (Oxford: Oxford University Press, 2011).

Tasso, Torquato, *Discourses on the Heroic Poem* ed. Mariella Cavalchini and Irene Samuel (Oxford: Clarendon Press, 1973).

— *Scritti sull'arte poetica*, ed. Einaudi Mazzali, 2 vols (Turin: Einaudi, 1977).

— *Discorsi del poema eroico*, ed. Ettore Mazzali and Francesco Flora (Milan: Ricciardi, 1959; repr. Rome: Biblioteca Italiana, 2004), http://www.bibliotecaitaliana.it/testo/bibit000856

— *The Liberation of Jerusalem*, transl. Max Wickert (Oxford: Oxford University Press, 2009).

Theodosius, Macrobius Ambrosius, *Commentarii in Somnium Scipionis*, transl. James Willis (Berlin: De Gruyter, 2013).

Tranquillus, C. Suetonius, *The Lives of the Twelve Caesars*, transl. Alexander Thomson ([n.p.]: Simon and Brown, 2013).

Trovato, Paolo. *Con ogni diligenza corretto. La stampa e le revisionieditoriali dei testi letterari italiani (1470–1570)* (Bologna: il Mulino, 1991).

Vasari, Giorgio, *Le Vite Vasari, Le vite de' più eccellenti pittori scultori e architettori*, ed. Gaetano Milanesi (Florence: Sansoni, 1878–1885).

— *Vasari on Technique* (New York: Dover, 1960).

— *La vita di Michelangelo nelle radazioni del 1550 e del 1568*, ed. Paola Barocchi (Milan-Naples: R. Ricciardi, 1962).

— *The Lives of the Artists*, transl. George Bull, 2 vols (London: Penguin Books, 1965).

— *Le vite de' più eccellenti pittori scultori e architettori: nelle redazioni del 1550 e 1568*, ed. Rosanna Bettarini and Paola Barocchi, 6 vols (Florence: Sansoni, 1966–1987).

— *The Lives of the Artists*, transl. Julia Conaway Bondanella and Peter Bondanella (New York: Oxford University Press, 1991).

Vergerio, Pier Paolo, *De ingenuis moribus ac liberalibus studiis* (Venice: [n.p.], 1472).

Virgil, *Georgics*, transl. Janet Lembke (New Haven: Yale University Press, 2005).

— *Aeneid*, transl. Frederick Ahl (Oxford: Oxford University Press, 2007).

Vitruvius, *I dieci libri dell'architettura di Marcus Vitruvio*, transl. Daniel Barbaro (Venice: Francesco de'Franceschi Senese & Giovanni Chrieger Alemano Compagni, 1567).

— *The Ten Books on Architecture*, transl. M. H. Morgan (New York: Dover, 1960).

Varagine, Jacobus de, *The Golden Legend: Readings on the Saints*, transl. William Granger Ryan, 2 vols (Princeton: Princeton University Press, 1993).

## Secondary Sources

Aiken, Jane Andrews, "Leon Battista Alberti's System of Human Proportions," *Journal of the Warburg and Courtauld Institutes*, 43 (1980), 68–96, https://doi.org/10.2307/751189

Barkan, Leonard, *Nature's Work of Art: The Human Body as Image of the World* (New Haven: Yale University Press, 1975).

Bartrum, Giulia, ed., *Albrecht Dürer and His Legacy: The Graphic Work of a Renaissance Artist* (Princeton: Princeton University Press, 2002).

Barzman, Karen, "The Florentine Accademia del Disegno: Liberal Education and the Renaissance Artist," in *Academies of Art between Renaissance and Romanticism*, ed. A. W. A. Boschloo (S'Gravenhage: SDU Uitgeverij, 1989), 14–30.

— "Perception, Knowledge, and the Theory of Disegno in Sixteenth-Century Florence," in *From Stuio to Studiolo: Florentine Draughtsmanship under the First Medici Grand Dukes*, ed. Larry J. Feinberg (Oberlin; Seattle: Allen Memorial Art Museum and University of Washington Press, 1991), 37–48.

— -edis, *The Florentine Academy and the Early Modern State: The Discipline of Disegno* (Cambridge, UK: Cambridge University Press, 2000).

Beekes, R. S. P., *Etymological Dictionary of Greek* (Leiden: Brill, 2009).

Bernheimer, Richard, "Theatrum Mundi," *The Art Bulletin*, 38.4 (1956), 225–47, https://doi.org/10.1080/00043079.1956.11408342

Białostocki, Jan, *Dürer and his Critics 1500–1971: Chapters in the History of Ideas Including a Collection of Texts* (Baden-Baden: V. Koerner, 1986).

Biggiogero, G. M., "Luca Pacioli e la sua 'Divina proportione,'" *Rendiconti dell'Istituto lombardo di scienze e lettere*, 94 (1960), 3–30.

Bleek-Bryne, Gabriele, "The Education of the Painter in the Workshop," in *Children of Mercury: The Education of Artists in the Sixteenth and Seventeenth Centuries*, ed. Jeffrey M. Muller (Providence, RI: Brown University, 1984), 28–39.

Blois, Lukas de, *The Policy of Emperor Gallienus* (Leiden: Brill, 1976).

Blunt, Anthony, "Poussin's Notes on Painting," *Journal of the Warburg Institute*, 1.4 (1938), 344–51, https://doi.org/10.2307/750002

— *Artistic Theory in Italy 1450–1600* (Oxford: Oxford University Press, 1962).

— *Nicolas Poussin* (London: Pallas Athene, 1967).

Bohern, H., "A Special Copy of G.'s Theatrum Mundi," *The Book Collector*, 18.1 (1969), 92.

Boschloo, A. W. A, *Annibale Carracci in Bologna: Visible Reality in Art after the Council of Trent*, 2 vols (New York: The Hague, 1974).

Bottari, Giovanni, *Raccolta di lettere sulla pittura, scultura ed architettura scritte da' più celebri personaggi dei secoli XV, XVI, e XVII*, ed. Stefano Ticozzi, 8 vols (Milan: Giovanni Silvestri, 1822–1825).

Brunati, Giuseppe, *Dizionarietto degli uomini illustri della Riviera di Salò* (Milan: Pogliani, 1837), https://archive.org/details/bub_gb_v93CFmYBx4kC/page/n4/mode/2up

Castelnuovo, Enrico, "Dürer scrittore e scienziato," in *Dürer e l'Italia*, ed. Kristina Herrmann Fiore (Milan: Electa, 2007), 97–103.

Celenza, Christopher, "Pythagoras in the Renaissance: The Case of Marsilio Ficino," *Renaissance Quarterly*, 52.3 (1999), 667–711, https://doi.org/10.2307/2901915

— *Piety and Pythagoras in Renaissance Florence. The Symbolum Nesianum* (Leiden: Koninklijke Brill NV, 2001).

Chambers, David and Brian Pullan, eds, *Venice: A Documentary History 1450–1630* (Oxford: Blackwell, 1992).

Ciardi, Roberto P., "Le regole del disegno di Alessandro Allori e la nascita del dilettantismo pittorico", *Storia dell'arte*, 12 (1971), 267–84.

Clare, R., "Catullus 64 and the Argonautica of Apollonius Rhodius: Allusion and Exemplarity," *Proceedings of the Cambridge Philological Society*, 42 (1997), 60–88, https://doi.org/10.1017/s0068673500002042

Conford, Francis MacDonald, *Plato's Cosmology: The Timaeus of Plato* (Indianapolis: Hackett Publishing Company, 1997).

Crawford Luber, Katherine, *Albrecht Dürer and the Venetian Renaissance* (Cambridge: Cambridge University Press, 2005).

Damiani, Enrico, "Contributi del dr. Petar Kolendič allo studio delle fonti italiane nella letteratura serbo-croata," *Giornale storico della letteratura italiana*, 100 (1932), 163.

Davis, Margaret, "Beyond the 'Primo Libro' of Vincenzo Danti's 'Trattato delle perfette proporzioni,'" *Mitteilungen des kunsthistorischen Institutes in Florenz*, 26.1 (1982), 63–84.

Debus, Allen G., *The Chemical Philosophy: Paracelsian Science and Medicine* (New York: Science History Publications, 1977).

Dempsey, Charles, "Some Observations on the Education of Artists in Florence and Bologna in the Later Sixteenth Century," *The Art Bulletin*, 62 (1980), 557–669, https://doi.org/10.2307/3050053

Doob, Penelope Reed, *The Idea of the Labyrinth: From Classical Antiquity through the Middle Ages* (Ithaca, NY: Cornell University Press, 1992).

Ernst, Germana, "Gallucci, Giovanni Paolo," *Dizionario Biografico degli Italiani*, 56 vols (Rome: Instituto dell'Enciclopedia Italiana, 1925-present), LI (1998), 327–65, 366–74.

Evans, Elizabeth, "Physiognomics in the Ancient World," *Transactions of the American Philosophical Society*, 59.5, 1–101, https://doi.org/10.2307/1006011

Fichter, Paula S., *Emperor Maximilian II* (New Haven: Yale University Press, 2001).

Finucci, Valeria, ed., *Renaissance Transactions: Ariosto and Tasso* (Durham and London: Duke University Press, 1999).

Gibbon, Edward, *The History of the Decline and Fall of the Roman Empire* (London: Penguin, 2001).

Giusti, Enrico, *Luca Pacioli e la matematica del Rinascimento* (Florence: Giunti, 1994).

Grafton, Anthony, *Cardano's Cosmos: The Worlds and Works of a Renaissance Astrologer* (Cambridge, MA: Harvard University Press, 1999).

Grafton, Anthony and William Newman, eds, *Secrets of Nature: Astrology and Alchemy in Early Modern Europe* (Cambridge, MA: MIT Press, 2001).

Haight, Elizabeth Hazelton, "Horace on Art: Ut Pictura Poesis," *The Classical Journal*, 47.5 (1952), 157–62, 201–02.

Hahm, David E., *The Origins of Stoic Cosmology* (Columbus, OH: Ohio State University Press, 1977).

Hartt, Frederick and David G. Wilkins, *History of Italian Renaissance Art*, 7th ed. (Upper Saddle River, NJ: Pearson/Prentice Hall, 2011).

Hess, Jacob, "On Some Celestial Maps and Globes of the Sixteenth Century," *Journal of the Warburg and Courtauld Institutes*, 30 (1967), 406–09, https://doi.org/10.2307/750759

Holt, Elizabeth Gilmore, *Literary Sources of Art History* (Princeton: Princeton University Press, 1947).

Hughes, Michael, *Early Modern Germany, 1477–1806* (Philadelphia: University of Pennsylvania Press, 1992).

Jacob Jansen, Dirk, "The Instruments of Patronage: Jacopo Strada at the Court of Maximilian II, A Case Study," in *Kaiser Maximilian II. Kultur und Politik im 16. Jahrhundert*, ed. F. Edelmayer and A. Kohler (Vienna: Verlag für Geschichte und Politik, 1992), 182–202.

Johansen, T. K. *Aristotle on the Sense-Organs* (Cambridge, UK: Cambridge University Press, 1997).

Justi, Ludwig, *Konstruierte Figuren und Köpfe unter den Werken Albrecht Dürers* (Leipzig: K. W. Hiersemann, 1902).

Koerner, Joseph Leo, *The Moment of Self-Portraiture in German Renaissance Art* (Chicago: University of Chicago Press, 1993).

— "Albrecht Dürer: A Sixteenth-Century Influenza," in *Albrecht Dürer and His Legacy: The Graphic Work of a Renaissance Artist*, ed. Giulia Bartrum (Princeton: Princeton University Press, 2002), 18–38.

Kwakkelstein, Michael, "Leonardo's Grotesque Heads and the Breaking of the Physiognomic Mould," *Journal of the Warburg and Courtauld Institutes*, 54 (1991), 127–36, https://doi.org/10.2307/751484

Lee, Rensselaer, "Ut Pictura Poesis: The Humanistic Theory of Painting," *The Art Bulletin*, 22.4 (1940), 197–269, https://doi.org/10.1080/00043079.1940.11409319

— *Ut Pictura Poesis: The Humanistic Theory of Painting* (New York: Norton, 1967).

Little, Charles E, "The Italians and Their Schools," *Peabody Journal of Education*, 10.4 (1933), 206–44.

Lukehart, Peter, ed., *The Accademia Seminars* (New Haven; London: National Gallery of Art, Yale University Press, 2009).

Maccagni, Carlo, "Augusto Marioni, Luca Pacioli e Leonardo," in *Hostinato rigore: Leonardiana in memoria di Augusto Marinoni*, ed. Pietro C. Marani (Milan: Electa, 2000), 55–60.

Martin, John Jefferies, *The Renaissance World* (New York and London: Routledge, 2007).

Maylender, Michele, *Storia delle accademie d'Italia*, 5 vols (Bologna: Cappelli, 1926–1930).

MacHardy, Karen Jutta, *War, Religion and Court Patronage in Habsburg Austria* (New York: Palgrave Macmillan, 2003).

Montagu, Jennifer, *The Expression of the Passions: The Origin and Influence of Charles Le Brun's Conférence sur l'expression générale et particulière* (New Haven: Yale University Press, 1994).

Muller, Jeffrey M., ed., *Children of Mercury: The Education of Artists in the Sixteenth and Seventeenth Centuries* (Providence, RI: Brown University, 1984).

Murdoch, Adrian, *The Last Pagan: Julian the Apostate* (Stroud: Sutton Publishing, 2008).

Noehles, Karl, *La Chiesa dei SS. Luca e Martina nell'opera di Pietro da Cortona* (Rome: Ugo Bozzi Editore, 1970).

Olson, Roberta J. M., "And They Saw Stars: Renaissance Representations of Comets and Pretelescopic Astronomy," *Art Journal*, 44.3 (1984), 216–24, https://doi.org/10.1080/00043249.1984.10792549

Onians, Richard Broxton, *The Origins of European Thought about the Body, the Mind, the Soul, the World, Time and Fate* (Cambridge, UK: Cambridge University Press, 1954).

Pagel, Walter, *Paracelsus: An Introduction to Philosophical Medicine in the Era of the Renaissance* (Basel: S. Karger, 1958).

Panofsky, Erwin, *Studies in Iconology* (New York: Oxford University Press, 1939).

— *Idea: A Concept in Art Theory* (Columbia: University of South Carolina Press, 1968).

— *Meaning in the Visual Arts* (Chicago: Chicago University Press, 1982).

— *Dürers Kunsttheorie: vornehmlich in ihrem Verhältnis zur Kunsttheorie der Italiener* (Berlin: De Gruyter, 2011).

Pellegrino, Alba Ceccarelli, "Sacre Scritture, Divine Proportioni e Honnêteté nell'Architecture di Philibert de L'Orme," in *Il sacro nel Rinascimento: atti del XII convegno internationale. Chianciano-Pienza. 17–20 Luglio, 2002*, ed. Luisa Rotondi Secchi Tarugi (Florence: F. Cesati, 2002), 181–207.

Pörtner, Regina, *The Counter-Reformation in Central Europe: Styria 1580–1630* (Oxford: Clarendon Press, 2001)

Posèq, Avigdor W. G., "On Physiognomic Communication in Bernini," *Artibus et Historiae*, 27.54 (2006), 161–90, https://doi.org/10.2307/20067127

Riccardi, Pietro, *Biblioteca matematica italiana*, 3 vols (Modena: Società tipografica, 1870–1880).

Roccasecca, Pietro, "Teaching in the Studio," in *The Accademia Seminars*, ed. Peter Lukehart (New Haven; London: National Gallery of Art, Yale University Press, 2009), 123–60.

Rossi, Massimiliano, "Un metodo per le passioni negli Scritti d'arte del tardo Cinquecento," in *Il volto e gli affetti: fisiognomica ed espressione nelle arti del Rinascimento: atti del convegno di studi, Torino 28–29 novembre 2001*, ed. Alessandro Pontremoli (Florence: L. S. Olschki, 2003), 83–102.

Sarton, George, "Remarks on the Theory of Temperaments," *Isis*, 34 (1943), 205–08, https://doi.org/10.1086/347791

Scheicher, Elisabeth, *Die Kunst- und Wunder Kammer der Habsburger* (Vienna: Molden, 1979).

Schleif, Corine, "Albrecht Dürer between Agnes Frey and Willibald Pirckheimer," in *The Essential Dürer*, ed. Larry Silver and Jeffrey Chipps Smith (Philadelphia: University of Pennsylvania Press, 2010), 85–205.

Sider, David, "Plato's Early Aesthetics: 'The Hippias Major'," *Journal of Aesthetics & Art Criticism*, 35.4 (1977), 465–70, https://doi.org/10.2307/430612

Snowden, Jr., Frank M., *Blacks in Antiquity: Ethiopians in the Greco-Roman Experience* (Cambridge, MA: Belknap Press, 1971).

Sohm, Philip, *Pittoresco: Marco Boschini, His Critics, and Their Critiques of Painterly Brushwork in Seventeenth- and Eighteenth-Century Italy* (Cambridge, UK: Cambridge University Press, 1991).

— *Style in the Art Theory of Early Modern Italy* (Cambridge, UK: Cambridge University Press, 2001).

— *The Artist Grows Old: The Aging of Art and Artists in Italy, 1500–1800* (New Haven: Yale University Press, 2007).

Stahl, William Harris, transl., *Commentary on the Dream of Scipio by Macrobius* (New York: Columbia University Press, 1990).

Tatarkiewicz, Wladyslaw, "The Great Theory of Beauty and Its Decline," *The Journal of Aesthetics and Art Criticism*, 31.2 (1972), 165–80, https://doi.org/10.2307/429278

Thorndike, Lynn, *History of Magic and Experimental Science*, 8 vols (New York and London: Columbia University Press, 1923–1958).

Unglaub, Jonathan, *Poussin and the Poetics of Painting: Pictorial Narrative and the Legacy of Tasso* (Cambridge, UK: Cambridge University Press, 2006).

Van der Schoot, Albert, *De ontstelling van Pythagoras: Over de geschiedenis van de goddelijke proportie* (Kok Agora: Kampen, 1998).

Wallace, William E., "Michelangelo, Tiberio Calcagni, and the Florentine 'Pietà,'" *Artibus et Historiae*, 21.42 (2000), 81–99, https://doi.org/10.2307/1483625

Wayman, Alex, "The Human Body as Microcosm in India, Greek Cosmology, and Sixteenth-Century Europe," *History of Religions*, 22.2 (1982), 172–90, https://doi.org/10.1086/462918

Westfall, Carroll William, "Painting and the Liberal Arts: Alberti's View," *Journal of the History of Ideas*, 30 (1967), 487–506, https://doi.org/10.2307/2708607

Wittkower, Rudolf, "The Changing Concept of Proportion," *Daedalus*, 89.1 (1960), 199–215.

Wormald, Francis, "An Italian Poet at the Court of Henry VII," *Journal of Warburg and Courtauld Institutes*, 14 (1951), 118–19, https://doi.org/10.2307/750355

Yates, Frances, *The Art of Memory* (Chicago: University of Chicago Press, 1966).

# List of Illustrations

| | | |
|---|---|---|
| Fig. 1 | Giovanni Paolo Gallucci, Title page, 1594. Woodcut from *Della simmetria dei corpi humani, libri quattro* (Venice: Roberto Meietti, 1594), https://archive.org/details/dialbertodurero00gallgoog/page/n4 | 2 |
| Fig. 2 | Leonardo da Vinci, *Vitruvian Man*, ca.1485–1490. Pen and ink, 13 ½ x 9 5/8 in. Gallerie dell'Accademia, Venice. Wikimedia, Public Domain, https://commons.wikimedia.org/wiki/File:Leonardo_da_Vinci-_Vitruvian_Man.JPG | 5 |
| Fig. 3 | Leonardo da Vinci, *Proportions of the Human Face*, 1509. Woodcut from Luca Pacioli, *De divina proportione* (Venice: Paganini, 1509), [n.p.]. Wikimedia, Public Domain, https://commons.wikimedia.org/wiki/File:Divina_proportione.png | 7 |
| Fig. 4 | Albrecht Dürer, *The Fall of Man*, 1504. Engraving, 9 7/8 x 7 5/8 in. Museum of Fine Arts, Boston. Wikimedia, Public Domain, https://upload.wikimedia.org/wikipedia/commons/9/90/Albrecht_D%C3%BCrer_-_The_Fall_of_Man_%28Adam_and_Eve%29_-_Google_Art_Project.jpg | 9 |
| Fig. 5 | Giovanni Paolo Gallucci (after Albrecht Dürer), *Proportions of a Man*, 1591. Woodcut from *Della simmetria dei corpi humani, libri quattro* (Venice: Roberto Meietti, 1594), First Book, 4vr, https://archive.org/details/dialbertodurero00gallgoog/page/n21 | 12 |
| Fig. 6 | Giovanni Paolo Gallucci (after Albrecht Dürer), *Proportions of a Woman*, 1591. Woodcut from *Della simmetria dei corpi humani, libri quattro* (Venice: Roberto Meietti, 1594), First Book, 6vr, https://archive.org/details/dialbertodurero00gallgoog/page/n25 | 12 |
| Fig. 7 | Giovanni Paolo Gallucci (after Albrecht Dürer), *Proportions of a Man*, 1591. Woodcut from *Della simmetria dei corpi humani, libri quattro* (Venice: Roberto Meietti, 1594), First Book, 11vr, https://archive.org/details/dialbertodurero00gallgoog/page/n35 | 13 |

Fig. 8    Giovanni Paolo Gallucci (after Albrecht Dürer), *Proportions of a Hand*, 1591. Woodcut from *Della simmetria dei corpi humani, libri quattro* (Venice: Roberto Meietti, 1594), First Book, 24r, https://archive.org/details/dialbertodurero00gallgoog/page/n61    13

Fig. 9    Giovanni Paolo Gallucci (after Albrecht Dürer), *Proportions of a Foot*, 1591. Woodcut from *Della simmetria dei corpi humani, libri quattro* (Venice: Roberto Meietti, 1594), First Book, 26v, https://archive.org/details/dialbertodurero00gallgoog/page/n65    14

Fig. 10    Giovanni Paolo Gallucci (after Albrecht Dürer), *Proportions of a Child*, 1591. Woodcut from *Della simmetria dei corpi humani, libri quattro* (Venice: Roberto Meietti, 1594), First Book, 29r, https://archive.org/details/dialbertodurero00gallgoog/page/n71    14

Fig. 11    Giovanni Paolo Gallucci (after Albrecht Dürer), *Proportions of a Man*, 1591. Woodcut from *Della simmetria dei corpi humani, libri quattro* (Venice: Roberto Meietti, 1594), First Book, 31vr, https://archive.org/details/dialbertodurero00gallgoog/page/n75    15

Fig. 12    Giovanni Paolo Gallucci (after Albrecht Dürer), *Proportions of a Man with Arms Outstretched*, 1591. Woodcut from *Della simmetria dei corpi humani, libri quattro* (Venice: Roberto Meietti, 1594), First Book, 46vr, https://archive.org/details/dialbertodurero00gallgoog/page/n105    16

Fig. 13    Giovanni Paolo Gallucci (after Albrecht Dürer), *Proportions of a Man*, 1591. Woodcut from *Della simmetria dei corpi humani, libri quattro* (Venice: Roberto Meietti, 1594), First Book, 75vr, https://archive.org/details/dialbertodurero00gallgoog/page/n161    17

Fig. 14    Giovanni Paolo Gallucci (after Albrecht Dürer), *Faces of a Man*, 1591. Woodcut from *Della simmetria dei corpi humani, libri quattro*, Roberto Meietti, Venice 1594, First Book, 84vr, https://archive.org/details/dialbertodurero00gallgoog/page/n177    18

Fig. 15    Giovanni Paolo Gallucci (after Albrecht Dürer), *Proportions of a Man and a Woman*, 1591. Woodcut from *Della simmetria dei corpi humani, libri quattro* (Venice: Roberto Meietti, 1594), First Book, 94vr, https://archive.org/details/dialbertodurero00gallgoog/page/n197    19

## List of Illustrations 203

| | | |
|---|---|---|
| Fig. 16 | Giovanni Paolo Gallucci (after Albrecht Dürer), *Proportions of a Woman*, 1591. Woodcut from *Della simmetria dei corpi humani, libri quattro* (Venice: Roberto Meietti, 1594), First Book, 100v, https://archive.org/details/dialbertodurero00gallgoog/page/n207 | 19 |
| Fig. 17 | Giovanni Paolo Gallucci (after Albrecht Dürer), *Proportions of a Man and a Woman*, 1591. Woodcut from *Della simmetria dei corpi humani, libri quattro* (Venice: Roberto Meietti, 1594), First Book, 113vr, https://archive.org/details/dialbertodurero00gallgoog/page/n231 | 21 |
| Fig. 18 | Giovanni Paolo Gallucci (after Albrecht Dürer), *Proportions of a Man and Body Parts*, 1591. Woodcut from *Della simmetria dei corpi humani, libri quattro* (Venice: Roberto Meietti, 1594), First Book, 113vr, https://archive.org/details/dialbertodurero00gallgoog/page/n241 | 21 |
| Fig. 19 | Robert Fludd, Title page, 1617. Engraving from *Utriusque cosmi historia* (Oppenheim: Johann Theodor de Bry, 1617). Wikimedia, Public Domain, https://commons.wikimedia.org/wiki/File:Robert_Fludd_Utriusque_cosmi.jpg#/media/File:Robert_Fludd_Utriusque_cosmi.jpg | 63 |

# Index of Proper Names

Achilles 116, 135, 136
Acosta, José de 36
Adonis 127
Aeneas 120, 136
Aesop 155
Ajax 128
Alberti 70, 78, 79, 81
Alberti, Leon Battista 3, 6, 15, 41, 42
Alcina 140, 154
Alcinous 162
Alexander the Great 94, 163, 178
Alexandros 45, 120
Allecto 148
Allori, Alessandro 80
Alzirdo 129
Amata 147
Amycus 130
Anacreon 44, 123, 125, 127
Angelica 124, 126, 142
Antonius Mariscottus, Jacobus 30
Apelles 94
Apollonius Rhodes 166
Aquinas, St. Thomas 74
Arachne 142
Archimedes 94
Ariosto 51, 54, 67, 109, 124, 126, 128, 129, 131, 132, 133, 134, 135, 136, 140, 142, 144, 145, 147, 148, 149, 150, 151, 154
Ariosto, Ludovico 44, 45
Aristotle 23, 28, 35, 41, 43, 52, 94, 105, 109, 110, 118, 119, 123, 134, 138, 139, 141, 183
Armenini, Giovanni Battista 76
Armida 124, 142, 148
Ashmole 64
Ashmole, Elias 60

Astolfo 128
Atlas 135
Augustus 168, 173, 178, 183
Augustus, Charles 98
Avicenna 29

Bacchus 127, 128, 165, 176, 180
Badoer, Federico 34
Bellini 101
Bellini, Giovanni 101
Bellori 69
Bellori, Giovan Pietro 49
Bocchi, Francesco 55
Borghini 73
Borghini, Raffaello 72
Borromeo, Carlo 47
Boselli, Orfeo ix, 56
Brunello 150

Cacus 149
Caesar 43
Caligula 146, 170, 171, 182
Cambiari, Luca 20
Camerarius 67
Camerarius, Joachim 8
Camilli, Camillo 28
Camillo, Giulio 25, 33, 66
Camillo, Guilio 36
Cardano, Girolamo 64
Carducci, Vincenzo 69
Castiglione 81
Catiline 151
Cato 43, 131
Catullus 44, 45, 99, 126, 154, 166
Charles V 93
Christ 66, 170

Cicero  43, 102, 109, 127
Ciotti, Giovan Battista  35
Clavius, Christopher  31
Condivi  71, 72, 73
Condivi, Ascanio  71
Costa, Luiz da  68
Cucina, Giovanni Battista  36

Daedalus  138
Dante  129
Dante Alighieri  44
Danti  71, 74, 80
Danti, Vincenzo  70
Dares  130
Degli Oddi, Marco  29
Della Porta  55
Della Porta, Giovanni Battista  55
Dido  136, 147
Dolce, Lodovico  42
Donatello  55
Dürer  51, 53, 58, 67, 68, 69, 70, 72, 74, 76, 78, 81, 92, 93, 97, 100, 101, 109, 118, 124, 151, 152, 155, 162, 166, 168, 169, 172, 173, 186
Dürer, Albrecht  xi, 3, 8, 10, 11, 15, 16, 20, 22, 26, 27, 30, 37, 38, 39, 46, 50

Erminia  127
Euclid  81, 94

Ficino  53, 58, 61, 62, 65, 183, 185
Ficino, Marsilio  25, 30, 32
Flavio  81
Fludd  62
Fludd, Robert  33
Foppa, Vincenzo  9
Formianus  166
Francavilla, Pietro  80

Galba  168
Galen  59, 64
Galilei, Galileo  40
Gallucci  51, 53, 54, 58, 65, 66, 67, 68, 69, 75, 76, 79, 80, 81
Gallucci, Giovanni Battista  27

Gallucci, Giovanni Paolo  ix, xi, 2, 20, 22, 23, 24, 25, 26, 27, 28, 30, 31, 32, 34, 37, 38, 39, 40, 41, 44, 45, 46, 48, 49, 50
Gaurico, Pomponoi  54
Gellius, Aulus  156
Ghiberti, Lorenzo  1, 40
Gradasso  134
Granada  123
Granada, Luis de  35, 36
Gregory XIII  31

Hector  130, 155
Helen  121, 128
Hephaistos  135
Hercules  105, 128, 155, 156, 164
Heron  81
Hippocrates  59, 97
Hollanda, Francisco de  55
Homer  44, 45, 54, 120, 128, 132, 135, 136, 139, 154, 162
Horace  40, 43, 44, 144, 154, 156

Icarus  139
Indagine, John  54

Jocondo  144, 145
Judas  67, 162
Julian the Apostate  94
Julius Caesar  177
Juno  162
Jupiter  133, 156
Juvenal  163, 172

Latinus  147
Laura  125
Le Brun, Charles  ix, 55
Leo  148
Leonardo  77, 79
Leonardo da Vinci  5, 6, 7, 8, 23, 24, 72
Lesbia  126
Lomazzo  53, 54, 61, 63, 70, 74, 76, 79, 81
Lomazzo, Gian Paolo  24, 25
Lomazzo, Giovan Paolo  ix, 8, 20
Lysippos  94

Macrobius  180
Maecenas  99, 144

Mancini, Giulio 75
Mantegna, Andrea 25, 101
Marino, Giambattista 35
Mars 123, 127
Marsus 99
Marsyas 172
Martial 146
Maximilian I 37, 81, 93, 98
Maximilian II 38
Maximilian III 3, 22, 68, 91
Maximillian III 37
Maximus Planudes 155
Meigret, Louis 67
Menelaus 132
Mercury 127, 133
Michelangelo 24, 37, 71, 79, 92
Milo of Croton 155
Minerva 139
Morosini, Francesco 30, 35
Muschio, Andrea 35

Naevolus 172
Nausicaä 162
Nero 153
Numanus 141

Olympia 128, 147, 148
Orlando 129, 131, 151, 155
Ovid 43, 44, 54, 81, 132, 140

Pacioli, Luca 6, 8, 72
Paggi, Giovanni Battista 77
Paleotti, Gabriele 47
Pannychus 146
Paris 45, 120, 122, 132
Parrhasius 47
Paul, St. 115
Paulus 127
Peckham, John 35, 36
Peleus 136
Peter, St. 115
Petrarch 44, 45, 121, 125, 171
Philomela 132
Pino, Paolo 54
Pirckheimer, Willibald 102

Pius IV 31
Plato 6, 43, 59, 94, 161, 171, 174, 183
Plautus 144
Pliny the Elder 44, 47, 109, 110, 185
Plutarch 44, 163
Pollux 127
Polygnotus 99
Porphyry 107
Poussin, Nicolas 48, 68
Priam 128
Pseudo-Aristotle xii, 52, 53, 55
Ptolemy 94

Quintia 126

Reisch, Gregor 34
Rinaldo 67, 132, 145
Ripa 81
Ruggiero 124, 134, 135, 140

Sallust 43, 44, 151
Samsonet 128
Sardanapalus 164
Seneca 43, 45, 126, 130, 134, 137, 143
Shakespeare, William 33
Sixtus V 30, 31, 65
Socrates 59
Stadius, Johannes 30
St Jerome 67
Strada, Jacopo da 38
Suetonius 146, 153, 168, 170, 171, 173, 178, 182, 183

Tasso 54, 117, 124, 127, 129, 133, 134, 135, 136, 137, 142, 148
Tasso, Torquato 44, 45, 47, 49
Terence 43
Thersites 155
Tiberius Caesar 178, 183
Trismegistus, Hermes 30, 65
Turnus 133

Valdes, Francisco 36
Valerius Maximus 43
Valverde, Juan 80
Vasari 70, 71, 75, 77

Vasari, Giorgio 1
Venus 123, 127
Vergerio, Pier Paolo 43
Vesalius, Andreas 80
Virdung von Hassfurt, Johann 30, 65
Virgil 43, 44, 54, 99, 120, 129, 130, 133, 136, 141, 147, 149, 153, 160, 167
Vitruvius 4, 40, 41, 109, 110
Vives 43

Vouet, Simon 81

Zabarella, Giacomo 29
Zerbin 142
Zeuxis 47, 121
Zlatarič, Dominko 28
Zuccaro 73, 74, 76
Zuccaro, Federico 73

# About the team

Alessandra Tosi was the managing editor for this book.

Adèle Kreager performed the copy-editing and proofreading. The author performed the indexing.

Anna Gatti designed the cover using InDesign. The image is by Albrecht Dürer, *Adam and Eve* (1507), sourced from Wikimedia, https://commons.wikimedia.org/wiki/File:Albrecht_D%C3%BCrer_-_Adam_and_Eve_(Prado)_2FXD.jpg. The cover was produced in InDesign using Fontin (titles) and Calibri (text body) fonts.

Luca Baffa typeset the book in InDesign. The text font is Tex Gyre Pagella; the heading font is Californian FB. Luca created all of the editions — paperback, hardback, EPUB, MOBI, PDF, HTML, and XML — the conversion is performed with open source software freely available on our GitHub page (https://github.com/OpenBookPublishers).

The complete manuscript of this work was 'single-blind' peer-reviewed by two experts in the field (meaning that the reviewers remain anonymous, although they know the identity of the author). For further details, please see the information for authors on our website: https://www.openbookpublishers.com/section/6/1

# This book need not end here...

## Share

All our books — including the one you have just read — are free to access online so that students, researchers and members of the public who can't afford a printed edition will have access to the same ideas. This title will be accessed online by hundreds of readers each month across the globe: why not share the link so that someone you know is one of them?

This book and additional content is available at:

https://doi.org/10.11647/OBP.0198

## Customise

Personalise your copy of this book or design new books using OBP and third-party material. Take chapters or whole books from our published list and make a special edition, a new anthology or an illuminating coursepack. Each customised edition will be produced as a paperback and a downloadable PDF.

Find out more at:

https://www.openbookpublishers.com/section/59/1

Like Open Book Publishers

Follow @OpenBookPublish

Read more at the Open Book Publishers BLOG

www.ingramcontent.com/pod-product-compliance
Lightning Source LLC
Chambersburg PA
CBHW071020240526
45469CB00006BD/2016